Securities

The Official Learning and Reference Manual

6th Edition, September 2010

This Workbook relates to syllabus version 10.0 and will cover examinations from 21 December 2010 to 20 December 2011

PROFESSIONALISM | INTEGRITY | EXCELLENCE

Securities

Welcome to the Chartered Institute for Securities & Investment's Securities study material.

This workbook has been written to prepare you for the Chartered Institute for Securities & Investment's Securities examination.

PUBLISHED BY:

Chartered Institute for Securities & Investment

8 Eastcheap
London
EC3M 1AE
Tel: +44 (0) 20 7645 0600
Fax: + 44 (0) 20 7645 0601

WRITTEN BY:
Clive Corcoran

A Learning Map, which contains the full syllabus, appears at the end of this workbook. The syllabus can also be viewed on the Institute's website at www.cisi.org and is also available by contacting Client Services on +44 (0)20 7645 0680. Please note that the examination is based upon the syllabus. Candidates are reminded to check the Candidate Commonroom area of the Institute's website (www.cisi.org/candidatecommonroom) on a regular basis for updates that could affect their examination as a result of industry change.

The questions contained in this manual are designed as an aid to revision of different areas of the syllabus and to help you consolidate your learning chapter by chapter. They should not be seen as a 'mock' examination or necessarily indicative of the level of the questions in the corresponding examination.

Workbook version: 6.1 (September 2010)

Foreword

Learning and Professional Development with the CISI

Formerly the Securities & Investment Institute (SII), and originally founded by members of the London Stock Exchange, the Institute is the leading examining, membership and awarding body for the securities and investment industry. We were awarded a royal charter in October 2009, becoming the Chartered Institute for Securities & Investment. We currently have around 40,000 members, who benefit from a programme of professional and social events, with continuing professional development (CPD) and the promotion of integrity very much at the heart of everything we do.

This learning manual (or 'workbook' as it is often known in the industry) provides not only a thorough preparation for the appropriate CISI examination, but is a valuable desktop reference for practitioners. It can also be used as a learning tool for readers interested in knowing more, but not necessarily entering an examination.

The CISI official learning manuals ensure that candidates gain a comprehensive understanding of examination content. Our material is written and updated by industry specialists and reviewed by experienced, senior figures in the financial services industry. Exam and manual quality is assured through a rigorous editorial system of practitioner panels and boards. CISI examinations are used extensively by firms to meet the requirements of government regulators. The CISI works closely with a number of international regulators that recognise our examinations and the manuals supporting them, as well as the UK regulator, the Financial Services Authority (FSA).

CISI learning manuals are normally revised annually. It is important that candidates check they purchase the correct version for the period when they wish to take their examination. Between versions, candidates should keep abreast of the latest industry developments through the Candidate Commonroom area of the CISI website. (The CISI also endorses the workbooks of 7City Learning and BPP).

The CISI produces a range of elearning revision tools such as Revision Express Interactive, Revision Express Online and Professional Refresher, which can be used in conjunction with our learning and reference manuals. For further details, please visit cisi.org.

As a Professional Body, around 40,000 CISI members subscribe to the CISI Code of Conduct and the CISI has a significant voice in the industry, standing for professionalism, excellence and the promotion of trust and integrity. Continuing professional development is at the heart of the Institute's values. Our CPD scheme is available free of charge to members, and this includes an online record-keeping system as well as regular seminars, conferences and professional networks in specialist subject areas, all of which cover a range of current industry topics. Reading this manual and taking a CISI examination is credited as professional development with the CISI CPD scheme. To learn more about CISI membership, visit our website at cisi.org.

We hope that you will find this manual useful and interesting. Once you have completed it, you will find helpful suggestions on qualifications and membership progression with the CISI at the end of this book.

With best wishes for your studies.

Ruth Martin
Managing Director

Contents

What next?
See the back of this book for details on CISI membership.

Need more support to pass your exam?
See our section on Accredited Training Providers and CISI elearning at the back of this book.

Want to leave feedback?
Please email your comments to learningresources@cisi.org

It is estimated that this workbook will require approximately 100 hours of study time.

CHAPTER ONE

SECURITIES

This syllabus area will provide approximately 24 of the 100 examination questions

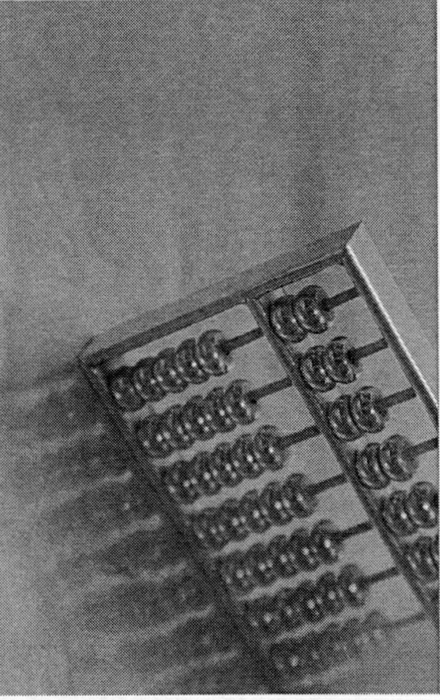

INTRODUCTION

SHARES AND BONDS

As a broad introduction to this chapter, it is useful to provide a reminder of the essential differences between the two major types of security: shares (or equities) and bonds.

Investors in **bonds** essentially hold an IOU (I owe you) from another organisation, such as a company. The bond investors:

- loan money to an organisation in return for an **agreed rate of interest**;
- have an **agreed date** on which they get their money back;
- can **sue** the issuer of the bond if the interest on the bond isn't paid;
- can **sue** the issuer of the bond if repayment doesn't occur.

Investors in **equities** hold a stake in the company. The equity investors:

- purchase a small piece, or **share**, of a company;
- cannot be certain that they will receive **dividend payments**;
- cannot be certain of the **amount of dividend** that they will receive;
- are liable to the **total amount** invested in fully paid shares.

Securities like shares and bonds take one of two main forms: registered and bearer. The form determines how an investor would prove ownership of a particular investment.

EXAMPLE

Mr X owns 100 shares in Marks and Spencer plc. If a burglar breaks into Mr X's house and steals Mr X's share certificates, can he pretend that he owns the Marks and Spencer shares and sell them?

Fortunately, the answer is no.

The answer to the above example is no because shares in the UK are held in **registered** form. This means that the certificate is simply evidence of ownership. The proof that counts is the name and address held on the company's share register.

Some securities come in **bearer** form. Unlike registered securities, with bearer-form securities the **physical possession** of the certificate is the proof of ownership.

Bearer securities are easier to transfer since there is no register. They can simply be handed over. However, this does raise a few problems:

- it is difficult for the authorities to monitor ownership, making them attractive investments for **money launderers**;
- the issuing company has difficulty knowing whom to send dividend or interest payments to;
- **physical security** of the certificates is of greater importance and can increase the cost of holding the investment.

Examples of securities that are usually held in bearer-form, which will be encountered later in this chapter, are **Eurobonds** and **American Depositary Receipts (ADRs)**.

1. SHARES

INTRODUCTION – TYPES OF SHARE

LEARNING OBJECTIVE

1.1.1 Know the principal features and characteristics of ordinary shares and non-voting shares: 'A' ordinary shares; 'B' shares; preference shares; bearer shares; partly paid shares and calls; ranking for dividends; ranking in a liquidation; voting rights; purpose of non-voting shares

Shares can be divided into two categories: ordinary shares and preference shares. Every company has ordinary shares in issue. In addition to the ordinary shares, some companies issue preference shares.

The performance of **ordinary shares** is closely tied to the fortunes of the company. Holders of ordinary shares have the right to **vote** on key decisions and receive **dividends**. Some companies have more than one class of ordinary shares (perhaps distinguishing between **A** ordinary shares and **B** ordinary shares), where one class of shares does not provide voting rights and is, therefore, referred to as non-voting shares.

Preference shares are less risky than ordinary shares and potentially less profitable. Holders generally do not have the right to vote on company affairs, but they are entitled to receive a fixed dividend each year (as long as the company feels they have sufficient profits). These dividends must be paid before any dividends to ordinary shareholders; hence the term preference. Although preference shares tend to be non-voting, it is common for preference shareholders to become entitled to vote in the event of no dividend being paid for a 'substantial' period of time. Precisely how long 'substantial' is will be detailed in the company's constitution.

Companies have an obligation to pay dividends to preferred shareholders before they pay a dividend, if any, to the ordinary shareholders. The ranking of dividend payments to the different kinds of preferred shareholders is addressed in section 1.2.

In the case of a winding-up or liquidation of a company, the priority and manner in which the owners of different tiers of the capital structure of that company are dealt with can be referred to as the 'liquidation ranking'.

The first and simple rule is that all shareholders or equity participants are subordinate to debt-holders. There are separate provisions for the priority of debt holders based upon the seniority of the debt, whether there is a fixed charge associated with the debt or a floating charge, and other covenants that were granted at the time of debt issuance.

Once the obligations to the debt-holders have been discharged, preferred shareholders will take priority over the ordinary shareholders in the case of liquidation. From the proceeds following a liquidation event (which may be defined to include events other than a winding-up of the company), the preferred shareholders will receive the par value of their shares before there is any distribution to the ordinary shareholders.

There is one further consideration which relates to the issuance of preference shares as part of early-stage or venture funding of a start-up company, and this is often referred to as 'liquidation preference'.

The liquidation preference is the amount that must be paid to the preferred stock holders, such as venture capital or 'angel' investors, before distributions may be made to common stock holders. The liquidation preference is payable on either the liquidation of a company, asset sale, merger, consolidation or any other reorganisation resulting in the change of control of the start-up.

It is usually expressed as a percentage of the original purchase price of the preferred, such as '2x'. Thus, if the purchase price of the preferred is £2 per share, a liquidation preference of 2x will be £4 per share. In effect, the preferred shareholders will receive twice the nominal value of their shares upon liquidation before there would be any distribution of the proceeds (if any) to the ordinary shareholders.

1.1 FEATURES OF ORDINARY SHARES

The ordinary shareholders of a company take the greatest risk. If the company is liquidated, they will only receive any pay-out if there is money remaining after satisfying all of the other claims from creditors, bondholders and preference shareholders.

If the company is sufficiently profitable, the ordinary shareholders may receive dividends. Dividends for ordinary shareholders are proposed by the directors and generally ratified by the shareholders at the Annual General Meeting (AGM). However, the ordinary shareholders will only receive a dividend after any preference dividends have been paid.

Each ordinary share is typically given the right to vote at AGMs and Extraordinary General Meetings (EGMs), although sometimes voting rights are restricted to certain classes of ordinary shares. Such different classes of shares (often called 'A' ordinary and 'B' ordinary shares), are created to separate ownership and control, as illustrated in the following example:

EXAMPLE

ABC plc is a small, successful, privately owned company with two founding directors each holding 500 of its total issue of 1,000 ordinary shares. ABC plc needs more investment for expansion and the company agrees to issue 200 new shares to venture capitalists. However, the venture capitalists require control over the company as a condition of their investment.

This is achieved by creating a second class of ordinary shares. The founding directors' shares become non-voting 'A' shares and the venture capitalists hold voting 'B' shares. The result is that, although the founding directors hold non-voting 'A' shares, they still own most of the company (1000 shares of the total 1200 shares), but control is now exercised by the venture capitalists since it is their 'B' shares that have votes.

If they do have voting shares, each shareholder may, if they so wish, appoint a third party, or proxy, to vote on their behalf. A proxy may be an individual or group of individuals appointed by the board of directors of the company to formally represent the shareholders who send in proxy requests, to vote the represented shares in accordance with the shareholders' instructions.

Each ordinary share has a **nominal value**, which represents the minimum amount that the company must receive from subscribers on the issue of the shares. Occasionally the company may not demand all of the nominal value at issue, with the shares referred to as being **partly paid**. At some later date, the company will call on the shareholders to pay the remaining nominal value.

Most ordinary shares are registered, meaning that the issuing company maintains a register of who holds the shares. Shares issued by a company that does not maintain a register are known as bearer shares – they can be transferred to other investors by simply handing over the certificate. For registered shares, a transfer requires a change of entry in the shareholders' register.

1.2 TYPES OF PREFERENCE SHARE

LEARNING OBJECTIVE

1.1.2 Understand the differences and principal characteristics of the following classes of preference shares: cumulative; participating; redeemable; convertible

Preference shares can come in a variety of forms.

- **Cumulative** – a cumulative preference shareholder will not only be paid this year's dividend before any ordinary shareholders' dividends, but also any unpaid dividends from previous years.
- **Redeemable** – these are preference shares that enable the company to buy back the shares from the shareholder at an agreed price in the future. The shares, from the company's perspective, are similar to debt. The money provided by the preference shareholders can be repaid, removing any obligation the firm has to them.
- **Participating** – one drawback of preference shares, when compared to ordinary shares, is that, if the company starts to generate large profits, the ordinary shareholders will often see their dividends rise, whereas the preference shareholders still get a fixed level of dividend. To counter this, some preference shares offer the opportunity to participate in higher distributions.
- **Convertible** – in this case, the preference shareholder has the right, but not the obligation, to convert the preference shares into a predetermined number of ordinary shares, eg, perhaps one preference share can be converted into two ordinary shares. This is another method of avoiding the lack of upside potential in the preference shares, compared to ordinary shares.

Note that a particular preference share may exhibit more than one of these features.

1.3 STOCK INDICES

LEARNING OBJECTIVE

1.1.3 Know the broad composition and geographical scope and use of the following stock indices: DJ STOXX; FTSE Eurofirst 300; MSCI World; FTSE 100; Dow Jones Industrial Average; Nikkei Stock 225; Hang Seng; CAC 40; DAX; S&P 500; FTSE All Share; NASDAQ

There are thousands of companies that are listed and traded on various stock exchanges around the world. Stock indices such as the FTSE 100 and the Dow Jones Industrial Average are produced so that existing and potential investors can get a snapshot of the way share prices are generally moving. These stock indices are calculated by specialist firms such as FTSE International (which originated as a joint venture between the *Financial Times* and the London Stock Exchange) and Dow Jones Indexes (part of the Dow Jones Company, which also publishes the *Wall Street Journal*). Each index can be thought of as an 'average' share price of its constituents, as illustrated below.

EXAMPLE – THE FTSE 100

The FTSE 100 is a stock index based on the share prices of the largest 100 companies listed on the London Stock Exchange. It started at a base level of 1000 points in January 1984, meaning that the value of the 100 constituent companies at that time equated to 1000 index points. As the value of the constituent companies increases (or decreases), the FTSE 100 will increase (or decrease). So, if the value of the constituents grew by 10% in the first nine months following the index publication date, the index would have risen to 1100 index points. At the time of writing (17 August 2010), the FTSE 100 stands at 5324 index points.

The following indices are covered within the syllabus, and the following table provides their broad composition and geographical scope.

Index name	Composition	Geographical Scope
FTSE 100	Largest 100 UK companies listed on the LSE and measured by market capitalisation	UK and multi-nationals
Dow Jones Industrial Average	30 large US companies selected by the editors of the *Wall Street Journal*	US-domiciled multi-nationals
Nikkei Stock 225	225 large and regularly traded Japanese companies traded on the Tokyo Stock Exchange	Japanese corporations

(continued overleaf)

Index name	**Composition**	**Geographical Scope**
Hang Seng	33 companies listed on the Hong Kong Stock Exchange selected on the basis of market value, turnover and financial performance	Hong Kong/China
DJ STOXX	A family of indices, based around the DJ STOXX Global 1800 index that consists of 600 largest capitalisation companies from each of 3 regions – Europe, Americas and Asia/Pacific	Global developed markets
MSCI World	A market capitalisation-based index including companies from 23 countries, totalling approximately 1,700 companies	Global developed markets
FTSE Eurofirst 300	300 largest listed companies by market capitalisation from across Europe	European-domiciled corporations
CAC 40	The CAC 40 (CAC *quarante*) represents a capitalisation-weighted measure of the 40 most significant values among the 100 highest market caps on the Paris Bourse (now Euronext Paris)	French-domiciled companies, about 45% of its listed shares are owned by foreign investors, more than any other main European index
DAX	The DAX (*Deutscher Aktien IndeX*) includes the 30 major German companies trading on the Frankfurt Stock Exchange	The Base date for the DAX is 30 December 1987 and it was started from a base value of 1,000. The Xetra system calculates the index
S&P 500	Standard & Poor's manages the composition of the index. The 500 constituents are selected by S&P from the largest cap stocks traded in the US	US-traded stocks which are multi-national companies operating in global markets
FTSE All Share	The **FTSE All Share Index**, originally known as the **FTSE Actuaries All Share Index**, is a capitalisation-weighted index, comprising around 600 of more than 2,000 companies traded on the LSE	To qualify, companies must have a full listing on the LSE with a sterling or euro-dominated price on SETS
NASDAQ	The **Nasdaq Composite** covers issues listed on the NASDAQ stock market with over 3,200 components, of which around 300 are non-US stocks. It is an indicator of the performance of stocks of technology companies and growth companies	Since both US and non-US companies are listed on the NASDAQ stock market, the index is not exclusively a US index
NASDAQ 100	The **NASDAQ 100 index** consists of the largest non-financial companies listed on the NASDAQ. It is a modified market value-weighted index	It does not contain financial companies, and includes companies incorporated outside the US

These stock market indices are used both as a gauge of the market and as a 'performance benchmark'. If the index is going up, the prices of the constituents will generally be increasing, and the market will be described as going through a 'bullish' phase. In contrast, if the index is falling, the prices of the constituents will generally be decreasing and the market will be described as going through a 'bearish' phase.

The use of an index as a performance benchmark is illustrated in the example below:

EXAMPLE

An investor holds a small number of large listed Japanese shares. Over the course of the year, the value of her shares has increased by 8%. The investor considers this a good performance because, over the same period, the Nikkei 225 has only increased by 5%. The investor's portfolio has 'outperformed' the market.

1.4 TAX CREDITS ON UK DIVIDENDS

LEARNING OBJECTIVE

1.1.4 Understand the use of a tax credit on a dividend

If a UK resident receives dividends on shares held, he will probably be subject to UK income tax. However, dividends received are deemed to have already suffered tax at 10% before they are received. This is called the 'tax credit' on the dividends and means that the investor only has to pay further income tax if he is a higher-rate (40%) taxpayer.

The effect of this credit under the applicable rules is that no income tax is payable by any recipient of dividends whose total income is below the higher-rate tax level, after adding in the grossed-up value of those dividends. It is not a proper credit because a non-taxpayer cannot recover it.

Where the dividends are received by higher-rate payers, then additional tax of 25% of the amount paid becomes payable, equivalent to 32.5% of the grossed up value minus the tax credit. Note that it is not 40%.

This is illustrated in the following example:

EXAMPLE

Mr X Ample is a higher-rate (40%) taxpayer and has 100 shares in ABC plc. ABC pays a dividend of 90p on each share. Mr Ample will receive £90 (90p x 100 shares) and, as far as the tax authority is concerned, he will be considered as having received £100 and having paid tax of £10 already. The £100 is referred to as the 'gross dividend' and the £90 received is the 'net dividend'. Since he is a higher-rate taxpayer, Mr Ample will have to pay a further 25% of the net dividend to complete his tax due and payable.

In summary, Mr X Ample:

Received 90p x 100 shares the 'net dividend'	=	**£90**
Tax credit = 10/100 of the net dividend	=	**£10**
'Gross dividend' entitlement	=	**£100**
Tax due = 32.5% (10% tax credit + 25% of net dividend payment received) x £100	=	**£32.50**
Deemed paid by way of the tax credit	=	**(£10)**
Remaining to be paid	=	**£22.50**

1.5 FREE-FLOAT AND MARKET CAPITALISATION

LEARNING OBJECTIVE

1.1.5 Know the implications of free-float on market capitalisation

The free-float of a public company is an estimate of the proportion of shares that are not held by large owners and that are not stock with sales restrictions (restricted stock that cannot be sold until it becomes unrestricted stock).

The free-float or a public float is usually defined as being all shares held by investors other than:

- shares held by owners owning more than 5% of all shares (those could be institutional investors, strategic shareholders, founders, executives, and other insiders' holdings);
- restricted stocks (granted to executives who can be, but don't have to be, registered insiders);
- insider holdings (it is assumed that insiders hold stock for the very long term).

Under market-capitalisation-weighted indices, the total market capitalisation of a company is included irrespective of who is actually holding the shares and whether they are freely available for trading.

1.5.1 Free-Float Factor

The free-float factor represents the proportion of shares that is free-floated as a percentage of issued shares and then is rounded to the nearest multiple of 5% for calculation purposes. To find the free-float capitalisation of a company, first find its market cap (number of outstanding shares x share price) then multiply by its free-float factor. A free-float adjustment factor is introduced in the calculations of most of the major global equity indices.

For example, the following press release from STOXX ltd which maintains the various EURO STOXX indices reflects the adjustment to the free-float factor for Volkswagen in 2008, and the changes that this had on various indices.

EXAMPLE

ZURICH (October 28, 2008) – STOXX ltd., the leading provider of European equity indexes, today announced to change Volkswagen's free-float factor to 0.3732 from 0.4963. This decision reflects the changes in the shareholder structure of Volkswagen and results in a lower weighting of Volkswagen in the respective indexes.

Indexes affected are the Dow Jones EURO STOXX 50, Dow Jones STOXX 600 Large, Dow Jones STOXX Total Market Large, Dow Jones STOXX Sustainability and its respective sub- and sector-indexes. The adjustment will be effective as of the opening of trading on Friday, October 31, 2008

In essence, 'free-float market cap' equates to the total cost of buying all the shares of a particular company which are traded in the open market.

The free-float method is seen as a better way of calculating market capitalisation because it provides a more accurate reflection of market movements. When using a free-float methodology, the resulting market capitalisation is smaller than what would result from a full market capitalisation method. This is useful for performance measurement, as it provides a benchmark more closely related to what money managers can actually buy.

2. DEBT INSTRUMENTS

2.1 FEATURES AND CHARACTERISTICS

LEARNING OBJECTIVE

1.2.1 Know the principal features and characteristics of debt instruments

As seen at the start of this chapter, a bond is essentially an IOU issued by an organisation (the borrower, or issuer), in return for money lent to it.

The **nominal value** (or par value) of a bond is the amount that the borrower will pay back to the holder of the bond on maturity.

The **issuer** of a bond is important. If a company issuing a bond is considered high-risk, it will need to offer a high rate of interest on the bond to attract investors.

The **redemption date** of a bond is the date on which the borrower agrees to pay back the nominal value of the bond. It is also referred to as the date on which the bond matures, ie, the **maturity date**.

A bond's **coupon** is the interest rate that the borrower pays to the bondholder, expressed as a percentage of the nominal value. In diagrammatic form:

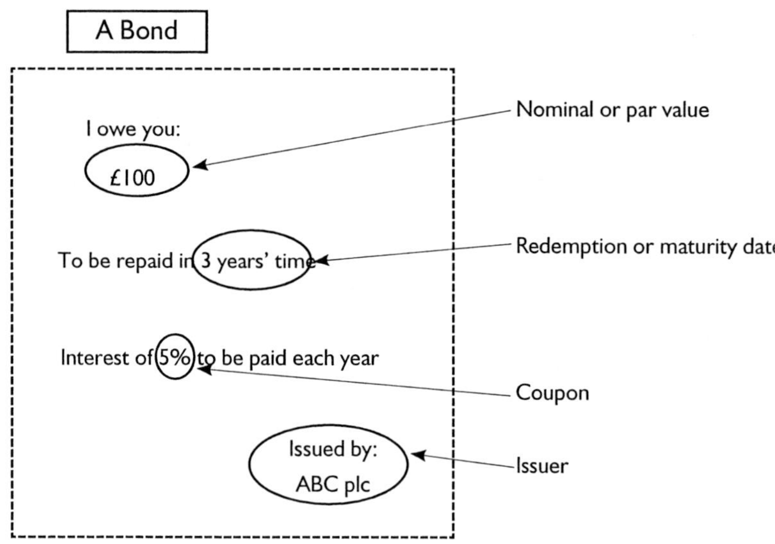

2.2 YIELDS

LEARNING OBJECTIVE

1.2.2 Understand the uses and limitations of the following: flat yield; gross redemption yield (using internal rate of return); net redemption yield; modified duration; calculation of price change; convexity

The yield is a measure of the percentage return that an investment provides. For a bond, there are three potential ways yields can be calculated: the flat yield (also known as the interest or running yield), the gross redemption yield and the net redemption yield.

2.2.1 Flat Yield

The flat yield only considers the coupon and ignores the existence of any capital gain (or loss) through to redemption. As such, it is best suited to short-term investors in the bond, rather than those investors who might hold the bond through to its maturity and benefit from the gain (or suffer from the loss) at maturity.

The calculation of the flat yield is as follows:

Flat yield = (annual coupon/price) x 100

For example, the flat yield on a 5% gilt, redeeming in six years and priced at £104.40, would be:

(5/104.40) x 100 = 4.79%.

EXERCISE 1

i. **Calculate the flat yield on a 4% gilt, redeeming in eight years and priced at £98.90**
ii. **Calculate the flat yield on a 7% gilt, redeeming in three years and priced at £108.60**

The answers can be found at the end of this chapter.

Using the flat yield, it is simple to see how a change in interest rates will impact bond prices. If interest rates increase, investors will want an equivalent increase in the yield on their bonds. However, because the coupon is fixed for most bonds, the only way that the yield can increase is for the price to fall. This is the inverse relationship between interest rates and bond prices. **When interest rates rise, bond prices fall and vice versa.**

2.2.2 Gross Redemption Yield (GRY)

The gross redemption yield is a fuller measure of yield than the flat yield, because it takes both the coupons and any gain (or loss) through to maturity into account. As such, it is more appropriate for long-term investors than the flat yield. In particular, because it ignores the impact of any taxation (hence gross redemption yield), this measure of return is useful for non-taxpaying, long-term investors such as pension funds and charities.

The calculation of the GRY utilises the approach covered in section 2.6 of this chapter to arrive at the present value of a bond. It is the 'internal rate of return' of the bond. The internal rate of return is simply the discount rate that, when applied to the future cash flows of the bond, produces the current price of that bond.

2.2.3 Net Redemption Yield (NRY)

The net redemption yield is similar to the gross redemption yield, in that it takes both the annual coupons and the profit (or loss) made through to maturity into account. However, it looks at the after-tax cash flows rather than the gross cash flows. As a result it is a useful measure for tax-paying, long-term investors.

The coupon received from gilts is generally taxable, but any gain made on redemption (or subsequent sale) is not taxable. This makes gilts with a low coupon attractive to higher-rate taxpayers, as the price will be lower than par, resulting in a substantial part of the return coming in the form of a tax-free capital gain.

2.2.4 Modified Duration

It is clear that if interest rates rise the price of fixed-rate debt instruments (eg, most gilts and many corporate debt issues) falls, and vice versa.

If an investor thinks that interest rates are going to fall in the future, then investing in fixed-interest securities is a good idea because, if the investor is correct, their price will rise.

However, some fixed-interest securities will be more responsive to a movement in interest rates than others. They will all rise in value when interest rates fall, but some will probably rise by more than others. The ones that rise the most are the more **volatile** securities.

All other things being equal, a lower-coupon bond will be more volatile to a change in interest rates than a higher coupon bond. Similarly, all other things being equal, a longer-dated bond will be more responsive than a shorter-dated bond.

To identify which bonds are more volatile, **volatility measures** can be used.

The one measure of volatility required for this examination is **modified duration**.

The modified duration of a particular debt instrument shows the **expected change in its price**, given a **specified change in interest rates**. The higher the modified duration, the more the price of that instrument will move. The modified duration is the approximate percentage change in the price of a bond brought about by a 1% change in the interest rate.

EXAMPLE

If a bond is priced at £95.84 and its modified duration is 1.02, what is the approximate price after an increase in interest rates by one percentage point?

If interest rates increase by one percentage point, the bond's price will fall by 1.02/100 x £95.84 = £0.98

If interest rates rise by one half of a percentage point, the bond price will fall by 1.02/100 x £95.84 x 0.5 = £0.49.

2.2.5 Convexity

If market interest rates (and, therefore, required yields) move by a small amount, then modified duration is fairly accurate in predicting the change in a bond's price. However, when rate changes are large, modified duration tends to underestimate the rise in prices (if rates fall) and overestimate price falls (when rates increase).

These errors are due to the relationship between yields and prices being curved rather than a straight line. Modified duration assumes a straight line relationship, and making the adjustment for convexity will refine the anticipated price change given a particular movement in yield.

Diagrammatically, the relationship between the modified duration-based estimate and the convexity adjustment can be seen in the following graph:

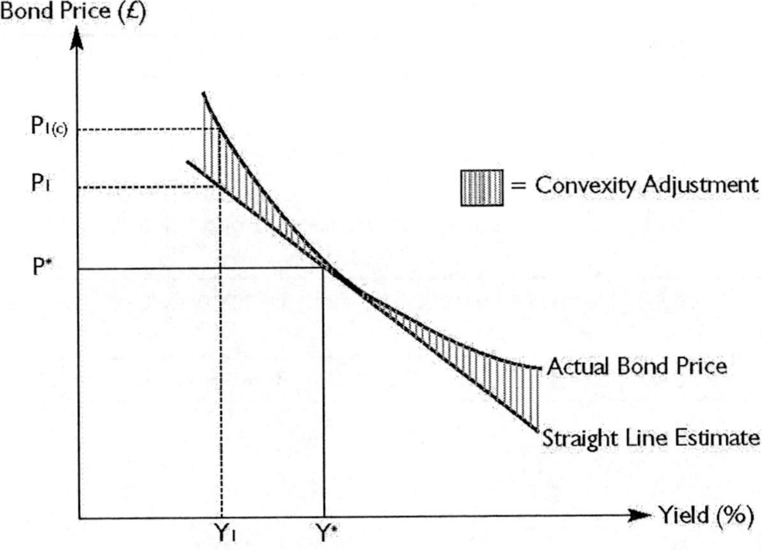

If a bond was currently priced at P* with a gross redemption yield of Y*, and the interest rates on the market and required yield fell to Y1, then modified duration would estimate the price would rise to P1. The actual price rise would be greater, and would be captured by applying the convexity adjustment to increase the price rise to P1(c).

The following example shows how to calculate the Macaulay Duration, modified duration and convexity for a five year coupon bond.

Using this method of calculation it is also possible to show the sensitivity of the price of the bond to a certain predicted change of yield by applying the modified duration and convexity adjustment.

Calculation of Modified Duration and Convexity				
Bond Price from NPV of Cash Flows	£102.58	Yield To Maturity – YTM	8.00%	
Face Value	£100.00	Coupon Frequency	1	
Coupon Rate	9.00%	Life in Years	3	
Period	**Cash Flow**	**PV Cash Flow**	**Duration Calculation**	**Convexity Calculation**
		Cash Flow/ [(1+YTM/Coupon Frequency) ^ Period]	PV Cash Flow* Period	1/(1+YTM/Coupon Frequency) ^ 2 *PV Cash Flow* (Period ^ 2+Period)
0				
1	£9.00	£8.33	£8.33	£14.29
2	£9.00	£7.72	£15.43	£39.69
3	£109.00	£86.53	£259.58	£890.20
	Totals	£102.58	£283.35	£944.18
Macaulay Duration	2.7623 [Total Of Duration Calculation/Bond Price]/Coupon Frequency			
Modified Duration	2.5577 Macaulay Duration/[1+Yield To Maturity/Coupon Frequency]			
Convexity	9.2046 [Total Convexity Calculation/Bond Price]/(Coupon Frequency ^ 2)			

2.3 CORPORATE DEBT

LEARNING OBJECTIVE

1.2.3 Be able to calculate: simple interest income on corporate debt; conversion premiums on convertible bonds; flat yield; accrued interest given details of the day count conventions

Corporate debt is simply money that is borrowed by a company that has to be repaid. Generally, corporate debt also requires servicing by making regular interest payments. Corporate debt can be subdivided into money borrowed from banks via loans and overdrafts, and money borrowed directly from investors in the form of IOU instruments, typically bonds.

Debt finance is less expensive than equity finance because investing in debt finance is less risky than investing in the equity of the same company. The interest on debt has to be paid and is paid before dividends, so there is more certainty. Additionally, if the firm were to go into liquidation, the holders of debt finance would be paid back before the shareholders received anything.

For investors in bonds, firms like Standard and Poor's capture the comparative riskiness of the issuer and the bond in their credit ratings.

However, raising money via debt finance does present dangers to the issuing company. The lenders are often able to claim some or all of the assets of the firm in the event of non-compliance with the terms of the loan – in the same way that a bank providing mortgage finance would be able to claim the property as security against the loan.

2.3.1 Interest on Corporate Debt

Interest on bonds is calculated by reference to the coupon rate, coupon frequency and nominal value. As seen, the flat yield is calculated using the coupon rate and the bond's price.

EXAMPLE

For example, XYZ plc has issued bonds paying an annual 8% coupon and maturing in 2020. The bonds are currently priced at 106 – meaning investors have to pay £106 for each £100 of nominal value.

If an investor were to buy £5,000 nominal value, the bonds would cost £5,300 (£5,000 x 106/100). The interest income for the investor each year would be nominal value times the coupon rate – £5,000 x 8% = £400.

The flat yield for the investor would be the coupon divided by the price expressed as a percentage, ie, 8/106 x 100 = 7.55%

If the interest was paid semi-annually, then the annual payment would be split into two portions.

2.3.2 Convertible Bonds

Some corporates issue bonds with conversion rights, known as 'convertible' bonds. Convertible bonds give the holder of the bond the right, but not the obligation, to convert into a predetermined number of ordinary shares of the issuer. Given this choice, the holder will choose to convert into shares if, at maturity, the value of the shares they can convert into exceeds the redemption value of the bond. Because there is this upside potential to the value of a convertible bond if the share price rises, and the downside protection of the redemption value if the shares do not perform well, convertible bonds generally trade at a **premium** to their share value. The calculation of the premium is shown by the following example:

EXAMPLE

A convertible bond issued by XYZ plc is trading at £114. It offers the holder the option of converting £100 nominal into 25 shares. The shares of XYZ are currently trading at £3.90. To calculate the premium, first work out the share value of the conversion choice.

For £100 nominal value, that is £3.90 x 25 shares = £97.50.

The bond is trading at £114, so the premium in absolute terms is £114 – £97.50 = £16.50.

It is more usual to express it as a percentage of the conversion value:

(£16.50/£97.50) x 100 = 16.9%

EXERCISE 2

The convertible bonds issued by ABC plc are trading at £110. Each £100 nominal value offers the holder the option of converting into 15 ordinary ABC plc shares. The ordinary shares of ABC plc are currently trading at £6.40. What is the conversion premium, expressed in percentage terms?

The answer can be found at the end of this chapter.

Convertible bonds enable the holder to exploit the growth potential in the equity whilst retaining the safety net of the bond. It is for this reason that convertible bonds trade at a premium to the value of the shares they can convert into. If there were no premium, then there would be an arbitrage opportunity for investors to buy the shares more cheaply via the convertible than in the equity market.

Usually, convertible bonds are issued where the price of each share is set at the outset, and that price will be adjusted to take into account any subsequent bonus or rights issues. Given the share price, it is simple to calculate the conversion ratio – the number of shares that each £100 of nominal value of the bonds can convert into.

$$\text{Conversion ratio} = \frac{\text{Nominal value}}{\text{Conversion price of shares}}$$

EXAMPLE

£100 nominal value of a convertible bond is able to convert into shares at £4.46 each.

The conversion ratio is £100/£4.46 = 22.42 shares

If the issuing company has a 1 for 1 bonus issue, then the conversion price would halve and the conversion ratio would double.

2.3.3 Flat Yield

The simplest measure of the return used in the market is the flat (interest or running) yield. This measure looks at the annual cash return (coupon) generated by an investment as a percentage of the cash price. In simple terms, what is the regular annual return that you generate on the money that you invest?

The calculation of the flat or running yield is provided by the formula:

$$\text{Flat Yield} = \frac{\text{Annual Coupon Rate}}{\text{Market Price}}$$

The flat yield only considers the coupon and ignores the existence of any capital gain (or loss) through to redemption. As such, it is best suited to short-term investors in the bond, rather than those investors that might hold the bond through to its maturity and benefit from the gain (or suffer from the loss) at maturity.

Limitations of Flat Yield

There are three key drawbacks for using flat yield as a robust measure in assessing bond returns.

Since it only measures the coupon flows and ignores the redemption flows, when applicable, it is giving an incomplete perspective on the actual returns from the bond. A bond that has been purchased at a price away from redemption will be significantly undervalued when the par value is excluded from the calculation.

The calculation completely ignores the timing of any cash flows and, because there is no discounted cash flow analysis, the time value of money is completely overlooked.

With floating rate notes, the return in any one period will vary with interest rates. If the coupon is not a constant, then using a flat yield basis for measuring returns becomes an arbitrary matter of selecting which coupon amount, amongst many possible values, to use for the calculation.

2.3.4 Accrued Interest

Listed bond prices are **flat prices**, which do not include accrued interest. Most bonds pay interest semi-annually. For settlement dates when interest is paid, the bond price is equal to the flat price. Between payment dates, the price of the bond will be the flat price + the accrued interest. **Accrued interest** is the interest that has been earned, but not paid, and is calculated by the following formula:

$$\text{Accrued Interest} = \text{Coupon payment x} \frac{\text{Number of days since last payment}}{\text{Number of days between payments}}$$

The graphic below shows how the 'dirty' price (ie, the flat price plus accrued interest) of a bond fluctuates over the lifetime of the bond, in this case two years. The assumption made is that the flat price remains constant over the two years, but this would actually fluctuate with interest rates, and because of other factors. The flat price is what is listed in bond tables for prices. The accrued interest must be calculated according to the above formula. Note that the bond price steadily increases each day until reaching a peak the day before an interest payment, then drops to minimum immediately following the payment.

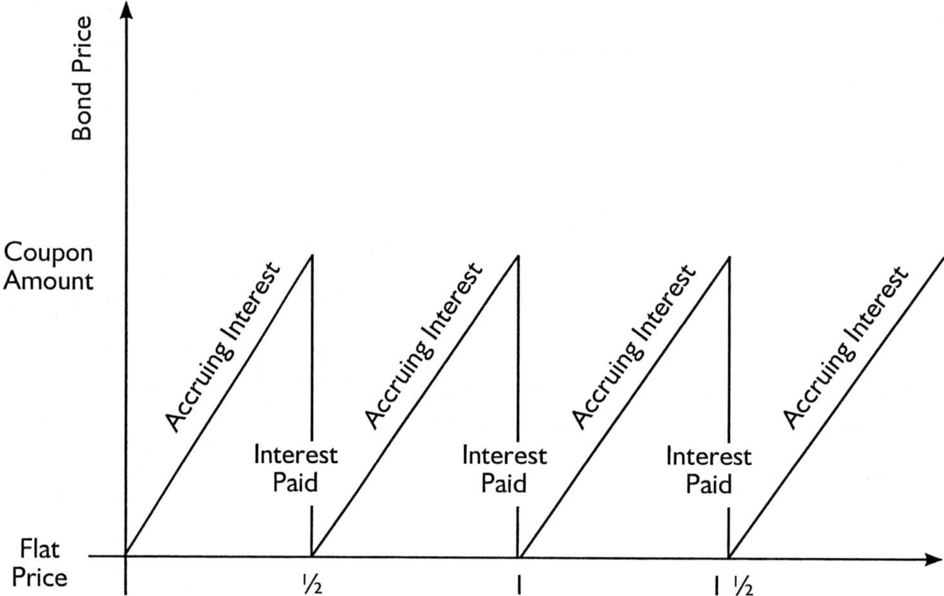

Calculating the Purchase Price for a Bond with Accrued Interest

EXAMPLE

An investor purchases a corporate bond with a settlement date on 15 September with a face value of £1,000 and a nominal yield of 8%, that has a listed price of 100.25, and that pays interest semi-annually on 15 February and 15 August. How much should the investor pay for the bond, or in other words what is its dirty price?

The semi-annual interest payment is £40 and there were 31 days since the last interest payment on 15 August. Assuming the settlement date fell on an interest payment date, the bond price would equal the listed price: 100.25 x £1,000.00 = £1,002.50.

Since the settlement date was 31 days after the last payment date, accrued interest must be added. Using the above formula, with 184 days between coupon payments, we find that:

$$\textbf{Accrued Interest} = £40 \text{ x } \frac{31}{184} = £6.74$$

Therefore, the actual purchase price for the bond will be £1,002.50 + £6.74 = £1,009.24.

Day Count Conventions

Historically, different day count conventions have evolved in calculating accrued interest to take into account of the fact that fixed income securities have different date of coupon payment characteristics, and to address issues related to the vagaries of the calendar system. The Julian calendar has uneven-length months and also has leap years where once every four years there are 366 days to a year rather than 365. This has given rise to a number of different ways of counting the intervals between payments and even the length in days of the year assumed in the calculations.

There is no central authority defining day count conventions, so there is no standard terminology. Certain terms, such as '30/360', 'Actual/Actual', and 'money market basis' must be understood in the context of the particular market. There has also been a move towards convergence in the marketplace, which has resulted in the number of conventions in use being reduced.

In the example just cited, the day count is what can be called Actual/Actual since the exact number of days between coupons and the actual days since the last payment have been used.

Other common day count conventions that affect the accrued interest calculation are:

- **Actual/360 (days per month, days per year)**
  Each month is treated normally and the year is assumed to be 360 days, eg, in a period from 1 February 2005 to 1 April 2005 T is considered to be 59 days divided by 360.

- **30/360**
  Each month is treated as having 30 days, so a period from 1 February 2005 to 1 April 2005 is considered to be 60 days. The year is considered to have 360 days. This convention is frequently chosen for ease of calculation: the payments tend to be regular and at predictable amounts.

- **Actual/365**
  Each month is treated normally, and the year is assumed to have 365 days, regardless of leap year status, eg, a period from 1 February 2005 to 1 April 2005 is considered to be 59 days. This convention results in periods having slightly different lengths.

- **Actual/Actual (ACT/ACT) – (1)**
  Each month is treated normally, and the year has the usual number of days, eg, a period from 1 February 2005 to 1 April 2005 is considered to be 59 days. In this convention leap years do affect the final result.

- **Actual/Actual (ACT/ACT) – (2)**
  Each month is treated normally, and the year is the number of days in the current coupon period multiplied by the number of coupons in a year, eg, if the coupon is payable 1 February and August then on 1 April 2005 the days in the year is 362, ie, 181 (the number of days between 1 February and 1 August 2005) x 2 (semi-annual).

2.4 SPREADS

LEARNING OBJECTIVE

1.2.4 Understand the concept of spreads and be able to convert spread over a government benchmark to a LIBOR-based spread

Commentators often refer to **spreads** in the bond markets. A spread is simply the difference between the yield available on one instrument and the yield available elsewhere. It is usually expressed in **basis points**, with each basis point representing 1/100 of 1%.

Spreads are commonly expressed as spreads over government bonds. For example, if a ten-year corporate bond is yielding 6% and the equivalent ten-year gilt is yielding 4.2%, the spread over the government bond is 6% – 4.2% = 1.8% or 180 basis points. This spread will vary, mainly as a result of the relative risk of the corporate bond compared to the gilt, so for a more risky corporate issuer the spread will be greater.

Spreads are also calculated against other benchmarks, such as the published interest rates represented by LIBOR (the London Inter-Bank Offered Rate). Because the government is less likely to default on its borrowings than the major banks (that provide the LIBOR rates), the spread of instruments versus LIBOR will generally be less than the spread against government bonds. If the equivalent LIBOR rate was 4.5%, the spread over LIBOR would be 6% – 4.5% = 1.5% or 150 basis points, compared to the 180 basis point spread over government bonds.

2.5 THE YIELD CURVE

LEARNING OBJECTIVE

1.2.5 Understand the role of the yield curve and the relationship between price and yield with reference to the yield curve (normal and inverted)

In the UK government bond market, there is a range of gilts available with various periods until maturity. By plotting the gross redemption yields of these gilts on a graph, with yields on the **Y** axis and time remaining on the **X** axis, a pattern emerges. The line of best fit across these points is the **yield curve**. It shows the yields available to investors in gilts over different time horizons. The yield curve provides a useful tool for comparison – eg, if ten-year gilts yield 4%, then a ten-year corporate bond should provide a higher yield to compensate investors for the additional default risk they face.

2.5.1 The Normal Yield Curve

Typically, the shape of the yield curve is upward sloping to the right, as shown in the following diagram:

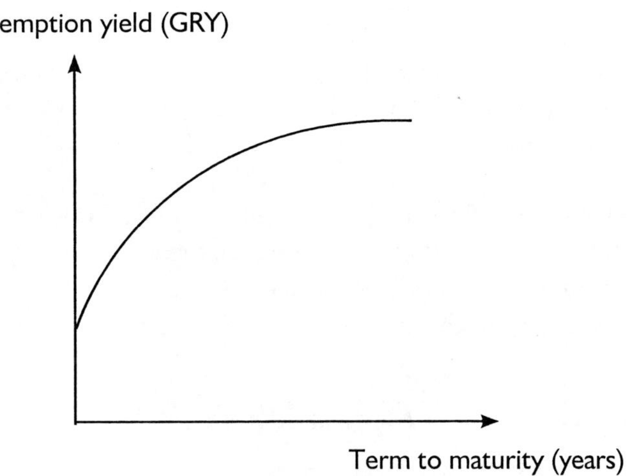

This is known as the normal yield curve, and its shape captures the fact that investors have a **liquidity preference**: they prefer more rather than less liquidity. As a result of this, they are willing to accept a lower yield on more liquid, short-dated gilts, and demand a higher yield on less liquid, longer-dated gilts. Given the same coupon rate, the price of a short-dated gilt will be higher than a longer-dated gilt, resulting in a higher yield for the longer-dated gilt than the equivalent shorter-dated gilt.

2.5.2 The Inverted Yield Curve

Occasionally, the yield curve may not exhibit its normal, upward sloping to the right shape. Instead, it might be downward sloping to the right, known as the inverted yield curve.

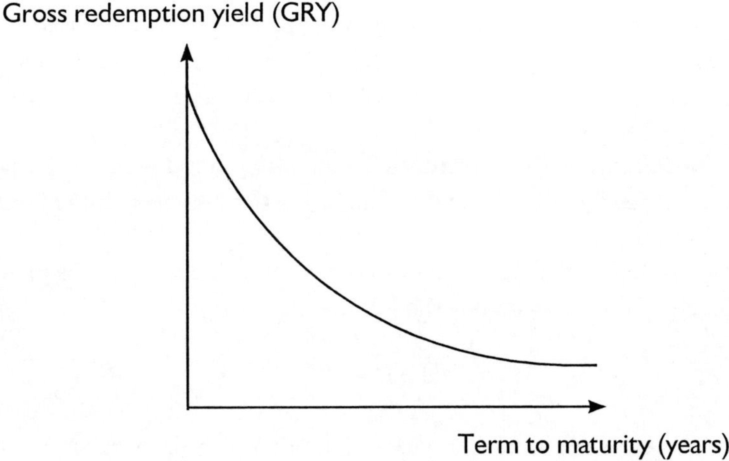

Clearly, in an inverted yield curve scenario, yields available on short-term gilts exceed those available on long-term gilts. This occurs when there is an expectation of a significant reduction in interest rates at some stage in the future. The consequence of this is that, when investing in longer-term gilts that will be outstanding when the interest rates fall, the investor is willing to accept a lower yield. For shorter-term gilts that will not be outstanding when the interest rate falls, the investor is demanding a higher yield.

The existence of an inverted yield curve does not remove any liquidity preference, but the impact of the anticipated interest rate fall outweighs the effect of the liquidity preference.

2.5.3 Inflation and the Yield Curve

Within the required yields on bonds is the investors' anticipation of inflation. If inflation is expected to increase, then the yields demanded by investors need to reward them for the anticipated inflation – so the yield curve would be expected to rise.

Paradoxically, when the Bank of England is concerned about inflationary pressures and increases short-term interest rates to counter the danger, the impact on medium and long-dated bonds can be that the yields fall. This is because the investors have confidence that, in the medium term, inflationary pressures will be removed by the pre-emptive actions of the Bank of England Monetary Policy Committee.

2.6 THE PRESENT VALUE OF A BOND

LEARNING OBJECTIVE

1.2.6 Be able to calculate the present value of a bond (maximum 2 years) with annual coupon and interest income

Money has a **time value**. That is, money deposited today will attract a rate of interest over the term it is invested. £100 invested today at an annual rate of interest of 5% becomes £105 in one year's time. The addition of this interest to the original sum invested acts as compensation to the depositor for forgoing £100 of consumption for one year.

The time value of money can also be illustrated by expressing the value of a sum receivable in the future in terms of its value today, again by taking account of the prevailing rate of interest. This is known as the sum's **present value**. So, £100 receivable in one year's time, given an interest rate of 5%, will be worth £100/1.05 = £95.24 today, in present value terms. This process of establishing present values is known as **discounting**, the interest rate in the calculation acting as the discount rate.

In other words, the value today, or the present value, of a lump sum due to be received on a specified future date can be established by discounting this amount by the prevailing rate of interest.

To arrive at the present value of a single sum, receivable after n years, when the prevailing rate of interest is r, simply multiply the lump sum by the following:

$$1/(1 + r)^n$$

Referring back to the earlier example, £100 receivable in one year's time, given an interest rate of 5%, would have a present value of:

$$£100 \times 1/(1+r)^n = £100 \times 1/(1+0.05)^1 = £100 \times 1/1.05 = £100 \times 0.9524 = £95.24$$

If £100 were due to be received in two years' time, then the present value would be:

$$£100 \times 1/(1+r)^2 = £100 \times 1/(1.05)^2 = £100 \times 1/1.1025 = £100 \times 0.907 = £90.70$$

The present value calculations can be used to derive the price of a bond, given the appropriate rate of interest and the cash flows.

EXAMPLE

Imagine £100 nominal of a two-year bond paying annual coupons of 10%. Given an appropriate rate of interest, the sum of the present values will provide the logical price for the bond.

Using an interest rate of 5% per annum, the following present values emerge:

Time	Cash flow	Discount factor	Present value
End of year one	£10	1/1.05	9.52
End of year two	£110	$1/1.05^2$	99.77
Sum of the individual present value = price of the bond			£109.29

EXERCISE 3

What would be the price of the bond if interest rates were:

(a) 6%?

(b) 4%?

The answers can be found at the end of this chapter.

3. GOVERNMENT DEBT

INTRODUCTION

Most developed countries have active markets for bonds issued by their government, eg, 'gilts' are bonds issued by the UK government. They are issued to cover the government's borrowing needs and the UK Treasury has created an executive agency called the Debt Management Office (DMO) to issue, service and manage gilts on its behalf.

As with other bonds, gilts are issued with a given nominal value that will be repaid at the bond's redemption date, and a coupon rate representing the percentage of the nominal value that will be paid to the holder of the bond each year. Obviously different gilts can have different redemption dates, and the coupon is payable at different points of the year (generally at semi-annual intervals).

EXAMPLE

Gilts are denoted by their coupon rate and their redemption date, for example 6% Treasury Stock 2028. The coupon indicates the cash payment per £100 nominal value that the holder will receive each year. This payment is made in two equal semi-annual payments on fixed dates, six months apart. An investor holding £1,000 nominal of 6% Treasury Stock 2028 will receive two coupon payments of £30 each, on 7 June and 7 December each year, until the repayment of the £1,000 on 7 December 2028.

3.1 CLASSES OF GOVERNMENT DEBT

LEARNING OBJECTIVE

1.3.1 Know the principal features and characteristics of the following classes of government debt: short-, medium-, long-dated; dual-dated; undated

Government debt, such as UK gilts, can be divided into three classes:

- Short-, medium- and long-dated;
- Dual-dated;
- Undated.

3.1.1 Short-, Medium- and Long-dated Gilts

These are the simplest form of UK government bonds and constitute the largest proportion of the gilts in issue. They are fixed coupon gilts with fixed redemption dates and are subdivided by the Debt Management Office into three, based on the period of time that remains until the gilt matures:

- Short – less than seven years to redemption;
- Medium – between seven and fifteen years to redemption;
- Long – over fifteen years to redemption.

For example, 6% Treasury Stock 2028 would be classified as a long-dated gilt because more than 15 years remain until it reaches its redemption date of 7 December 2028.

3.1.2 Dual-dated Gilts

These gilts have two specified redemption dates and the Debt Management Office can choose to repay the gilt at any point between the two dates. The maturity classification applied to dual-dated gilts is short-, medium- or long-dated depending upon the time remaining to the later of the two dates.

EXAMPLE

For example, 5% Treasury 2020–2024 would enable the DMO to choose to redeem the gilt at the earliest in 2020, and at any time up to the later date of 2024.

What would make the government redeem early or late?

The answer is dependent upon the interest rates at the time. If in 2020 the interest rate that the DMO would have to pay to provide the funds for redemption were only 4%, then it would redeem at the earliest point – saving 1% per annum. By contrast, if the interest rate were greater than 5%, the DMO would not redeem, potentially, until it was forced to in 2024.

3.1.3 Undated Gilts

There are a small number of gilts for which the redemption is at the discretion of the government. Examples include 3.5% War Loan and 2.5% Consolidated Loan Stock (commonly referred to as 2.5% Consol's). They are some of the oldest gilts outstanding and, because they all have comparatively low coupons, there is little incentive for the government to redeem them. On issue, these gilts did have a date attached to them, but it was followed by 'aft', meaning that it is the date on, or after, which the government can choose to redeem. If the government issued a gilt with a date of 2022 aft, it could choose to redeem the gilt at any stage after 2022, effectively making the gilt undated.

3.2 INTEREST RATES AND ACCRUED INTEREST

LEARNING OBJECTIVE

1.3.2 Understand the following features and characteristics of government debt: redemption price; interest payable; accrued interest; effect of changes in interest rates

As seen, government bonds such as UK gilts specify a redemption value (the nominal value of the bond) that will be repaid at the end of the bond's life and a coupon. The coupon is the amount of interest paid to the holder of the bond each year.

Gilts are quoted on the basis of the price a buyer would pay for £100 nominal value.

EXAMPLE

For example, Treasury 6% 2028 might be trading at 108, so a buyer would have to pay £108 for each £100 nominal value. Why would the buyer be willing to pay more than £100? The answer lies in the available interest rate across the financial markets. If the interest rate available on deposited funds were lower than the coupon rate on the gilt, then that gilt would be a relatively attractive investment and its price would be pushed upwards until the return it offered was in line with other investments.

As interest rates across the financial markets decrease, the quoted price of gilts will increase. Conversely, if interest rates increase, the quoted price of gilts will decrease. In summary, there is an inverse relationship between gilts prices and interest rates.

Bonds' quoted prices are **clean prices**, ie, they are exclusive of interest. If a gilt is purchased between interest payments, an adjustment is made to arrive at the amount of cash required to cover the interest element as well. This is known as the **accrued interest** and it is the amount of interest earned by the bond's seller since the last coupon payment. The price including the accrued interest is the **dirty price**.

Accrued interest is paid to compensate the seller for the period during which the seller has held the gilt, but for which they receive no interest from the bond's issuer. Having only held the gilt for part of the interest-earning period, the seller receives a pro-rata share of the next coupon from the purchaser.

EXAMPLE

If the £5,000 nominal of 6% Treasury 2028 mentioned above were sold by the original owner exactly halfway between the semi-annual coupon payments at a clean price of £126.46, the settlement would involve the following sum:

Clean price: £126.46 x £5,000/£100 = £6,323

Accrued interest: £5,000 x 6% x 6/12 x ½ = £75

Dirty price paid by the buyer to the seller = £6,398

The accrued interest in the gilts market is calculated using the **actual/actual day count convention**. In other words, the seller is compensated for the interest on the basis of the actual number of days that have elapsed since the last coupon was paid, divided by the total number of days in the actual period.

The DMO will pay the coupons to the registered holder of the gilt at each coupon payment date. However, because of the possibility of ownership changes just before the coupon payment date, there is a period prior to each coupon payment date when a gilt is dealt without entitlement to the impending coupon payment. This is known as the **ex-dividend** period. For most gilts this period is **seven working days** prior to the coupon payment date. For the remainder of the year the gilt is described as trading **cum-dividend.**

3.3 INDEX-LINKED DEBT

LEARNING OBJECTIVE

1.3.3 Understand the following features and characteristics of index-linked debt: index-linking; the retail price index and index-linking; effect of the index on price, interest and redemption; return during a period of zero inflation

Index-linked bonds (such as index-linked gilts) differ from conventional bonds in that the coupon payments and the principal are adjusted in line with a published index of price inflation, such as the UK Retail Prices Index (RPI). This means that both the coupons and the principal on redemption paid by these bonds are adjusted to take account of inflation since the bond's issue. Assuming inflation is positive, the nominal amount outstanding of an index-linked bond is less than the redemption value the government will pay on maturity.

To calculate the inflation adjustment, two index figures are required: that applicable to the stock when it was originally issued, and that relating to the current interest payment. For UK gilts, the RPI figures used are those applicable eight months before the relevant dates (eg, for a December coupon, the previous April RPI data is used). This indexation lag is required so that the size of each forthcoming interest payment is known at the start of the coupon period, thereby allowing accrued interest to be calculated.

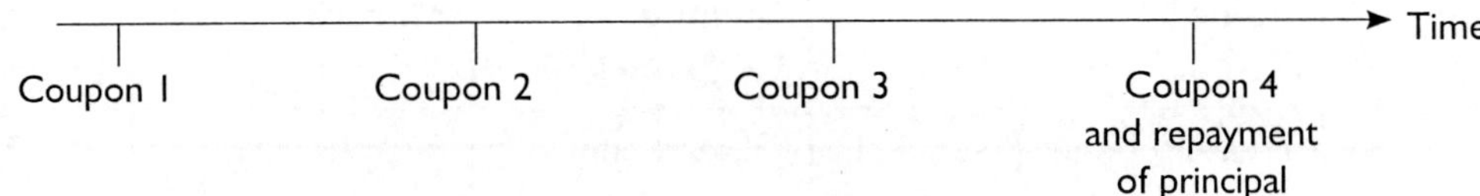

Each payment is uplifted by multiplying by:

$$\frac{\text{RPI 8 months previously}}{\text{RPI 8 months prior to issue}}$$

Every six months the coupon payment on an index-linked gilt consists of two elements:

- half of the annual real coupon; and
- an adjustment factor to uplift the real coupon to take into account inflation (as measured by RPI increases post-issue).

The uplifted redemption payment is calculated in a similar fashion, using the RPI eight months earlier and the RPI applicable to the original issue date.

EXAMPLE

A 2% index-linked 2035 pays semi-annual coupons on 26 January and 26 June each year. An investor holding £20,000 nominal will receive 2% of £20,000 x 6/12 = £200 each half-year plus the RPI uplift.

At the redemption date in 2035, the investor will receive £20,000 uplifted by the RPI increases since issue.

Because these bonds are uplifted by increases in the relevant price index, they are effectively inflation-proof. In times of inflation, they will increase in price and preserve the purchasing power of the investment.

In a period of zero inflation, index-linked bonds will pay the coupon rate with no uplift and simply pay back the nominal value at maturity.

3.4 INTERNATIONAL GOVERNMENT BONDS

LEARNING OBJECTIVE

1.3.4 Know the features and characteristics of French, German, Japanese and US bonds: settlement periods; coupons; terms and maturities

The following table highlights the way government bonds are referred to and classified across the major economies of the world, and the settlement period for any market transactions that might take place after the bonds are issued.

The coupon payment is the periodic payment that is made by the bond issuer to the bond holder, and the maturity represents the time period during which the coupon payments will be paid, at the conclusion of which the principal amount of the bond will be repaid to the holder.

Country	Name	Coupon Frequency	Maturity	Settlement Period
US	Treasury bonds (T-bonds)	semi-annual	over 10 years	T+1
	Treasury notes (T-notes)	semi-annual	2 to 10 years	T+1
	Treasury bills (T-bills)	no coupon paid	Less than 1 year	Trade date
France	OAT	annual	7 to 30 years	T+3
	BTAN	annual	2 to 5 years	
Germany	Bund	annual	over 10 years	T+3
	Bobl	annual	5 years	
	Schatz	annual	up to 2 years	
Japan	Japanese Government Bond (JGB)	semi-annual	long (10 years, most common), super-long (20 years)	T+3

4. CORPORATE DEBT

4.1 SECURED DEBT

LEARNING OBJECTIVE

1.4.1 Understand the principal features and uses of secured debt: fixed charges and floating charges; asset-backed securities; mortgage-backed securities; securitisation processes

Investors in corporate debt face the risk that the issuer will not be able to pay the interest and/or the principal amount. If this were to happen, it is known as default. One way for the corporate borrower to lessen the risk of default is to issue secured debt, where the debt offers the company's assets as a guarantee. There are two ways of doing this:

- **fixed charge** – the debt carries a fixed charge over a particular company asset, eg, a building;
- **floating charge** – the debt is secured against a group of the company's assets. In the event of default, a floating charge crystallises over the available assets.

Bonds issued with a fixed charge are generally referred to as 'debentures'.

4.1.1 Asset-Backed Securities

Asset-backed securities are bonds that are backed by a particular pool of assets. These assets can take several forms, such as mortgage loans, credit card receivables and car loans. The rock star David Bowie issued asset-backed securities on the future royalties that would be generated from his music.

The assets provide the bondholders' security, since the cash generated from them is used to service the bonds (pay the interest), and to repay the principal sum at maturity. Such arrangements are often referred to as the **securitisation** of assets. The name 'securitisation' reflects the fact that the resulting financial instruments used to obtain funds from the investors are considered, from a legal and trading point of view, as securities.

Diagrammatically:

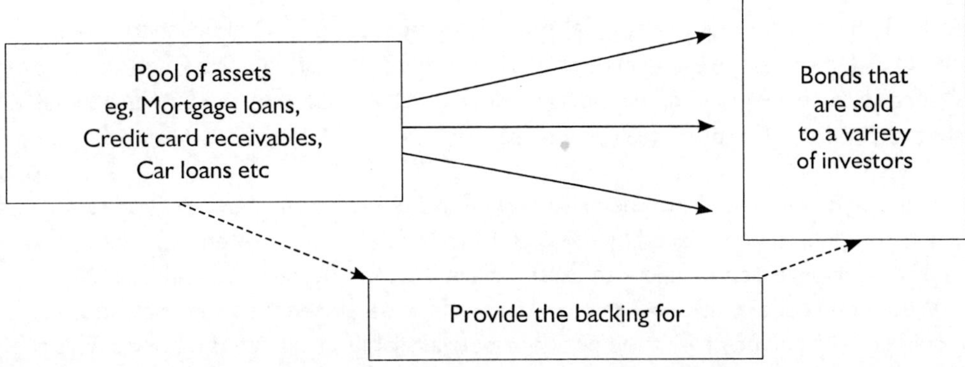

4.1.2 Mortgage-Backed Securities

Mortgage-backed securities are one example of asset-backed securities. They are created from mortgage loans made by financial institutions like banks and building societies. Mortgage-backed securities are bonds that are created when a group of mortgage loans are packaged (or pooled) for sale to investors. As the underlying mortgage loans are paid off by the homeowners, the investors receive payments of interest and principal.

The mortgage-backed securities market began in the US, where the majority of issues are made by (or guaranteed by) an agency of the US government. The Government National Mortgage Association (commonly referred to as 'Ginnie Mae'), the Federal National Mortgage Association ('Fannie Mae') and the Federal Home Loan Mortgage Corporation ('Freddie Mac') are the major issuers. These agencies buy qualifying mortgage loans, or guarantee pools of such loans originated by financial institutions, then they securitise the loans and issue bonds. Some private institutions, such as financial institutions and house builders, issue their own mortgage-backed securities.

As with other asset-backed securities, mortgage-backed securities issues are often subdivided into a variety of classes (or 'tranches'), each tranche having a particular priority in relation to interest and principal payments. Typically, as the underlying payments on the mortgage loans are collected, the interest on all tranches of the bonds is paid first. As loans are repaid, the principal is first paid back to the first tranche of bondholders, then the second tranche, third tranche, etc. Such arrangements will create different risk profiles and repayment schedules for each tranche, enabling the appropriate securities to be held according to the needs of the investor. Traditionally, the investors in such securities have been institutional investors, like insurance companies and pension funds, although some are attracting the more sophisticated individual investor.

4.1.3 Further Details in Relation to Asset-Backed Securities

As mentioned above, the investors in asset-backed securities have recourse to the pool of assets, although there may be an order of priority between investors in different tranches of the issue.

The precise payment dates for interest and principal will be dependent on the anticipated and actual payment stream generated by the underlying assets and the needs of investors. Asset-backed securities based on a pool of mortgage loans are likely to be longer-dated than those based on a pool of credit card receivables. Within these constraints, the issuers of asset-backed securities do create a variety of tranches to appeal to the differing maturity and risk appetites of investors.

Many asset-backed securities utilise a **special purpose vehicle** (or **SPV**) in order to lessen the default risk that investors face when investing in the securities. This SPV is often a trust, and the originator of the assets, such as the bank granting the mortgage loans, sells the loans to the SPV and the SPV issues the asset-backed bonds. This serves two purposes:

1. The SPV is a separate entity from the originator of the assets, so the assets leave the originator's financial statements to be replaced by the cash from the SPV. This is often described as an 'off balance sheet' arrangement because the assets have left the originator's balance sheet.
2. The SPV is a standalone entity, so if the originator of the assets were to suffer bankruptcy, the SPV would still remain intact with the pool of assets available to service the bonds. This is often described as 'bankruptcy remote' and enhances the creditworthiness of asset-backed securities, potentially giving them a higher rating than the originator of the assets.

Diagrammatically:

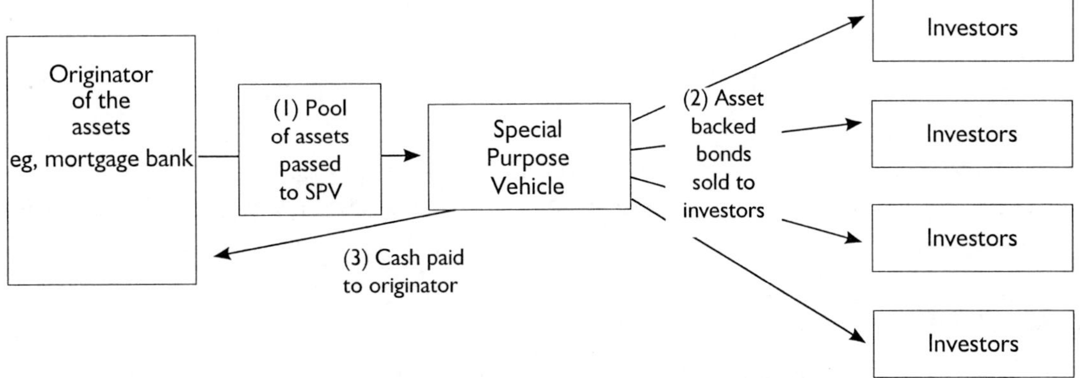

4.1.4 Role of Trustee in Secured Debt

LEARNING OBJECTIVE

1.4.2 Understand the role of the Trustee, rating agency, cash manager and servicer in a secured debt transaction

Trustee for Secured Debt Issues

In the UK a secured debt transaction is called a debenture, whereas the term is not so widely used in the US; the term 'asset-backed security' or ABS is more commonly used.

When a corporation either in the UK or US issues a secured debt, it is invariably the case that a trustee will be appointed when debenture stock is issued to a large number of persons.

The mechanics of the process are that, under the terms of the trust deed, the property of the company is mortgaged to the debenture holders to secure payment of the money owing under the debenture(s). However, there is a contract or deed of trust put in place between the company and the trustees. The trustee holds the benefit of the covenant by the company to repay the monies on trust for the holders of the debenture stock.

Under English law, the trustee has wide discretionary powers, whereas under US law its responsibilities are usually clearly defined. Below are the main trustee roles for a UK debenture trustee:

- **Note Trustee**
  The Note Trustee is appointed to represent the interests of holders of issues of securities, while providing guidance to the issuer.
- **Security Trustee**
  For issues secured by a pledge of securities or other properties, the security is charged in favour of the trustee for the benefit of the various secured parties. The governing documents dictate the order of priority of payments among the entitled parties.

- **Share Trustee**
  The share trustee holds the shares in an issuing Special Purpose Vehicle (SPV) in order to ensure off-balance-sheet treatment for the originator of the transaction. Sometimes these SPVs are domiciled in offshore jurisdictions.

- **Successor Trustee**
  This role played by a trustee is provided for banks which need to resign because of conflicts of interest (especially in connection with defaulted or bankrupt issues) on when work requirements exceed the bank's capacity.

Benefits of a Trust Deed

The security and all enforcement powers in respect of the trust deed are vested in the trustee as a single entity acting on behalf of all the debenture holders. This enables a coherent enforcement procedure rather than a series of disparate actions by different debenture holders. This is an advantage to the individual holders as it ensures organised action and parity of treatment. The trust deed would usually provide that all holders are paid proportionately and one action by the trustee prevents some holders recovering and not others. It is an advantage to the company as it means it does not have to defend a series of actions for what might be a trifling breach of any one provision.

Costs

Administration and enforcement by the trustee will be less costly than numerous parties dealing with the company.

Representation of the Interests of the Bondholders

To make bonds a marketable security, a trustee is assigned to represent the interests of the bondholders. The corporate trustee is usually a bank or a trust company, and, although the trustee is paid by the issuing corporation, the trustee represents the interests of the bondholders.

Before marketing a debenture the issuer, often using the corporate trustee as its agent, will engage the services of a credit rating agency to assess the creditworthiness of the issuer and the likelihood that all of the terms of the debenture offering are likely to be fulfilled. This engagement is to represent the interest of the bondholders as just stated above, but in this instance there is more cause for a potential conflict of interest, as the credit ratings agency will be paid by the issuer but its ratings are provided to advise the bondholders of the security risk of the offering. Credit ratings agencies will never specifically recommend any particular offering but the ratings which are provided (these are discussed in Section 4.3) are relied upon by many investors.

The corporate trustee must keep track of all bonds sold, verifying that the amount issued is not greater than what is stated in the indenture and making sure that the corporation complies with all covenants—which are the terms of the indenture—while the bond issue is outstanding.

For instance, the indenture may stipulate that the corporation maintain a certain percentage of assets over liabilities, or that the corporation does not take on too much debt. Adherence to the covenants of the indenture is one of the principal roles of the trustee.

The trustee may either provide services for the payment of dividends and the cash management function or it may appoint a separate custodian for the purpose.

4.2 UNSECURED DEBT

LEARNING OBJECTIVE

1.4.3 Understand the principal features and uses of unsecured debt: subordinated; guaranteed; convertible bonds

Unsecured debt is not secured against any of the company's assets, so the holder has no special protection against default. To compensate the holder for the additional risk, the coupon on an unsecured bond, or the interest on unsecured bank borrowing, will be higher than on equivalent secured borrowings.

Subordinated debt is not secured and the lenders have agreed that, if the company fails, they will only be reimbursed when other creditors have been paid back, and then only if there is enough money left over. Interest payments on subordinated borrowings will be higher than those on equivalent unsecured borrowings that are not subordinated. This is simply because of the additional default risk faced by subordinated lenders.

Guaranteed debt is where a guarantee is provided by someone other than the issuer. The guarantor is typically the parent company, or another company in the same group of companies as the issuer.

As seen earlier, **convertible bonds** give the holder of the bond the right, but not the obligation, to convert into a predetermined number of ordinary shares of the issuer.

The following table summarises the characteristics of subordinated, guaranteed and convertible bonds as compared to an unsecured bond issued by the same company:

	Subordinated bond	**Guaranteed bond**	**Convertible bond**
Normal life	No difference: Typically seven to 30 years to maturity		
Ranking in a liquidation	Below unsecured bonds	Alongside other unsecured bonds	Alongside other unsecured bonds
Risk and rating	Greater risk of default, so a lower credit rating	Risk dependent upon the guarantors own financial standing, so a higher credit rating	No difference to unsecured bonds
Coupon	Likely to be higher than unsecured bonds	Likely to be lower due to the guarantee	Potentially lower due to the upside potential of the share price
Benefits to the issuer	Attractive regulatory treatment for financial institution issuers	Guarantor is lowering the cost of the debt finance	Upside potential of the shares restricts the cost of the debt and the possibility of conversion lowers the risk of eventual repayment

Fixed-coupon bonds are issued with a fixed rate of coupon. If interest rates rise, the fixed coupon becomes less attractive and the price of the bond falls. The opposite is true of an interest rate fall. As for government bonds, the interest is always calculated by reference to the nominal value of the bond, so a £1,000 nominal 5% ABC corporate bond will pay £50 per annum to the holder.

Floating rate bonds are bonds where the coupon rate varies. The rate is adjusted in line with published, market interest rates. The published interest rates that are normally used are based on London Inter-Bank Offered Rates (LIBOR). LIBORs are the average rates at which banks in London offer loans to other banks. The British Bankers' Association (BBA) publishes LIBORs for different currencies and time periods each day. Typically, a margin is added to the LIBOR rate, measured in basis points, each basis point representing one hundredth of one percent. A corporate issuer may offer floating rate bonds to investors at 3-month sterling LIBOR plus 75 basis points. If LIBOR were at 4%, then the coupon paid would be 4.75%, with the additional 75 basis points compensating the investor for the higher risk of payment default.

4.3 CREDIT RATINGS

LEARNING OBJECTIVE

1.4.4 Understand the principal features and uses of credit ratings: rating agencies; impact on price; use of credit enhancements; difference between investment grade and sub-investment grade bonds

Bondholders face the risk that the issuer of the bond might default on their obligation to pay interest and the principal amount at redemption. This so-called 'credit risk' – the probability of an issuer defaulting on their payment obligations and the extent of the resulting loss – can be assessed by reference to the independent credit ratings given to most bond issues.

The three most prominent credit rating agencies that provide these ratings are Standard & Poor's, Moody's and Fitch. Bond issues subject to credit ratings can be divided into two distinct categories: those accorded an investment grade rating and those categorised as non-investment grade or speculative. The latter are also known as 'high-yield' or 'junk' bonds. Investment grade issues offer the greatest liquidity. The table below provides a comprehensive survey of the credit ratings available from the three agencies.

Although the three rating agencies use similar methods to rate issuers and individual bond issues, essentially by assessing whether the cash flow likely to be generated by the borrower will comfortably service, and ultimately repay, its debts, the rating each gives often differs, though not usually significantly so.

Moody's	S&P	Fitch	Description
Aaa	AAA	AAA	Prime
Aa1	AA+	AA+	
Aa2	AA	AA	High grade
Aa3	AA–	AA–	
A1	A+	A+	
A2	A	A	Upper medium grade
A3	A–	A–	
Baa1	BBB+	BBB+	
Baa2	BBB+	BBB+	Lower medium grade
Baa3	BBB–	BBB–	
Ba1	BB+	BB+	Non-investment grade
Ba2	BB	BB	Speculative
Ba3	BB–	BB–	
B1	B+	B+	
B2	B	B	Highly speculative
B3	B–	B–	
Caa1	CCC+		Substantial risks
Caa2	CCC		Extremely speculative
Caa3	CCC–	CCC	In default with little prospect for recovery
Ca	CC		
	C		
C		DDD	
	D		In default

Occasionally, issues such as asset-backed securities are credit-enhanced in some way to gain a higher credit rating. The simplest method of achieving this is through some form of insurance scheme that will pay out should the pool of assets be insufficient to service or repay the debt.

In 2007/2008 a financial crisis arose from asset-backed securities such as mortgage-backed securities (MBSs). The credit ratings agencies were criticised for the generous ratings they had attached to some of these securities. As a result, it is likely that there will be increased regulatory oversight of the credit rating process in the future.

4.4 COMMERCIAL PAPER

LEARNING OBJECTIVE

1.4.5 Know the principal features and uses of Commercial Paper: issuers, including CP Programmes; investors; discount security; unsecured; asset-backed; rating; normal life, method of issuance; role of dealer

Zero coupon bonds pay no interest. Instead, they promise to pay just the nominal value at redemption. Because there is no other possible form of return, investors will pay less than the nominal value when they buy zero coupon bonds, with their return coming in the form of the difference between the price they pay for the bond and the amount they receive when the bond is redeemed. The bond is said to be issued at a discount to its face value, with the discount providing all of the return on a zero coupon bond.

Discount securities, such as zero coupon bonds, are attractive investments for an investor looking for a fixed sum at some set date in the future. Because the investor is looking for a set, single sum, he does not want to worry about reinvesting regular interest payments.

Commercial paper is a money market instrument, issued by a company. The money market is the term for the market involving cash deposits and short-term instruments that are issued with less than one year to their maturity. Commercial paper is the corporate equivalent of a government's Treasury bill. Commercial paper is issued at a discount to its nominal value and can have a maturity of up to one year in Europe and 270 days in the USA; however, it is common to find in both territories that commercial paper will be issued for three months.

Large companies issue commercial paper to assist in the management of their liquidity. Rather than borrowing directly from banks, these large entities run commercial paper programmes that are placed with institutional investors.

The various companies' commercial paper is differentiated by credit ratings – where the large credit rating agencies assess the stability of the issuer.

Asset-backed commercial paper is a short-term investment vehicle with a maturity that is typically between 90 and 180 days. The security itself will be issued by a bank or other financial institution, and the notes are backed by physical assets such as trade receivables.

Finance companies will typically provide consumers with home loans, unsecured personal loans and retail automobile loans. These receivables are then used by the finance company as collateral for raising money in the commercial paper market. Some finance companies are wholly owned subsidiaries of industrial firms that provide financing for purchases of the parent firm's products.

A major activity of General Motors Acceptance Corporation (GMAC) is the financing of purchases and leases of General Motors' vehicles by dealers and consumers.

It is perhaps important to mention that a missed payment by an issuer of a commercial paper for as little as one day can lead to bankruptcy proceedings. Issuers take great care to repay the principal on the due day.

Commercial Paper Issuance and Role of Dealers

There are two methods of issuing commercial paper. The issuer can market the securities directly to a buy and hold investor such as most money market funds. Alternatively, it can sell the paper to a dealer, who then sells the paper in the market. The dealer market for commercial paper involves large investment banks and other financial services firms such as gilt dealers and other participants in the money markets.

Unlike bonds or other forms of long-term indebtedness, a commercial paper issuance is not all brought to market at once. Instead, an issuer will maintain an ongoing commercial paper programme. It advertises the rates at which it is willing to issue paper for various terms, so buyers can purchase the paper whenever they have funds to invest. Programmes may be promoted by dealers, in which case the paper is called dealer paper. Larger issuers, especially finance companies, have the market presence to issue their paper directly to investors. Their paper is called **direct paper**.

Direct issuers of commercial paper are usually financial companies that have frequent and sizeable borrowing needs and find it more economical to sell paper without the use of an intermediary. In the US, direct issuers save a dealer fee of approximately 5 basis points, or 0.05% annualised, which translates to $50,000 on every $100 million outstanding. This saving compensates for the cost of maintaining a permanent sales staff to market the paper. Dealer fees tend to be lower outside the US.

Commercial paper entails credit risk, and programmes are rated by the major rating agencies. Because commercial paper is a rolling form of debt, with new issues generally funding the retirement of old issues, the main risk is that the issuer will not be able to issue new commercial paper. This is called **rollover risk**. Many issuers obtain credit enhancements for their programmes. These may include a line of credit or other alternative source of financing.

Since the banking crisis of 2008, the primary issuance of commercial paper and the secondary market for commercial paper have been severely curtailed, and it has been difficult to persuade dealers to 'make a market' in commercial paper.

5. MONEY MARKETS

LEARNING OBJECTIVE

1.5.1 Understand the features and characteristics of Treasury bills: issuer; purpose of issue; minimum denomination; normal life; no coupon and redemption at par; redemption

As well as issuing bonds to fund the government's long-term borrowing needs, developed countries also manage the liquidity needs of the government. This is done primarily through issuing short-term IOUs known as '**Treasury bills**'.

5.1 DEFINITION, USES AND PRINCIPAL FEATURES

Treasury bills (T-bills) are short-term loan instruments, guaranteed by the government, with a maturity date of less than one year at issue. Generally, they are issued with either one month (28 days), three months (91 days) or six months (182 days) to redemption, with the three month T-bill the most common. They pay no coupon, and consequently are issued at a discount to their nominal value, the discount representing the return available to the investor.

In the UK, Treasury bills are issued at weekly auctions, known as 'tenders', held by the DMO at the end of the week (usually a Friday). These tenders are open to bids from a group of eligible bidders which include all of the major banks. The bids are tendered competitively – only those bidding a high enough price will be allocated any Treasury bills and they will pay the price that they bid. The bids must be for a minimum of £500,000 nominal of the Treasury bills, and above this level bids must be made in multiples of £50,000. In subsequent trading, the minimum denomination of T-bills is £25,000.

Since they are guaranteed by the government, Treasury bills provide a very secure investment for market participants with short-term investment horizons. The return on a Treasury bill is wholly dependent upon the price paid.

For example, if a purchaser paid £990,000 for £1,000,000 nominal of a three-month Treasury bill, the return will be the gain made of £10,000. As a percentage of invested funds the return is: £10,000/£990,000 x 100 = 1.01% over three months.

5.2 REPO MARKETS

LEARNING OBJECTIVE

1.5.2 Understand the basic purpose and characteristics of the repo markets: sale and repurchase at agreed price, rate and date; reverse repo – purchase and resale at agreed price and date; documentation; benefits of the repo market

A repo is a **sale and repurchase agreement**. It is legally binding for both buyer and seller. For example, a gilt repo is a contract in which the seller of gilts agrees to buy them back at a future specified time and price. In effect, a gilt repo is a means of borrowing using the gilt as security, as illustrated in the following diagram:

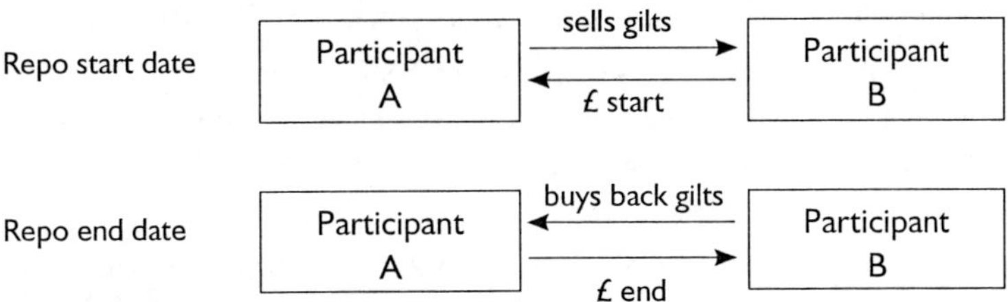

In the above diagram, both parts of the repo transaction are agreed between the participants at the outset: Participant A has entered into a repo transaction, Participant B has entered into a 'reverse repo' agreement.

The amount of cash paid over by Participant B at the start of the repo will be less than the amount paid over to Participant B at the end of the repo period. The difference between the two amounts, expressed as a percentage, is the effective interest rate on the repo transaction. It is usually referred to as the 'repo rate'.

The obvious benefit to Participant A is that they are able to raise finance against the security of the gilts that they hold – potentially a relatively cheap source of short-term finance. If Participant B is considered a conventional bank simply providing finance, then the benefit of using the repo is the security gained by holding the gilts. However, Participant B may be a Gilt Edged Market Maker (GEMM) that has sold gilts that it does not hold. The repo transaction enables the GEMM to access the gilts that it requires to meet its settlement obligations. In this way, gilt repo facilitates the smooth running of the secondary market in gilts.

The smooth running of the gilts market is further assisted by the DMO's 'Standing Repo Facility'. This enables any GEMM, or other DMO counterparty, to enter into a reverse repo arrangement with the DMO, perhaps to cover a short position in gilts. They must first sign the relevant documentation provided by the DMO and then are able to request any amount of a gilt above £5 million nominal. This facility is for next-day settlement, and the facility can be rolled forwards for up to two weeks. The DMO does charge a slightly higher than normal repo rate for firms accessing the Standing Repo Facility.

Although the gilt market has been used as an example, it should be noted that the use of repos is an important liquidity provider for the debt markets as a whole.

6. EUROBONDS

6.1 PRINCIPAL FEATURES AND USES

LEARNING OBJECTIVE

1.6.1 Understand the principal features and uses of Eurobonds: issued through syndicates of international banks; concept of continuous pure bearer; immobilised in depositories; ex-interest date; accrued interest; interest payments

Essentially, Eurobonds are international bond issues. They are a way for an organisation to issue debt without being restricted to their own domestic market. They are generally issued via a syndicate of international banks. Generally, Eurobond issuers do not keep a record of the holders of their bonds; the certificates themselves are all that is needed to prove ownership. This is the concept of bearer documents, where the holder of the certificates (the bearer) has all the rights attached to ownership. Eurobonds are issued in bearer form and, because they are issued internationally, they are largely free of national regulation. Eurobonds have been innovative in their structure to accommodate the needs of issuers and investors. There are 'plain vanilla', fixed coupon bonds that normally pay the coupons once a year. Additionally, there are zero-coupon bonds and other forms of eurobond such as floating rate bonds and bonds with coupons that increase over time ('stepped bonds').

An absence of national regulation means that Eurobonds can pay interest gross, making the buyer responsible for paying their own tax and avoiding 'withholding tax' (tax being withheld in the country of origin). Initially, Eurobonds were aimed at wealthy individuals, but as the market has grown they have increasingly become investments held by institutional investors.

As bearer documents, it is important that Eurobonds are kept safe, and this is often achieved by holding the bonds in depositaries, particularly those maintained by Euroclear and Clearstream. When the bonds are deposited in these organisations they are described as being 'immobilised'. Immobilisation does not mean that the bonds cannot be transferred in secondary market transactions, it simply means that the bonds are safely held within a reputable depositary and a buyer is likely to retain the bonds in their immobilised form.

As the Eurobond market has grown, a self-regulatory organisation has been formed that oversees the market and its participants – the International Capital Market Association (ICMA).

Settlement and accrued interest conventions have been established for the secondary market. Settlement is on a 'T+3' basis and accrued interest is calculated on the basis of 30 days per month and 360 days per year ('30/360' basis).

The following table highlights the major features of Eurobonds:

Feature	Detail
Form	Bearer
Interest payments	Gross
Tax	Taxable but untaxed at source
Trades matched through	TRAX system
Trades settled through	Euroclear or Clearstream
Settlement period	Trade day plus three
Trading mechanism	Over-the-counter (OTC)

7. OTHER SECURITIES

7.1 DEPOSITARY RECEIPTS

LEARNING OBJECTIVE

1.7.1 Know the principal features and characteristics of Depositary Receipts: American Depositary Receipts; Global Depositary Receipts; transferability; means of creation including pre-release facility; how registered; rights attached; dividends; transfer to underlying shares

Depositary Receipts (DRs) come in two broad forms – American Depositary Receipts (ADRs) and Global Depositary Receipts (GDRs).

The US is a huge pool of potential investment. Therefore, substantial non-US companies may want to attract US investors to raise funds. **American Depositary Receipts** (ADRs) facilitate this process; indeed, they were created to make it easier for Americans to invest in overseas companies. **Global Depositary Receipts** (GDRs) are depositary receipts that are identical to ADRs, except that they are marketed to appeal to a broader base of investors, some of whom may be based outside America. Both ADRs and GDRs are negotiable certificates evidencing ownership of shares in a corporation from a country outside the US. Each DR has a particular number of underlying shares, or is represented by a fraction of an underlying share.

EXAMPLE

Volkswagen AG (the motor vehicle manufacturer) is listed in Frankfurt. It has two classes of shares listed – ordinary shares and preference shares. There are separate ADRs in existence for the ordinary shares and preference shares. Each ADR represents 0.2 individual Volkswagen shares.

DRs are typically created (or 'sponsored') by the foreign corporation (Volkswagen in the above example). They will liaise with an investment bank regarding the precise structure of the DR, such as the number or fraction of shares represented by each DR. A 'depositary' bank will then accept a certain number of underlying shares from the issuer, create the DRs to represent the shares and make these DRs available to US, and potentially other, investors, probably via local brokers. This creation process for an ADR is illustrated by the following diagram:

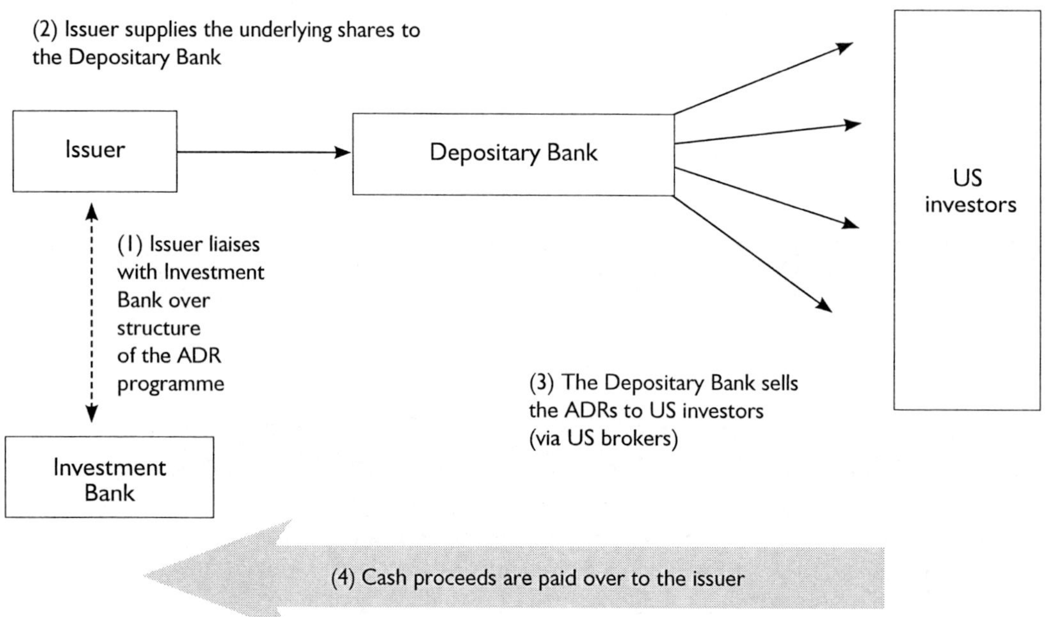

One characteristic of DRs that must also be considered is **pre-release trading** (or **grey market trading**). When an DR is being created, the depositary bank receives notification that, in the future, the shares will be placed on deposit. As long as the depositary bank holds cash collateral, even though the shares are not yet on deposit, the depositary bank can create and sell the receipt (the DR) at this time. Effectively, investors are buying a receipt that entitles them to all the benefits of a share that will, in the future, be held on deposit for them. The DR can be treated in this way for up to three months before the actual purchase of the underlying shares.

The shares underlying the DR are registered in the name of the depositary bank, with the DRs themselves transferable as bearer securities. The DRs are typically quoted and traded in US dollars and are governed by the trading and settlement procedures of the market on which they are traded.

The **depositary bank** acts as a go-between for the investor and the company. When the company pays a dividend, it is paid in the company's domestic currency to the bank, which then converts the dividend into dollars and passes it on to the DR holders. The US investor therefore need not concern himself with currency movements. Furthermore, when an DR holder decides to sell, his DRs will be sold on in dollars. This removal of the need for any currency transactions for the US investor is a key attraction of the DR.

DR holders are entitled to vote, just like ordinary shareholders, only the votes will be exercised via the depositary bank.

If the DR represented a UK company's shares, there are tax ramifications in the form of **stamp duty**. The UK tax authority, Her Majesty's Revenue & Customs (HMRC, formerly the Inland Revenue) levies a tax known as stamp duty on share purchases, at 0.5% of the price paid to purchase shares.

However, because DRs may trade outside the UK, in the US, there is **no stamp duty charged on the purchase of a DR**. Instead, HMRC charges a **one-off fee for stamp duty of 1.5%**, when the DR is created.

If an investor wanted to sell his DRs, he could do so either by selling them to another investor as a DR, or by selling the underlying shares in the home market of the company concerned. The latter route would involve cancelling the DR by delivering the certificates to the depositary bank. The depositary bank would then release the appropriate number of shares in accordance with the instructions received.

7.2 WARRANTS

LEARNING OBJECTIVE

1.7.2 Know the rights, uses and differences between warrants and covered warrants: benefit to the issuing company and purpose; issuer; right to subscribe for capital; effect on price of maturity and the underlying security; detachability; exercise and expiry; the calculation of the conversion premium (discount) on a warrant (warrant price plus exercise price minus the share price)

Traditionally, a warrant is an instrument issued by a company that allows the holder to subscribe for shares in that company at a fixed price over a fixed period. A typical warrant might have a life of several years.

Warrants are listed and traded on stock exchanges. If the holder decides to exercise, the company will issue new shares.

EXAMPLE

Warrants are available in a (fictional) investment company, Cambridge Investment Trust plc. Cambridge Investment Trust plc shares are currently trading at 77p each, and warrants are available giving the investor the right to buy shares at £1 each, up until 2010. The warrants are trading at 4p each.

In the above example, the warrant's 'expiry' date is in 2010 and its 'exercise price' is 100p.

What are the advantages to the company, such as the fictional Cambridge Investment Trust plc encountered above, that persuade them to issue warrants? Clearly, the sale of warrants for cash will raise money for the company, and if the warrants are exercised, then further capital will be raised by the company. Similarly to call options, holding the warrant does not entitle the investor to receive dividends or to vote at company meetings, so the capital raised until the warrant is exercised could be considered as free.

Obviously warrants offer a highly geared investment opportunity for the investor, and warrants are often issued alongside other investments, rather than sold in their own right.

EXAMPLE

CBC plc is attempting to raise finance by issuing bonds. Their advisors inform them that they could issue bonds paying a coupon of 6% pa, or lower it to 5% pa if they give away a single warrant with each £100 nominal of the bonds. The warrants are detachable from the bonds – in other words, the investors could decide to sell their warrants or keep them, regardless of whether they retain the bonds.

Another type of warrant is a covered warrant. These are warrants issued by firms (usually investment banks), rather than the company whose shares the warrant enables the investor to buy. They are offered in the form of call warrants (giving the investor the right to buy), or put warrants (giving the investor the right to sell). In the UK, covered warrants are traded on the London Stock Exchange.

7.2.1 Warrant Price Behaviour

Warrants (including covered warrants) are highly geared investments. A modest outlay can result in a large gain, but the investor can lose the value of his/her entire stake in the warrant Their value is driven by the length of time for which they are valid (their 'maturity' or period until expiry) and the value of the underlying security.

There is a relatively simple method of looking at the price of one warrant relative to other warrants – using the **conversion premium**. The conversion premium is the price of the warrant plus the exercise price required to buy the underlying share less the prevailing share price.

For example, calculating the conversion premium for the Cambridge Investment Trust encountered above:

Warrant price	=	4p
Plus exercise price	=	100p
Less share price	=	77p
Conversion premium	=	27p

Note that if the resultant figure was a negative, the warrant would be trading at a 'conversion discount'.

8. FOREIGN EXCHANGE

8.1 INTRODUCTION

LEARNING OBJECTIVE

1.8.1 Know the principal features and uses of spot, forward and cross rates: quotation as bid-offer spreads; forwards quoted as bid-offer margins against the spot; quotation of cross rates

The foreign exchange market (or 'forex' or 'FX') is the collective way of describing all the transactions in which one currency is exchanged for another, anywhere in the world. There is no physical exchange for the currency market in London, it is purely **over-the-counter (OTC)** and dominated by the banks.

There are two types of transaction conducted on the foreign exchange market:

- **spot transactions** are immediate currency deals that are settled within two working days;
- **forward transactions** involve currency deals that are agreed for a future date at a rate of exchange fixed now.

As we will see in the next section, both spot and forward rates are quoted by dealers in the form of a buying rate (the bid) and a selling rate (the offer). The spread between these two prices enables the foreign exchange dealer to make a profit.

The users of the foreign exchange market fall into two broad camps.

First, the foreign exchange transactions driven by international trade. If a Japanese company sells goods to a US customer, they might invoice the transaction in US dollars. These dollars will need to be exchanged for Japanese yen by the Japanese company and this is the foreign exchange transaction. The Japanese company may not be expecting to receive the dollars for a month after submission of the invoice. This gives them two choices:

i. They could wait until they receive the dollars and then execute a 'spot' transaction.
ii. They could enter into a forward transaction to sell the dollars for yen in a month's time. This would provide them with certainty as to the amount of yen they will receive and assist in their budgeting efforts.

The second reason for foreign exchange transactions is for speculative transactions. If an investor felt that the US dollar was likely to weaken against the euro, he could buy euros in either the spot or forward market to profit if he is right.

Generally, exchange rates around the world are quoted against the US dollar. A **cross rate** is any foreign currency rate that does not include the US dollar, eg, the GBP/JPY (Great Britain pound/ Japanese yen) is a cross rate. Obviously such a cross rate will be of particular interest to companies doing international business between the constituent countries, eg, a UK company selling goods or services to Japanese consumers, and receiving payment in yen.

8.2 SPOT AND FORWARD TRANSACTIONS

LEARNING OBJECTIVE

1.8.2 Be able to calculate spot and forward settlement prices using: premiums or discounts; interest rate parity

A typical sterling/dollar spot quote might look something like this:

GBP\USD spot rate 1.8055–1.8145

Buyer's rate: £1 buys $1.8055
Seller's rate: $1.8145 buys £1

The buyer's rate and seller's rate refer to buying and selling dollars respectively. The difference between the buyer's and seller's rates is generally referred to as the bid-offer spread. It enables the bank offering the deals to make money.

How much would an investor expect to get if the above spot rate is applied? If the investor wanted to sell $50,000 for pounds sterling, he would get £27,556. This is based on the seller's rate of $1.8145:£1.

EXERCISE 4

Using the same spot rates as above:

i. How much would Mr A receive in £s for $100,000?

ii. How much would Mr X receive in $s for £70,000?

The answers can be found at the end of this chapter.

The forward market is almost exactly the same as the spot market, except that currency deals are agreed for a future date, but at a rate of exchange fixed now. These rates of exchange are not directly quoted. Instead, quotes on the forward market state how much must be added to, or subtracted from, the present spot rate.

For example, the three month GBP/USD quote might be as follows:

spot $1.805 –$1.8145

three month forward 1.00–0.97c pm

pm stands for **premium**. It is used when the dollar is going to be more expensive relative to £ sterling in the future. It is deducted from the quoted spot rate in order to arrive at the forward rate. So your £1 will buy fewer dollars in three months' time and if you have dollars in three months' time, the bank will sell you more £ sterling per dollar than they will now. The premium is quoted in cents, unlike the spot rate, which is quoted in dollars. So 1.00 pm is a premium of 1 cent or 0.01 dollars. And 0.97 pm is a premium of 0.97 cents or 0.0097 dollars.

The three-month forward quote is, therefore:

three-month forward $1.7955–$1.8048

Alternatively the three-month forward rate might exhibit a discount, rather than a premium, for example:

spot 1.8055–1.8145

three-month forward 0.79–0.82c dis

dis stands for **discount**. The discount is used when the dollar is going to be cheaper relative to £ sterling in the future. It needs to be added to the quoted spot rate to arrive at the forward rate. £1 will buy more dollars in three months' time and, if you have dollars in three months' time, the bank will sell you less £ sterling per dollar than they will now. The three month forward quote is therefore:

three-month forward $1.8134–$1.8227

EXERCISE 5

i. Using the same spot rate of $1.8055–$1.8145, what would the one-year forward rate be given the following:

one-year forward 3.98–3.85c pm

ii. How many dollars would an investor receive in a year's time, if he were to agree to sell £1m in a one year forward transaction?

The answers can be found at the end of this chapter.

8.2.1 Interest Rate Parity

The quoted forward rate premium or discount is not a random view of where the market thinks the exchange rate will be in the future. It is driven by its relationship with interest rates available for deposits and borrowings in the respective currencies. If the so-called 'interest rate parity' relationship does not hold, then there is a potential for arbitrageurs to exploit the forward rates to make guaranteed profits.

This is best illustrated by looking at the following:

EXAMPLE

The spot rate between US dollars and £ sterling is currently £1 equivalent to $1.80 (ignoring the bid-offer spread). The annual interest rate available for borrowing or depositing cash is 2% in the US and 4.5% in the UK. What is the one-year forward rate?

The forward rate should be based on the spot rate ($1.80 = £1), adjusted for the interest rates.

$1.80 now attracts interest at 2% pa, so in a year it will become $1.80 x 1.02 = $1.836.

£1 now attracts interest at 4.5% pa, so in a year it will become £1.00 x 1.045 = £1.045.

The forward rate should be based on $1.836 being equivalent to £1.045, or 1.836/1.045 = $1.757 per £1.

If the forward rate were not at this level, then arbitrageurs could exploit the inequality between spot, interest rates and forward rates.

9. PRIME BROKERAGE AND EQUITY FINANCE

9.1 PRIME BROKER SERVICES

LEARNING OBJECTIVE

1.9.1 Know the main services provided by an equity and fixed income prime broker, including: securities lending and borrowing; leverage trade execution; cash management; core settlement; custody; rehypothecation

'Prime brokerage' is the term given to a collection of services provided by investment banks to their hedge fund clients. **Hedge funds** are investment funds that are typically only open to a limited range of investors. They tend to follow complex investment strategies, often involving derivatives. However, amongst the more straightforward strategies adopted is the equity long/short strategy. This involves taking both long positions in equities (in other words, buying shares) and, at the same time, committing to sell equities that are not held by the fund (described as selling short). The hope is that the gain in one half of the strategy (the long or the short) will more than cover the loss on the other half of the strategy (the short or the long). Selling short inevitably means that the fund will need to 'borrow' the securities it has sold until the position is unwound.

The typical services that are provided by a prime broker include the following:

1. **Securities lending and borrowing** – eg, to cover short positions in a long/short strategy.
2. **Leveraged trade execution** – in other words, undertaking trades on the fund's behalf that are partly financed by borrowed funds.
3. **Cash management** – maximising the return that is generated from cash held by the fund.

4. **Core settlement** – taking the necessary steps to make sure that any securities purchased become the property of the fund, and the appropriate cash is received for any sales made of the fund's securities in a timely manner.
5. **Custody** – keeping safe the securities held by the fund, and processing any corporate actions promptly and in accordance with its targets.
6. **Rehypothecation** – in addition to holding collateral and having a charge over the fund's portfolio, the prime broker might also require a right to re-charge, dispose of or otherwise use the customer's assets which are subject to the security, including disposing of them to a third party. This is commonly described as a 'right of rehypothecation'. When assets have been rehypothecated, the assets become the property of the prime broker as and when the prime broker uses them in this way, for instance by depositing rehypothecated securities with a third-party financier to obtain cheaper funding, or by lending the securities to another client.

9.2 SOURCES OF EQUITY FINANCE

LEARNING OBJECTIVE

1.9.2 Know the use of the main sources of equity financing: stock borrowing and lending; repurchase agreements; collateralised borrowing; tri-party repos; synthetic financing

In order to finance and create positions in equity required by their hedge fund clients, prime brokers have a number of possibilities:

1. **Stock borrowing and lending**. Prime brokers can arrange for the appropriate shares to be borrowed to cover the hedge fund's short positions and also use the fund's long positions to lend to others and provide additional returns to the fund as a result.
2. **Repurchase agreements**. Repurchase agreements (or repos) are essentially where the prime broker arranges the sale of securities owned by the fund for cash, while agreeing to buy back the equivalent securities later for a slightly inflated price. The increase in price is effectively the borrowing cost of the cash, and is often referred to as the 'repo rate'.
3. **Collateralised borrowing**. Prime brokers advance cash to the customer against the security of a first fixed charge over the customer's portfolio. In the event of the customer's default, this gives the prime broker a right of recourse against the charged assets for the amounts owing to it. The availability of the portfolio as collateral in this way should enable the bank to provide loans at more competitive rates than would be the case with an unsecured loan.
4. **Tri-Party Repos**. In the case of a tri-party repo a custodian bank or clearing organisation acts as an intermediary between the two parties to the repurchase or repo agreement outlined above. The tri-party agent is responsible for the administration of the transaction including collateral allocation, the marking to market, and, where required, the substitution of collateral. The lender and the borrower of cash both enter into tri-party transactions in order to avoid the administrative burden of the simpler form of bi-lateral repos. Moreover, there is an added element of security in a tri-party repo because the collateral is being held by an agent and the counterparty risk is reduced.
5. **Synthetic financing**. This is where the prime broker will create exposure to particular securities by using derivatives, like swaps, rather than directly buying and holding the securities themselves. This route is generally substantially cheaper than outright purchases.

9.3 STOCK LENDING

LEARNING OBJECTIVE

1.9.3 Know the uses of, requirements and implications of stock lending: what is stock lending; purpose for the borrower; purpose for the lender; function of market makers and stock borrowing and lending intermediaries; effect on the lender's rights; lender retains the right to sell; collateral

Stock lending is the temporary transfer of securities, by a lender to a borrower, with agreement by the borrower to return equivalent securities to the lender at pre-agreed time. There are two main motivations for stock lending: securities-driven, and cash-driven. In securities-driven transactions, borrowing firms seek specific securities (equities or bonds), perhaps to facilitate their trading operations. In the cash-driven trades, the lender is able to increase the returns on an underlying portfolio by receiving a fee for making its investments available to the borrower. Such transactions may boost overall income returns, enhancing, for example, returns on a pension fund.

The terms of the securities loan will be governed by a 'Securities Lending Agreement', which requires that the borrower provide the lender with collateral, in the form of cash, government securities, or a Letter of Credit of value equal to or greater than the loaned securities. As payment for the loan, the parties negotiate a fee, quoted as an annualised percentage of the value of the loaned securities. If the agreed form of collateral is cash, then the fee may be quoted as a 'rebate', meaning that the lender will earn all of the interest which accrues on the cash collateral, and will 'rebate' an agreed rate of interest to the borrower.

9.3.1 Benefits of Stock Lending

The initial driver for the securities lending business was to cover settlement failure. If one party fails to deliver stock to you, it can mean that you are unable to deliver stock that you have already sold to another party. In order to avoid the costs and penalties that can arise from settlement failure, stock could be borrowed at a fee, and delivered to the second party. When your initial stock finally arrived (or was obtained from another source) the lender would receive back the same number of shares in the security they lent.

The principal reason for borrowing a security is to cover a short position. As you are obliged to deliver the security, you will have to borrow it. At the end of the agreement you will have to return an equivalent security to the lender. Equivalent in this context means fungible, ie, the securities have to be completely interchangeable. Compare this with lending a ten euro note. You do not expect exactly the same note back, as any ten euro note will do.

Securities lending and borrowing is often required, by matter of law, in order to engage in short selling. In fact, regulations enacted in 2008 in the US, Australia and the UK, among other jurisdictions, required that, before short sales were executed for specific stocks, especially banks and financial services companies, the sellers first pre-borrow shares in those issues. There is an ongoing debate amongst global policymakers and regulators about how to impose new restrictions on short selling, and Germany took a unilateral step in banning the naked short selling of CDSs (ie, where the short seller had no interest in the underlying security for the credit default swap) in June 2010, during a period of turbulence for the Eurozone.

The FSA lists the following positive aspects of stock lending in its guidance to the investment community:

- It can increase the liquidity of the securities market by allowing securities to be borrowed temporarily; thus reducing the potential for failed settlements and the penalties this may incur.
- It can provide extra security to lenders through the collateralisation of a loan.
- It can support many trading and investment strategies that otherwise would be extremely difficult to execute.
- It allows investors to earn income by lending their securities on to third parties.
- It facilitates the hedging and arbitraging of price differentials.

9.3.2 Risks of Stock Lending

Many feel that securities lending could aid market manipulation through short selling, which can potentially influence market prices. Short selling as such is not wrong (although market manipulation certainly is), and stock lending can assist those that have sold stock short, thus adding liquidity to the market.

As already noted, the debate about the merits and validity of 'short selling' is sometimes emotion-charged, and features in the rhetoric of politicians in populist attacks on the financial services industry. It probably is fair to say that for most investment professionals who actually work in the financial markets the notion that short selling in itself is an abusive practice is not palatable. There may be times when the activity can be disruptive, but markets have a tendency to over-react in either direction and the periodic focus given to short selling when a market is moving down should be counter balanced by the tendency for markets to become too frothy and for long investors to become exuberant when markets are going up.

Another alleged potential abuse is that of tax evasion. However, the act of stock lending itself does not lead to tax evasion.

In the UK those involved in securities lending will generally be supervised by the Financial Services Authority (FSA). They will be subject to the FSA's Handbook, including the Inter-professional Conduct Chapter of the Market Conduct Sourcebook; and also subject to the provisions of the Financial Services and Markets Act on, among other things, market abuse.

They will also have regard to the provisions of the Stock Borrowing and Lending Code, produced by the Stock Lending and Borrowing Committee, a committee of market participants, chaired by the Bank of England and including a representative of the FSA.

9.3.3 Legalities

Securities lending is legal and clearly regulated in most of the world's major securities markets. Most markets mandate that the borrowing of securities be conducted only for specifically permitted purposes, which generally include:

1. to facilitate settlement of a trade;
2. to facilitate delivery of a short sale;
3. to finance the security; or
4. to facilitate a loan to another borrower who is motivated by one of these permitted purposes.

Effect on a Lender's Rights and Corporate Actions

When a security is loaned, the title of the security transfers to the borrower. This means that the borrower has the advantages of holding the security, just as though they owned it. Specifically, the borrower will receive all coupon and/or dividend payments, and any other rights such as voting rights. In most cases, these dividends or coupons must be passed back to the lender in the form of what is referred to as a 'manufactured dividend'.

If the lender wants to exercise its right to vote it should recall the stock in good time so that a proxy voting form can be completed and returned to the registrar by the required deadline.

Similar issues are involved in other corporate actions such as a capitalisation issue. Technically, the consequences arising from any corporate action by the issuer of a security, such as a capitalisation matter or rights issue, which has been lent to another would *prima facie* be to the benefit/cost of the borrower. Under the terms of the security agreement it is customary that these costs/benefits should flow back to the lender, and the exact manner in which this will be implemented should be reflected in the securities lending agreement.

The term 'securities lending' is sometimes used erroneously as a synonym of 'stock loan'. The latter is used in private hedged portfolio stock collateralised loan arrangements, where the underlying securities are hedged so as to convert the variable asset to a relatively stable asset against which a usually non-recourse or limited-recourse loan can be placed.

Legal Underpinnings for Stock Lending

Parties to a stock lending transaction generally operate under a legal agreement such as the Global Master Securities Lending Agreement which sets out the obligations of the borrower and lender. In securities lending the lender effectively retains all the benefits of ownership, other than the voting rights. The borrower can use the securities as required – perhaps by lending them on to another party – but is liable to the lender for all the benefits such as dividends, interest, or stock splits.

The Global Master Securities Lending Agreement (GMSLA)

The Global Master Securities Lending Agreement (GMSLA) has been developed as a market standard for securities lending. It was drafted with a view to compliance with English law and covers the matters which a legal agreement ought to cover for securities lending transactions.

The Global Master Securities Lending Agreement is referred to in this Code as the 'Securities Lending Legal Agreement'. This agreement is kept under review, and amendments are made from time to time, although parties to an existing agreement would need to agree that those amendments would apply to their agreement.

Stock Lending versus Repo

While stock lending and sales/repurchase agreements, repos are similar, the difference is that a stock lender charges a fee to the borrower, whereas a repo counterparty pays (or receives) a rate of interest.

EXAMPLE

A large pension fund manager with a position in a particular stock agrees that the security can be borrowed by a securities lender. The securities lender, a prime broker or investment bank, would then allow a hedge fund client to borrow the stock and sell it short. The short seller would like to buy the stock back at a lower price and realise a profit when returning the security to the broker from whom it has been borrowed.

Once the shares are borrowed and sold, cash is generated from selling the stock. That cash would become collateral for the borrower. The cash value of the collateral would be marked-to-market on a daily basis so that it exceeds the value of the loan by at least 2%. The pension fund manager would have access to the cash for overnight investment and this would enable the pension fund to maintain a long position in the stock. The pension fund manger is able to earn additional income from lending the stock, and the hedge fund manager is able, providing that his/her prediction that the price of the security is going to decline is correct, is able to profit from the short sale. In addition, the prime broker earns a spread from facilitating the transaction and also by providing this prime brokerage service to the hedge fund client.

EXERCISE ANSWERS

Exercise 1

(i) Calculate the flat yield on a 4% gilt, redeeming in eight years and priced at £98.90.

(4/98.90) x 100 = 4.04%

(ii) Calculate the flat yield on a 7% gilt, redeeming in three years and priced at £108.60.

(7/108.60) x 100 = 6.45%

Exercise 2

The share value of the conversion choice is currently 15 x £6.40 = £96.

The bond is trading at £110, so the premium is £14 per £100 nominal value.

Expressed as a percentage 14/96 x 100 = 14.6%.

Exercise 3

(a)

Time	Cash flow	Discount factor	Present value
End of year one	£10	$1/1.06$	9.43
End of year two	£110	$1/1.06^2$	97.90
Sum of the individual present value = Price of the bond			£107.33

(b)

Time	Cash flow	Discount factor	Present value
End of year one	£10	$1/1.04$	9.62
End of year two	£110	$1/1.04^2$	101.70
Sum of the individual present value = Price of the bond			£111.32

Exercise 4

Using the spot rate $1.8055–$1.8145:

(i) How much would Mr A receive in £s for $100,000?

Using the seller's rate of $1.8145, Mr A would receive: 100,000/1.8145 = £55,111.60

(ii) How much would Mr X receive in $s for £70,000

Using the buyer's rate of $1.8055, Mr X would receive 70,000 x 1.8055 = $126,385

Exercise 5

(i) Spot rate $1.8055–$1.8145

One-year forward	3.98–3.85c pm
One-year forward rate	$1.7657–$1.7760

(ii) How many dollars would an investor receive in a year's time, if he were to agree to sell £1 million in a one-year forward transaction?

Using the buyer's rate = $1.7657 x £1m = $1,765,700

CHAPTER TWO

NEW ISSUES

This syllabus area will provide approximately 26 of the 100 examination questions

1. THE PRIMARY AND SECONDARY MARKETS

LEARNING OBJECTIVE

2.1.1 Know the principal characteristics of, and the differences between, the primary and secondary markets. In particular: the role of the listing authority; users of the primary market and why; users of the secondary market and why

Stock exchanges, like the London Stock Exchange (LSE) in the UK and NYSE Euronext in the US, are simply organised marketplaces for issuing securities and then trading those securities via their members. All stock exchanges provide both a primary and a secondary market.

1. The **primary market**, or the new issues market, is where securities are issued for the first time. The primary markets exist to enable issuers of securities, such as companies, to raise capital, and to enable the surplus funds held by potential investors to be matched with investment opportunities the issuers offer. It is a crucial source of funding. The terminology often used when companies 'float' on the Stock Exchange is that they first access the primary market. The process that the companies go through when they float is often called the 'initial public offering' (or IPO). As we will see later in this chapter, companies can use a variety of ways to achieve flotation, such as offers for investors to subscribe for their shares (offers for subscription).
2. The **secondary market** is where existing securities are traded between investors, and the stock exchanges provide a variety of systems to assist in this, such as the LSE's SETS system that is used to trade the largest companies' shares. These systems provide investors with liquidity, giving them the ability to sell their securities if they wish. Trading activity in the secondary market also results in the ongoing provision of buy and sell prices to investors via the exchange's member firms.

Each jurisdiction has its own rules and regulations for companies seeking a listing, and continuing obligations for those already listed. In the UK, there is the **United Kingdom Listing Authority (UKLA)** which is a division of the Financial Services Authority (FSA). The formal description of the UKLA is that it is the **competent authority for listing** – making the decisions as to which companies' shares and bonds (including gilts) can be admitted to be traded on the LSE. The rules are contained in a rulebook called the **Listing Rules**, often referred to as the purple book because it has a purple cover.

It is the UKLA that sets the rules relating to becoming listed on the LSE, including the implementation of any relevant EU directives. The LSE is responsible for the operation of the exchange, including the trading of the securities on the secondary market, although the UKLA can suspend the listing of particular securities and, therefore, remove their secondary market trading activity on the exchange.

In a similar way in the US, the Securities and Exchange Commission (SEC) requires companies seeking a listing on the US exchanges (such as NYSE Euronext and NASDAQ) to register certain details with the SEC first. Once listed, companies are then required to file regular reports with the SEC, particularly in relation to their trading performance and financial situation.

2. STOCK EXCHANGES

2.1 PURPOSE AND ROLE

LEARNING OBJECTIVE

2.2.1 Know the purpose, role and main features of the major stock exchanges. In particular: scope: provision of liquidity, price formation; brokers versus dealers; different types of stock exchanges: electronic, open outcry; major exchanges: Deutsche Börse, London Stock Exchange; NASDAQ; NYSE Euronext; Tokyo Stock Exchange

As seen above, stock exchanges provide trading systems to enable listed securities to be bought and sold in the secondary market. Primarily these exchanges provide liquidity to existing and potential investors, enabling existing investors to sell their securities and allowing potential investors to become actual investors by purchasing securities. Furthermore, because these exchanges concentrate trading activity on their systems, the prices at which trades are executed is the 'market price' at any given time. This is described as the 'price formation' process.

Stock exchanges offer membership to investment banks and firms of stockbrokers. Becoming a member of an exchange enables these banks and stockbrokers to be involved in secondary market trades. This involvement will be in one of two ways:

1. **Brokers**. Brokers simply arrange deals for their clients, as well as potentially giving advice to their clients as to which securities they should buy, sell or retain. In return for arranging (and potentially advising), the brokers will earn a commission that is typically calculated as a set percentage of the value of the deal. Acting as a broker is often described as 'dealing as agent', and firms of stockbrokers tend to act as brokers on the stock exchanges.
2. **Dealers**. In contrast to brokers, dealers actually buy or sell securities. If a client wants to sell shares, a dealer may buy those shares; if another client wants to buy shares, a dealer may sell those shares. Acting as a dealer is often described as 'dealing as principal', because the dealer is taking a principal position by either buying, or selling the securities. It is the investment banks that tend to act as dealers on the stock exchanges.

Historically, stock exchanges were physical locations where the members would gather. The brokers would bring orders from their clients and arrange deals with the dealers on the floor of the exchange. Where the deals are arranged verbally on the floor of the exchange, the method of trading is described as 'open outcry'. However, stock exchanges have introduced electronic systems to execute deals, and the physical exchange floor is increasingly unusual. Today the majority of the world's major stock exchanges run secondary market trading systems that are solely 'electronic'.

The major exchanges around the world are detailed in the following table alongside the country (or countries) they operate within, and a brief outline of their trading systems:

Exchange	Country/Countries	Trading System
Deutsche Börse	Germany	Electronic
London Stock Exchange	UK	Electronic
NASDAQ	US	Electronic
NYSE Euronext	US and Europe	Electronic plus some open outcry in Wall Street
Tokyo Stock Exchange	Japan	Electronic

3. ADVISERS

LEARNING OBJECTIVE

2.2.2 Know the role of advisers: Listing Agent; Corporate Broker

2.2.3 Know the Issuer's obligations: corporate governance; reporting

In order to have its securities listed, the company concerned will have to appoint certain advisers. The precise requirements and roles are laid down in the local regulations that apply to the particular exchange. Generally, the advisers will include both a listing agent (at the initial public offering (IPO) stage) and a corporate broker (both at IPO and afterwards).

The **listing agent** is alternatively referred to as the 'sponsor'. The role is to ensure that the company is suitable for a listing, as well as advising the company generally in relation to the listing, and liaising with the exchange and the listing authority on the company's behalf. Additionally, the listing agent will co-ordinate the activities of other advisers working on behalf of the company, such as accountants and solicitors. The firm acting as listing agent is typically an investment bank or a firm of stockbrokers.

The **corporate broker** may be the same firm as the listing agent. The responsibilities of the corporate broker are to act as an interface between the company on the one hand, and the stock market and investors in the company's securities on the other. In particular, the corporate broker advises the company on 'market conditions' – the way existing and potential investors are viewing the company in relation to its peers, and the general direction of the market.

An issuer that is planning to have its securities listed will have to undertake certain obligations. Like the requirements for advisers, the precise obligations can vary across jurisdictions, but they always include obligations in relation to corporate governance and reporting.

Corporate governance is the way a company (the corporate) manages and controls its activities (governs itself). In particular, it is expected (and, in some jurisdictions, required) that the listed companies have put in place appropriate corporate and management structures. Examples include reducing the influence of a single individual by splitting the roles of chairman and chief executive of the company, appointing a reasonable proportion of non-executive directors to the board, and having a suitably qualified finance director.

Reporting requirements are designed to make sure that existing and potential investors are kept informed of progress and developments at the listed company. It is particularly important that financial information is provided regularly and that the information is reliable and so listed companies are generally required to provide audited annual accounts and less detailed half-yearly, or perhaps quarterly, reports.

4. LONDON STOCK EXCHANGE

LEARNING OBJECTIVE

2.3.1 Know the regulatory framework for the LSE: Companies Act; FSA; Exchange Rule Book

The regulatory framework that lies behind the way that the LSE operates includes three major constituents: the law (in particular the Companies Act), the requirements of the Financial Services Authority (FSA) and the rules laid down by the exchange itself (in its rule book).

The **Companies Act** details the requirements for companies generally, such as the requirement to prepare annual accounts, the need to have accounts audited and for Annual General Meetings. Of particular significance to the LSE are the Companies Act requirements to enable a company to be a public limited company (plc), since one of the requirements for a company to be listed and traded on the Exchange is that the company is a plc.

The **Financial Services Authority** has to give its recognition before an exchange is allowed to operate in the UK. It has granted recognition to the LSE and, by virtue of this recognition, the exchange is described as a recognised investment exchange (RIE). In granting recognition, the FSA assesses whether the exchange has sufficient systems and controls to run a market. Furthermore, the FSA (through its division – the UK Listing Authority, or UKLA) lays down the detailed rules that have to be met before companies are admitted to the official 'list' that enables their shares to be traded on the exchange.

The London Stock Exchange also has its own rules in relation to who can access its systems and become members of the exchange, as well as how those members must behave when trading on the exchange.

4.1 CRITERIA FOR LISTING: THE OFFICIAL LIST

LEARNING OBJECTIVE

2.3.2 Know the admissions criteria for listing: trading record; amount raised; percentage in public hands; market

The LSE has established two markets for company securities: the **Official List** and the **Alternative Investment Market (AIM)**. The official (or full) List is the senior market, indeed often it is referred to as the 'main market' – entry rules are stringent, ensuring that only companies of a high quality can be involved. AIM was created to provide a market for smaller, less well-established companies. As we will see later in this chapter, the admission requirements of AIM are less stringent.

The criteria for admission to the official list are set out in the Listing Rules and, as we have seen, this rulebook is maintained by the UK Listing Authority, itself a division of the FSA.

The main rules contained in the Listing Rules for admission to the full list are:

- Every company applying for a listing must be a public limited company (a plc) and must be represented by a **sponsor** (alternatively referred to as a 'listing agent'), which will usually be an investment bank, stockbroker, law firm or accountancy practice. The sponsor provides a link between the company and the UKLA, guiding the company through the listing process.
- The expected market capitalisation of the company should be at least £700,000.
- The company should have a trading record of at least three years.
- At least 25% of the company's shares should be in public hands, or be available for public purchase. The term 'public' excludes directors and their associates and anyone who holds 5% or more of the shares.
- The company and its advisers must publish a **prospectus**, a detailed document providing potential investors with the information required to make an informed decision on the company and its shares.
- The company must restrict its ability to issue warrants to no more than 20% of the issued share capital.
- Listing is not free, and a further requirement before a company's shares can be admitted to the Official List is that the appropriate fee has been paid.

Once listed, companies are expected to fulfil certain **continuing obligations**: they are obliged to issue a **half-yearly report** in addition to annual accounts, and they have to notify the market of any new, price-sensitive information.

4.2 AIM

LEARNING OBJECTIVE

2.4.1 Know the admissions criteria: appointment and role of a nominated adviser; appointment and role of a broker; transferability of shares; no minimum shares in public hands; no trading record required; no shareholder approval needed; no minimum market capitalisation

In contrast to the Official List, where access is via application to the UKLA and the UKLA's listing rules must be complied with, AIM companies' application and regulations are set by the LSE. AIM companies are usually smaller than their fully listed counterparts, and the rules governing their listing are much less stringent. There is no restriction on market value, percentage of shares in public hands or trading history and no shareholder approval is required.

The main requirements for a company's shares to be admitted to the AIM are two-fold:

1. That there is no restriction of the transferability of the shares.
2. That the AIM company appoints two experts to assist them:
   a) the **nominated adviser**. The nominated adviser can be thought of as an exchange expert, advising the company on all aspects of AIM listing rules and compliance;

b) the **broker**. AIM companies' shares are usually less liquid than those of fully listed companies; it is the broker's job to ensure that there is a market in the company's shares, to facilitate trading in those shares and to provide ongoing information about the company to interested parties. (As with the full market, the LSE imposes similar continuing obligations on AIM companies).

There are also certain other aspects in relation to AIM companies and the broker and nominated adviser:

- the broker and adviser can be the same firm; they are often firms of stockbrokers or accountants;
- if a company ceases, at any time, to have a broker or adviser, then the firm's shares are suspended from trading;
- if the company is without a broker or adviser for a period of one month they are removed from AIM.

LEARNING OBJECTIVE

2.4.2 Know the issuer's obligations: corporate governance; reporting

Companies considering admission onto the AIM must meet the **corporate governance requirements** of the market. Broadly, the companies are required to have independent non-executive directors on the board to represent the interests of outside shareholders.

Once a company has been admitted onto the AIM market, that company takes on certain **reporting requirements**. These require the preparation and distribution of both annual and interim (half-yearly) accounts to shareholders, as well as announcing any price-sensitive information in an orderly manner.

LEARNING OBJECTIVE

2.4.3 Know the regulatory framework for AIM: London Stock Exchange; AIM Rules; Companies Act; FSA

As with the overall exchange, there are three major constituents to the regulatory framework for AIM: the law (in particular, the Companies Act), the requirements of the FSA, and the rules established by the exchange itself (in its own rulebook).

As we have seen, the **Companies Act** details the requirements for companies generally, such as the requirement to prepare annual accounts, the need to have accounts audited and for Annual General Meetings. As with the LSE generally, the Companies Act requirements to enable a company to be a plc are particularly important because one of the requirements for a company to be listed and traded on AIM is that the company is a plc.

The **Financial Services Authority**'s recognition of the LSE as an RIE enables the LSE to set up the submarket that is AIM. However, the nominated adviser role removes the need for any UK Listing Authority involvement.

The **London Stock Exchange** also has its own rules in relation to AIM. There is a rulebook for the companies admitted to the market ('the AIM rules for companies'), and a rulebook for the nominated advisers ('the AIM rules for nominated advisers').

5. LISTING SECURITIES

Deciding to list (or 'float') securities on a stock exchange such as the London Stock Exchange is a significant decision for a company to take. Flotations have both pros and cons – the fact that the company can gain access to capital and enable their shares to be readily marketable are often-quoted positives. The most often quoted negatives are the fact that the original owners may well lose control of the company and that the ongoing disclosure and attention paid to the company after listing is much greater than previously.

5.1 THE ORIGINATION TEAM

LEARNING OBJECTIVE

2.5.1 Understand the role of the Origination Team

Once the decision has been made to list, the company will have to find and appoint a **sponsor**. As seen earlier in this chapter, the sponsor is likely to be an investment bank, a stockbroking firm or a professional services firm like an accountancy practice. The role of the sponsor includes assessing the company's suitability for listing, the best method of bringing the company to the market, and co-ordinating the production of the 'prospectus'. The prospectus is a detailed document about the company, including financial information that should enable prospective investors to decide on the merits of the company's shares.

The sponsor is only part of the **origination team** helping the company in the flotation. In addition to the sponsor, the issuing company will appoint a variety of other advisers, such as reporting accountants, legal advisers, public relations (PR) consultants and a corporate broker.

The reporting accountants will attest to the validity of the financial information provided in the prospectus. The **legal advisers** will make sure that all relevant matters are covered in the prospectus and the statements made are justified. The combination of the reporting accountants and the legal advisers is said to be providing 'due diligence' for the prospectus – making sure the document is accurate and complies with the regulations.

A **public relations consultant** is generally appointed to optimise the positive public perception of the company and its products and services in the run-up to listing.

Finally, the origination team may require a **corporate broker** to ensure that there is a market in the company's shares, to facilitate trading in those shares and to provide ongoing information about the company to interested parties. This role will probably be provided by the sponsor, if the sponsor is an investment bank or a stockbroking firm.

5.2 THE SYNDICATE GROUP

LEARNING OBJECTIVE

2.5.2 Understand the role of the syndicate group: different roles within a syndicate: bookrunner, co-lead, co-manager; marketing and bookbuilding

For large listings, where the issuing company is planning to issue substantial quantities of shares to interested investors, the sponsor will gather together a **syndicate** of investment banks and stockbrokers to market the share issue to their clients. These clients may be a mixture of both institutional clients (such as insurance companies and asset management firms) and retail clients. The sponsor will generally act as the **lead manager** of the syndicate, appointing a host of **co-managers** to assist. Sometimes the issue may be large enough to warrant the appointment of more than one lead manager, perhaps with each **co-lead manager** taking responsibility for particular geographical areas – for example, one lead manager for Europe, another for the US.

The process of finding buyers for the issuing company's shares is known as '**bookbuilding**', and the lead managers co-ordinate the overall level of demand across the syndicate. This role is commonly referred to as that of the '**book runner**'.

During the bookbuilding, the syndicate will gather the willingness of investors to purchase the shares, which will be sensitive to the price at which the shares are sold. Usually, the bookbuilding begins with an indicative range of prices; the finalisation of the price will come just prior to listing. This is illustrated in the following example.

EXAMPLE

Cauldron Stanley is a large investment bank. It is acting as lead manager and sponsor for a new issue of shares for a client, Wizard Enterprises plc, which is looking to raise several billion pounds. Because of the size of the issue, Cauldron Stanley sets up a syndicate of 10 investment banks to assist in the marketing and act as co-managers.

The syndicate initially markets the shares at an indicative price range of £2 to £2.20 each. The strength of demand is strong so that, as listing approaches, the final price is set at the top of the range, at £2.20 per share.

5.3 UNDERWRITING

LEARNING OBJECTIVE

2.5.3 Understand the purpose and practice of underwriting, rights and responsibilities of the underwriter: benefits to the issuing company; risks and rewards to the underwriter

In circumstances where a company is attempting to sell shares to the investing public, there is a danger that the demand is not sufficient, perhaps because of a general fall in share prices near to the flotation date. This could lead to the flotation failing, so it is usual to 'underwrite' new issues of shares. Underwriting is agreeing with financial institutions, such as banks, insurance companies and asset managers, that, if the demand is insufficient, the financial institutions will buy the shares. Effectively, underwriting creates an insurance policy that the issue will happen because, in the worst case, the underwriters (the financial institutions that have agreed to underwrite the offer) will buy the shares.

In such circumstances the price at which the underwriters guarantee to buy is generally at a discount to the share price at which the shares are offered to the public, eg, shares offered to the public at £5 each might be underwritten at £4.75 each.

The benefits to the issuing company of an underwriting arrangement are obvious – the sale of the shares and minimum proceeds are guaranteed. For the underwriters, the risk is that they may end up buying shares for more than they are worth. However, in return for accepting this risk, the underwriters will be paid fees, regardless of whether or not there is a lack of demand for the shares from the public.

5.4 STABILISATION

LEARNING OBJECTIVE

2.5.4 Understand stabilisation and its purpose: governing principles and regulation with regard to stabilisation activity; who is involved in stabilisation; what does stabilisation achieve; benefits to the issuing company and investors

Stabilisation is the process whereby, to prevent a substantial fall in the value of securities when a large number of new securities are issued, the lead manager of the issue agrees to support the price by buying back the newly issued securities in the market if the market price falls below a certain, pre-defined level. This is done in an attempt to give the market a reasonable chance to adjust to the increased number of securities that have become available, by stabilising the price at which they are traded.

By increasing the demand for the securities in the market at the same time as more securities become available, the price should remain more stable. This will mean the issuing company's securities appear less volatile, and existing investors will be less likely to begin panic-selling, creating a downward spiral in the security's price. The securities that are bought back by the lead manager of the issue will then be sold back into the market over time.

There are strict rules laid down by regulators regarding stabilisation practices. For example, the FSA restricts the stabilisation period and requires disclosure to the market that stabilisation is happening, and that the market price may not be a representative one because of the stabilisation activities.

5.5 IPOs

LEARNING OBJECTIVE

2.5.5 Understand the use of an initial public offering: why would a company choose an IPO; structure of IPO – base deal plus greenshoe; stages of an IPO; underwritten versus best efforts

The key advantages of initial public offers (IPOs) over other capital-raising methods are that IPOs can raise substantial sums of capital and create a great deal of publicity for the issuing companies. The money raised in the form of an IPO is known as **risk capital** and the company assets are not encumbered or hypothecated in the same manner as they would be if the capital were raised from a debt offering.

An IPO is usually structured with a base number of shares that the company is planning to issue. However, the issuing company may also reserve the right to increase the number of shares it issues, if significant levels of demand would remain unsatisfied if only the base number of shares were issued. The option to increase the number of shares is referred to as a **green shoe**.

As seen, there are three broad stages to an IPO:

1. **The decision**. The issuing company (in conjunction with its advisers, particularly the investment bank) makes a decision to raise capital via an IPO. This will involve careful consideration of the pros and cons of a public offer.
2. **The preparation of the prospectus**. This is the necessary document that must accompany an IPO, involving the whole team of advisers, including the investment bank, reporting accountants and legal advisers.
3. **The sale of securities**. The investment bank will lead manage the sale and may well establish a syndicate of co-managers to assist in selling the securities to their clients.

Underwriting the offer is generally the responsibility of the investment bank(s) and they typically arrange 'firm' underwriting where there are guarantees in place to buy the securities. Investment banks may not provide a 'firm' undertaking to place all of the securities on behalf of their clients. Instead the lead underwriter along with the co-managers of the offer may provide a '**best efforts**' underwriting, in which they will do their best to sell the shares involved in the offering but where there is no formal guarantee that this will be achieved. In practice this would mean that the managers of the underwriting are not committing to purchase any unplaced securities for their own account in an unconditional manner. By an underwriter and the co-managers inserting the 'best efforts' conditionality, should there be a failure to fully complete a sale of the offering, there is less risk to the underwriter of reputational damage and not being invited to participate in future IPO's.

5.6 FOLLOW-ON OFFERINGS

LEARNING OBJECTIVE

2.5.6 Understand the use of follow-on offerings: why would a company choose a follow-on offering; structure of follow-on – base deal plus greenshoe; stages of follow-on offering; underwritten versus best efforts

An already-listed company looking to raise more capital can choose to go through a follow-on offering. A follow-on offering is alternatively referred to as a 'secondary' offer. Clearly, issuing more shares in a follow-on offering would only be considered if the equity markets were sufficiently robust – in a bear market there is unlikely to be sufficient demand for the shares at the price the issuing company is looking for.

Like an initial public offering, a follow-on offering will be structured with a base number of shares that the company is planning to issue. Again, the issuing company may also retain a greenshoe option to increase the number of shares that it issues, if significant levels of demand would otherwise remain unsatisfied.

A secondary offering will inevitably be quicker, easier and cheaper than an IPO, simply because the company has been through the stages before in its IPO. The broad stages of a follow-on offer are the same as an IPO:

1. **The decision**.
2. **The preparation of the prospectus**. This should be relatively easy, since the issuing company has prepared a prospectus before when it first became a listed entity.
3. **The sale of securities**. As in an IPO, the appointed investment bank will lead manage the sale and may well establish a syndicate of co-managers to assist in selling the securities to their clients.

As with an IPO, the follow-on offering may also be underwritten, with a potential combination of firm underwriting by the investment bank(s) and best efforts underwriting by clients such as stockbroking firms.

As with an IPO, a follow-on offering is said to be underwritten when there is a firm undertaking by the investment bank(s) that is conducting the offering that all of the offering will be fully subscribed. In other words, the underwriting bank(s) will guarantee that any shortfall by subscribers will be purchased by the bank(s) for its own account.

A best efforts agreement provides no such guarantee. In this case the underwriting bank(s) agree to use their best efforts to sell as much of an issue as possible to the public. If the underwriter is unable to sell all of the offering because of adverse market conditions, he does not take responsibility for placing any of the unsold inventory. Arrangements that are made on a 'best efforts' basis are often found with high-risk securities.

5.7 OPEN OFFERS AND OFFERS FOR SUBSCRIPTION

LEARNING OBJECTIVE

2.5.7 Understand the use of open offers and offers for subscription: why would a company choose an open offer; structure of offer; stages of offer; tenders; strike price; who is involved in the offer process

As seen in the previous sections, a company applying for admission to the Official List in the UK needs to have at least 25% of its ordinary shares in the hands of the public. In order to achieve this, and to raise capital through their listing, a company can have an IPO of ordinary shares by making an **offer for subscription**.

An offer for subscription involves the company sending a prospectus (including the share price) and an application form to potential investors. The company's sponsor along with reporting accountants and legal advisers will assist in the preparation of the prospectus. Those potential investors who want to invest in the company apply for shares. The company then issues **allotment letters** to successful applicants.

Only new (not previously issued) shares may be issued in this way.

This method is rare in large IPOs, mainly because issuing companies like to use the expertise of the investment banks to facilitate their IPOs, in particular their ability to price and sell shares to their substantial client base. As a result, large IPOs tend to follow the offer for sale route outlined in the next section.

Diagrammatically:

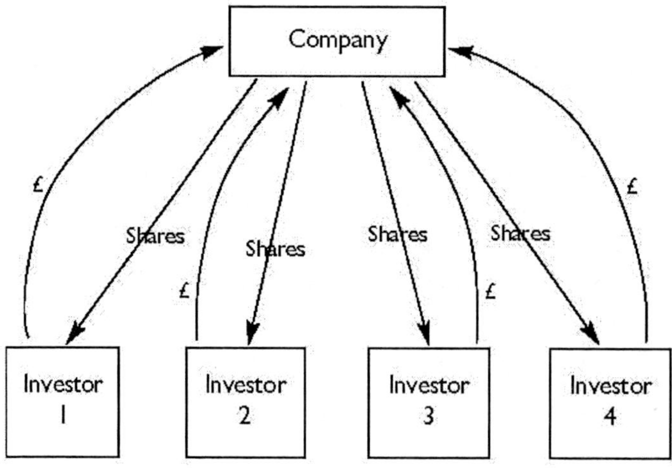

An **open offer** is similar in that it is an invitation to subscribe for new shares. However, open offers are follow-on offers that only offer the new shares to the existing shareholders, in proportion to their existing shareholding. This meets the pre-emptive rights of the shareholders, but it differs from a rights issue in that the rights are not able to be sold 'nil paid'. The offer is simply open for the existing shareholders to take up, or not.

5.8 OFFERS FOR SALE

LEARNING OBJECTIVE

2.5.8 Understand the use of offers for sale: why would a company choose an offer for sale; structure of a offer for sale; stages of a offer for sale; tenders, strike price, who may receive an allotment, who is involved in the offer process

Offers for sale are a much more common way of achieving a listing. The company seeking to sell the shares approaches an **issuing house** (usually an investment bank) that specialises in approaching potential shareholders and preparing the necessary documentation. The issuing company sells its shares to the issuing house (usually an investment bank), which then invites applications from the public at a slightly higher price than the issuing house has paid and on the basis of a detailed prospectus, known as the **offer document**. For a company applying for a full listing, this provides comprehensive information about the company and its directors and how the proceeds from the share issue will be applied. As seen, this document must be prepared by the company's directors and assessed by their sponsor to satisfy the UKLA of the company's suitability to obtain a full listing.

5.8.1 Offering Allotments

In conjunction with an offer for sale an issuer may also tender a **Provisional Allotment Letter**. This is especially true in the case of a rights issue, when a company returns to the market to raise additional equity capital. Existing ordinary shareholders of a company will receive a provisional allotment of new shares as part of the new offering. After being granted such an allotment, one may decide to exercise the rights to add to one's holding but there is no obligation to take up such an offer.

Companies decide to raise more money for a variety of reasons but usually it is to fund expansion, perhaps to take over a rival or to diversify into a new business area. Rights issues are almost always offered to existing investors, and the amount they are offered depends on how many shares they already own. They could, for example, decide to issue two new shares for every one held.

Shares offered under a rights issue are usually offered at a discount to the current share price. Existing shareholders receive a Provisional Allotment Letter which tells them how many shares they are entitled to and what the price will be.

Should an existing shareholder decide to decline the right to purchase new shares, they can sell their rights under the Provisional Allotment letter onto another person who can subscribe for the shares instead. This is known as '**rights nil paid**'. Another option is to do nothing. In this case the company will sell the shares in the market, retain the subscription price and remit any excess proceeds from the sale to the person who has opted not to participate in the new offering.

Once a company has issued extra shares, the value of the shares to all existing shareholders will have been diluted. How much less will depend on how much other investors are prepared to pay for them.

A second kind of allotment provision is used in the case of an Initial Public Offering (IPO) and has become almost standard in the case of new offerings undertaken by US investment banks. It is known as the **green shoe option** because the term comes from a company founded in 1919 as Green Shoe Manufacturing Company, now called Stride Rite Corporation, which was the first company to permit this practice to be used in an offering.

More properly known by its legal title as an 'over-allotment option', the green shoe provision gives the underwriters of an IPO the right to sell additional shares in a registered securities offering if demand for the securities is in excess of the original amount offered. But it is also used as a tool in providing price stabilisation and a successful execution of the offering on behalf of the issuer. At the time of issuance the timing of the sale of shares can often be quite sensitive, and the underwriters have developed strategies which enable them to smooth out price fluctuations if demand surges on the one hand and to help support the initial offering price if there are adverse market conditions. By using the over-allotment provision the issuer may ensure a more successful marketing and distribution of the offering. However some issuers have refrained from providing their underwriters with a green shoe option.

The London Stock Exchange has ratified the requests from sponsoring member firms enabling them to exercise an over-allotment option for initial offerings conducted for issuers that wish to be listed on its exchange.

The situation is outlined in the following memorandum from the LSE:

'Green shoe arrangements are commonly agreed by a sponsoring member firm as part of the stabilisation and underwriting arrangements for an introduction to either the UKLA's Official List or AIM, as well as for further new issues of shares. Whether the option is ever exercised, and the extent to which it is utilised, will depend on the take up of the issue, the underlying share price in the market and the stabilisation transactions undertaken.'

The Exchange has agreed that such transactions can be brought on Exchange under the following circumstances:

- the terms of the green shoe option must be agreed and included in the circular or prospectus prior to sign-off, including confirmation that the option writer holds sufficient shares to meet any obligation under the option;
- at the point of exercise the shares to be delivered are admitted to trading; and
- a regulatory news announcement has disclosed that exercise has taken place.

Diagrammatically:

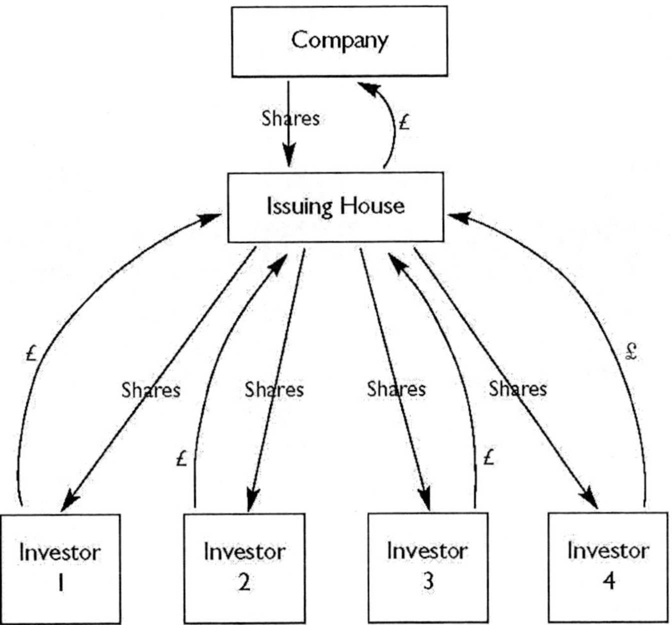

Offers for sale do not necessarily require the company to create new shares specifically for the share issue. Indeed, offers for sale are often used by a company's founders to release part, or all, of their equity stake in their company, and have also been the preferred route for government privatisation programmes, where former nationalised monopolies have been sold to the public. In both cases, existing shareholdings are disposed of, rather than new shares created, in order to obtain a listing.

An offer for sale, or an offer for subscription, can be made on either a fixed or a tender price basis:

1. Fixed price offer

When a fixed price offer is made, the price is usually fixed just below that at which it is believed the issue should be fully subscribed so as to encourage an active secondary market in the shares. Subscribers to a fixed price issue apply for the number of shares they wish to purchase at this fixed price. If the offer is oversubscribed, as it nearly always is given the favourable pricing formula, then shares are allotted either by scaling down each application or by satisfying a randomly chosen proportion of the applications in full. The precise method used will be detailed in the offer document.

2. Tender offer

Given the judgement required in setting the price at a level that does not lead to the issue being excessively oversubscribed but which leads to a successful new issue, and the fact that market sentiment can and often does change between the announcement of the IPO and the end of the offer period, offers for sale and offers for subscription can be made on a tender basis. By not stipulating a fixed price for the shares, but by inviting tenders for the issue, usually by setting a minimum tender price, investors state the number of shares they wish to purchase and state the price per share they are prepared to pay.

Once the offer is closed, a single strike price can then be determined by the issuing house or by the company, as appropriate, to satisfy all applications tendered at, or above, this price. Although this auctioning process is the more efficient way of allocating shares and maximising the proceeds from a share issue, tender offers are also more complex to administer and, as such, tend to be outnumbered by fixed price offers.

5.9 SELECTIVE MARKETING AND PLACING

LEARNING OBJECTIVE

2.5.9 Understand the basic process and uses of selective marketing and placing; advantages to the issuing company; what is a placing; what is selective marketing; how is a placing achieved; how is selective marketing achieved

In placing its shares, a company simply markets the issue directly to a broker, an issuing house or other financial institution, which in turn places the shares to selected clients. Although the least democratic of the three IPO methods, given that the general public does not initially have access to the issue, a placing is the least expensive as the prospectus accompanying the issue is less detailed than that required for the other two methods and no underwriting is required.

A placing is often referred to as a **selective marketing**, because the intermediary is selecting the clients to whom the offer is directed.

Diagrammatically:

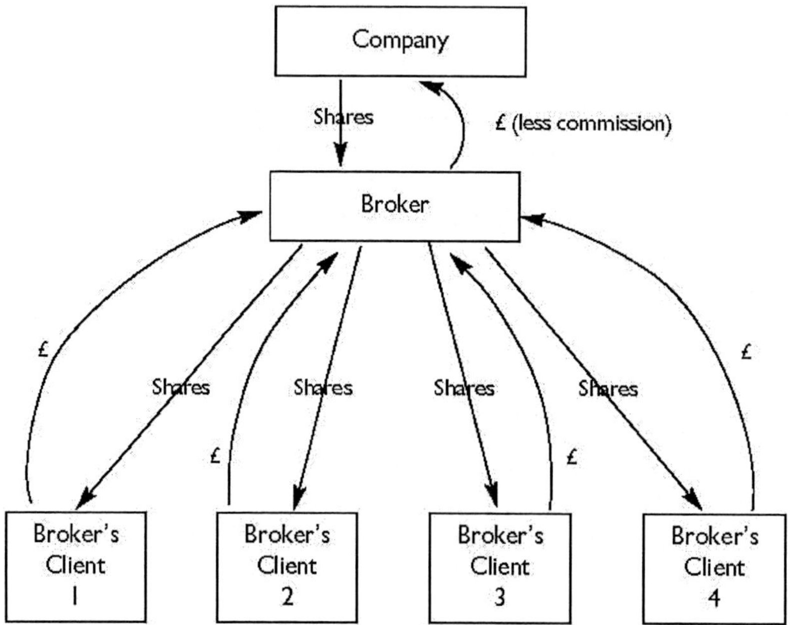

5.9.1 The Prospectus

For most public offerings of securities a vital pre-requisite is a prospectus or offering document which the issuer has to make available to all prospective investors and the exchanges upon which it intends to list its securities. Such a prospectus has to fully disclose all of the pertinent details regarding the offering including a detailed business plan, an explanation of how the proceeds from the offering will be used, details of all owners/directors of the entity, and most importantly a comprehensive disclosure of all of the risks associated with the investment.

There are however offerings of securities which are made, not to the general public, but a subset of so-called 'sophisticated investors', where the same rigorous kinds of disclosures that have to be made in an IPO prospectus can be avoided.

Changes brought about by the Prospectus Directive (see below), which forms a part of the EU initiatives known collectively as MiFID, has enabled the use of placements to so called 'sophisticated investors' and has allowed issuers, and the investment banks who advise them, to selectively market these offerings – often known as 'private placements' to a restricted class of investors.

In the US the SEC has special provisions for what are termed private placements. A private placement (or non-public offering) is a funding round of securities which are sold without an initial public offering, and without the formality of an approved prospectus, usually to a small number of chosen private investors.

In the US, although these placements are subject to the Securities Act of 1933, the securities offered do not have to be registered with the Securities and Exchange Commission if the issuance of the securities conforms to an exemption from registrations as set forth in the under the Rules know as Regulation D. Private placements may typically consist of stocks, shares of common stock or preferred stock or other forms of membership interests, warrants or promissory notes (including convertible promissory notes), and purchasers are often institutional investors such as banks, insurance companies or pension funds.

5.9.2 Prospectus Directive

Under the MIFID directives which were co-ordinated amongst members of the European Union a similar provision has been made for offerings made to a restricted class of investors in Europe where a formal prospectus is not statutorily required, or at least where the disclosures required are far less onerous than those required for a public offering.

The Prospectus Regulations 2005, implementing the EU Prospectus Directive 2003/71/EC, were made on 26 May 2005. The Statutory Instrument (No. 1433) was laid before Parliament on 27 May 2005.

The Prospectus Directive (PD) sets out the initial disclosure obligations for issuers of securities that are offered to the public or admitted to trading on a regulated market in the EU. It provides a passport for issuers which in turn enables them to raise capital across the EU on the basis of a single prospectus.

During 2010, the FSA in the UK has been in the process of finalising its Prospectus Directive and the new rules will apply to prospectuses for public offers of securities and admission of securities to trading on a regulated market. The key provisions of the new directives will be:

- **Prospectus Requirements** – prescribing the contents and format of prospectuses; allowing issuers to incorporate by reference; allowing the use of three part prospectuses; setting out the exemptions from the requirement to produce prospectuses;
- **Approval and Publication of Prospectus** – setting out procedures for approval or prospectuses and how and where they must be published;
- **Passport Rights** – introducing administrative measures to facilitate the passporting of prospectuses on a pan-European basis, making it easier for companies to raise capital across Europe;
- **Third Country Issuers** – prospectuses drawn up under a third country's law can be treated as equivalent to directive requirements. This will be determined on a case-by-case basis;
- **Other Provisions** – requiring issuers to produce annual information updates and the establishment of a Qualified Investors register (see below).

5.9.3 Qualified Investors

One very significant provision of the Prospectus Directive (PD), as implemented in the UK, is that issuers/offerors are exempt from the obligation to produce a prospectus where offers of securities are made only to Qualified Investors (QIs).

QIs are legal entities authorised to operate in the financial markets (eg, investment firms and insurance companies), governments, supranational institutions, as well as natural persons and small and medium-sized enterprises (SMEs) that certify that they meet the required criteria.

The PD allows the FSA to maintain a register of QIs, which must then be available to all issuers and offerors. The information held on the Qualified Investors Register (QIR) is solely to facilitate the issuance of securities without the requirement to publish a prospectus under the PD.

Natural persons and SMEs can only be recognised as QIs if they meet the criteria specified below and are registered on the QIR.

QIs will be removed from the QIR annually (30 June) and so QIs must specifically request that their details appear on the new register every year.

Investors wishing to register as a QI need to self-certify. At least two of the following three criteria to qualify for inclusion on the QIR must be met:

1. The investor must have carried out transactions of a significant size (at least €1,000) on securities markets at an average frequency of, at least, ten per quarter for the last four quarters.
2. The investor's security portfolio must exceeds €0.5 million.
3. The investor must work – or have worked for at least one year – in the financial sector in a professional position which requires knowledge of securities investment.

SMEs are also required to self-certify. However, at least two of the following three criteria must be fulfilled to qualify for inclusion on the QIR:

1. Average number of employees is less than 250.

2. Total balance sheet does not exceed €43,000,000.
3. Annual net turnover does not exceed €50,000,000.

The following information is included on the QIR for individuals:

1. QI's name;
2. QI unique reference number;
3. a contact address (this can be the address of their representative/legal, financial or other adviser or a P.O. Box address) or broker name and identification number with that broker.

5.10 INTRODUCTIONS

LEARNING OBJECTIVE

2.5.10 Understand the use of introductions: why would a company undertake an introduction; structure of an introduction; stages of an introduction

An introduction is not actually an issue at all. It is used by a company that wishes to become listed (eg, on the London Stock Exchange) to gain access to the secondary market that it provides.

An introduction is unusual because most companies use listing as an opportunity to raise extra funds and some companies are forced to issue more shares to comply with the listing rules.

An introduction is used by a company that does not need to raise extra capital through share issues, but wishes to gain the extra liquidity in its shares that a listing provides. This might be a company that is already listed on another, overseas stock exchange, a new company formed from two previously listed companies that have merged, or a demutualised organisation.

Because an introduction raises no funds, it is not a marketing operation in the same way as an offer for sale, offer for subscription or placing.

5.11 EXCHANGEABLE/CONVERTIBLE BOND OFFERINGS

LEARNING OBJECTIVE

2.5.11 Understand the use of exchangeable/convertible bond offerings: the difference between exchangeable and convertible bonds; structure of offering – base deal plus greenshoe; stages of offering; underwritten versus best efforts

Exchangeable bonds and convertible bonds are similar instruments – they both can be described as hybrid instruments, with characteristics of both equities and bonds. A **convertible bond** is a bond, paying a coupon and with a nominal value to be repaid on maturity, that offers the holder of the bond the right to convert the bond into a set number of ordinary shares of the company that issued the bond.

EXAMPLE

XYZ issues convertible bonds paying a 6% annual coupon and redeeming in 5 years' time. The holder of the convertible can choose to convert £100 nominal value of the bonds into 25 XYZ shares at redemption.

Clearly the holder of the bonds will convert as long as the shares are trading at more than £4 each at the redemption date.

An **exchangeable bond** is again a bond that pays a coupon and has a set redemption date. However, like a convertible, it gives the holder the right to exchange the bond for a set number of shares, but these shares are not those of the bond issuer, but of another company's shares that are held by the issuer.

EXAMPLE

XYZ plc holds ABC plc shares and issues exchangeable bonds paying a 6% annual coupon and redeeming in 5 years' time. The holder of the exchangeable can choose to convert £100 nominal value of the bonds into 20 ABC shares at redemption.

Clearly the holder of the bonds will exchange as long as the shares are trading at more than £5 each at the redemption date.

The holder of either a convertible or an exchangeable bond has the safety of coupons and repayment, combined with the potential upside of equity growth. The difference between the two instruments is simply that the convertible can be converted into the issuer of the bond's shares, whereas an exchangeable can be converted into the shares of a company other than the issuer of the bonds. Both types of bond will enable the issuer to raise borrowed funds more cheaply because the bonds have the upside potential of the conversion/exchange into shares.

The structure of an offering of a convertible or exchangeable bond mirrors that of equities – the issuer will set a base amount of bonds it wishes to issue and perhaps retain a green shoe, reserving the right to issue more if demand is strong.

The stages of the convertible/exchangeable offer are the same as an IPO:

1. **The decision**.
2. **The preparation of the prospectus**.
3. **The sale of securities**.

As with an IPO, the offer may also be underwritten, with a potential combination of firm underwriting by the investment bank(s) and best efforts underwriting by clients of the investment bank(s) such as stockbroking firms.

6. BOND OFFERINGS

6.1 TYPES OF ISSUER

LEARNING OBJECTIVE

2.6.1 Know the different types of issuer: supranationals; governments; agency; municipal; corporate; financial institutions and special purpose vehicle

As we have seen, bonds are essentially 'I owe you' (IOU) instruments that specify a face value, coupon rate and redemption date. They are issued by a variety of organisations including:

- **Supranationals**. Organisations like the World Bank raise money through issuing bonds.
- **Governments**. Most governments have a requirement to borrow money at some stage, and the long-term borrowing is generally financed by bond issues, such as the UK gilts and the US Treasury bonds.
- **Agencies**. Agencies (often backed by the government) issue bonds for particular purposes. These are common in the US where examples include the Federal National Mortgage Association ('Fannie Mae'), created to provide mortgage finance for the disadvantaged, and the Student Loan Marketing Association ('Sallie Mae') created to finance student education.

  Recent developments in the US credit markets have seen government sponsored entities such as Fannie Mae and Freddie Mac (Federal Home Loan Mortgage Corporation) come under the conservatorship of the US Treasury and a public underwriting of their entire obligations.
- **Municipalities**. Municipalities in the US issue municipal bonds to finance local borrowing. These municipal bonds are often tax efficient, particularly for investors who reside in that municipality.

  Municipal bonds are usually guaranteed by a third party, known in the US market as a monoline insurer, and their credit quality may be enhanced by such a guarantee which enables the municipality to secure funds on more advantageous terms. Some of the well known monoline insurers in the US extended their activities to providing a range of far more risky guarantees for asset-backed securities, and have since lost their own investment grade ratings.
- **Corporates**. Large companies often use bonds to finance borrowing needs.
- **Financial Institutions and Special Purpose Vehicles**. Like other corporates, financial institutions issue bonds to finance borrowing. These financial institutions also arrange borrowing for themselves and others by creating special purpose vehicles ('SPV') to enable money to be raised that does not appear within the accounts of that entity. This type of finance is often described as 'off balance sheet finance', because it does not appear in the balance sheet that forms of part of the company's accounts.

Owing to illiquidity and critical developments in the credit markets during 2008, many parent institutions have had to abandon special purpose vehicles including SIVs (structured investment vehicles) and have had to move these 'off balance sheet' accounts back on to the parent entity's balance sheet. In particular, Citigroup was forced to come to the rescue of certain funds within its own SIV, and this resulted in almost $50 billion being returned to the company's balance sheet.

6.2 DEBT SENIORITY

LEARNING OBJECTIVE

2.6.2 Understand the seniority of debt and how they rank in default: senior; subordinated; mezzanine; PIK

Debt issued by companies can come in a variety of forms including bonds and bank borrowing. When there are multiple forms of debt, the issuer will have to establish some sort of order as to which debt will be serviced and repaid first in the event of the company's encountering financial difficulties. In broad terms the seniority of the debt falls into three main headings:

- **Senior**. Senior debt or bonds have a claim that is above that of the more junior forms of borrowing and the equity of the issuer in the event of liquidation.
- **Subordinated**. Subordinated debt or bonds have accepted that their claim to the issuer's assets ranks below that of the senior debt in the event of a liquidation. As a result of accepting a greater risk than the senior debt, the subordinated borrowing will be entitled to a greater rate of interest than that available on the senior debt.
- **Mezzanine and PIK**. The mezzanine level of debt, if it exists at all, will be even more risky than the subordinated debt. It will rank below other forms of debt, but above the equity in a liquidation. As the most risky debt, the mezzanine debt will offer a greater rate of interest than the subordinated and senior levels of debt. Mezzanine borrowing can be raised in a variety of ways – one example is the issue of payment in kind notes (PIK notes). PIK notes are simply zero coupon bonds that are issued at a substantial discount to their face value. When they are repaid, the difference between the redemption value and the purchase cost will provide the investor's return.

It should be noted that each of the three main categories can themselves contain sub-categories such as **senior secured**, **senior unsecured**, **senior subordinated** and **junior subordinated**. In practice, the various rating agencies look at debt structures in these narrower terms. Seniority can be contractual as the result of the terms of the issue, or based on the corporate structure of the issuer.

6.3 PRICING BENCHMARKS

LEARNING OBJECTIVE

2.6.3 Understand the pricing benchmarks: spread over government bond benchmark; spread over/under LIBOR; spread over/under swap

As seen, the seniority of bonds is reflected in the returns that are available on those bonds – subordinated bonds pay a greater rate of return than senior bonds from the same issuer. In a similar way, bonds issued by different issuers will pay different levels of return to reflect investors' perceptions of the relative risks of default by those issuers. This is measured and assessed by looking at '**spreads**'. The spread is simply the difference between the rate of return (the yield) on one instrument compared to another. It is generally quoted in basis points, with each basis point representing one one-hundredth of a percentage point (ie, 0.01%).

The use of a particular pricing benchmark is generally determined by the type of debt asset class. Also, specific features of a bond can mean that pricing off a benchmark security/rate becomes more difficult eg, a ten-year corporate bond, with a put/call feature, is unlikely to price off the ten-year gilt but rather a benchmark curve, as the estimate of the maturity of the corporate bond is unlikely to coincide with the specific maturity of the given gilt because of the put/call feature. (The term 'pricing off' simply means the price/value of one thing – here a bond – being determined from the price/value of something else – here another bond).

The comparison tends to be against one of three yields:

1. **Government bond yields**, such as the yield on the ten-year US Treasury Note or the yield on long-dated gilts.
2. **LIBOR** (the London Inter Bank Offer Rate), which is the rate at which funds in a particular currency and for a particular maturity are available to one bank from other banks. LIBORs are gathered and published by the British Bankers Association (BBA) in London on a daily basis. At times of financial stress such as during the banking crisis in the autumn of 2008 the spread between LIBOR and the applicable base rates can widen dramatically which, in that instance reflected the incapacity or unwillingness of banks to engage in normal money market activities.
3. **Swap rates**. There is a very active market in exchanging floating rates for fixed rates in the so-called 'swaps market'. There is also an enormous market in credit default swaps (CDS) which are a form of insurance against the risk of borrowers defaulting on their debt.The rates available on swaps are also used as benchmarks against which to judge yields.

The spreads on a particular instrument could be above or below benchmarks as shown in the following example:

EXAMPLE

UBX Inc is a well-established and highly-rated company. It has bonds in issue that expire in approximately ten-years' time and are currently yielding 5.40%. Comparative government bonds (based on the ten-year Treasury Bond) are yielding 5.15%, and the ten-year swaps rate is 5.20%. Three month LIBOR is 5.54%.

The spreads can be summarised as follows:

UBX bonds spread above government bonds = 25 basis points (5.40%–5.15%)
UBX spread under LIBOR = 14 basis points (5.40%–5.54%)
UBX bonds spread over swap rates = 20 basis points (5.40%–5.20%)

6.4 BOND ISSUANCE

LEARNING OBJECTIVE

2.6.4 Know the methods of issuance: scheduled funding programmes and opportunistic issuance (eg, MTN); auction/tender; reverse inquiry (under MTN)

Traditionally, borrowing money via a bond issue had been only sensible when large sums of money were being raised in a single capital raising transaction. The sums had to be large enough to make the costs involved in issuance worthwhile. The details of the bond would be established, including its coupon and maturity, and the bonds would be marketed to potential investors. The investors would either be invited to bid for the bonds in an auction-type process, or a tender method was adopted. Both of these are illustrated in the examples that follow in relation to UK Government bonds.

The **Debt Management Office (DMO)** is the part of the **Treasury** that oversees gilt issues. It uses a number of different issue methods, depending on the circumstances. Most commonly used is the auction method, where the DMO announces the auction, receives bids and allocates the gilts to those that bid highest, at the price they bid. Gilt-Edged Market Makers (GEMMs) are expected to bid for gilts when the DMO makes a new issue, and the DMO reserves the right to take the gilts onto its own books if the auction is not fully taken up.

EXAMPLE

Auction example:

First, the DMO sets a minimum price. Applicants bid for the gilt and successful bidders pay the price at which they bid.

Imagine the auction is for £1m nominal and the DMO's minimum price is £100 for £100 nominal.

- **A offers to buy £0.5m nominal, willing to pay £101.50 for every £100 nominal.**
- **B offers to buy £0.5m nominal, willing to pay £100.75 for every £100 nominal.**
- **C offers to buy £0.5m nominal, willing to pay £100.50 for every £100 nominal.**

A and B are awarded the gilts for the prices that they bid and there is nothing left for C.

Up until 1987 the tender method was standard, where all bidders paid a common strike price.

EXAMPLE

Tender example:

A minimum price is set by the DMO and investors make bids. The gilts are awarded at the highest price at which they can all be sold.

Imagine the tender is for £1m nominal and the minimum price is £100 for £100 nominal. The bids submitted are:

- **A offers to buy £0.5m nominal, paying £101.50 for every £100 nominal.**
- **B offers to buy £0.5m nominal, paying £100.75 for every £100 nominal.**
- **C offers to buy £0.5m nominal, paying £100.50 for every £100 nominal.**

In this instance, A and B are awarded the gilts, but both pay the lower price: £100.75 (the highest price at which all the gilts could be sold).

Because many issuers, particularly companies, needed to borrow money regularly in line with the developments of their business, they tended to prefer to set up scheduled programmes with their banks under which they would be able to borrow money, instead of issuing bonds.

However, a US innovation has been introduced that has been subsequently adopted in many other jurisdictions which enables bond financing to be much more flexible. Traditionally, it was awkward and expensive to regularly raise bond finance because each bond issue had to be separately registered with the financial regulator (the SEC in the US). A process known as '**shelf registration**' was introduced that enabled a single registration to be used for a number of bond issues over a period of up to two years. This has been heavily used in the **medium-term note** (MTN) market for bonds with generally two to 10 years between issue and maturity. Shelf registration introduced flexibility to the bond market, allowing companies to issue smaller batches of bonds, with the coupons and maturity varying according to market demand at the time.

The process involves the bond issuer finding two or more dealers that are willing to offer their services to market the bonds to their clients on a best efforts basis. The issuer will then issue bonds as and when the money is required, with coupon rates and maturity in accordance with market demand. Indeed, it is not unusual for some MTNs to be issued in response to an enquiry from clients of the dealers that want a particular maturity and coupon. These are termed '**reverse inquiries**' in the US, and the issuer can decide whether to accept the terms and issue the bonds or not.

6.5 THE ROLE OF THE ORIGINATION TEAM

LEARNING OBJECTIVE

2.6.5 Understand the role of the origination team including: pitching; indicative bid; mandate announcement; credit rating; roadshow; listing; syndication

Many of the activities in originating bond issues are similar to those of originating equity issues, particularly if the bonds are going to be listed and therefore need a prospectus. In such cases there will be a whole '**origination team**' involving the issuer, its investment bank, reporting accountants, legal and PR advisers.

A typical new issue of bonds could contain any, or all of the following stages:

1. **Pitching**. The issuer of the bonds will need to decide that a bond issue is appropriate and which investment bank(s) it wants to assist in the issue. The final decision will be dependent upon an assessment of the qualities of the potential banks. A final decision is usually made on the basis of a presentation made by the banks, to the issuer. This is known as a 'pitch'.
2. **Indicative bid**. During the pitching stage, the banks will detail their views of how much finance the issuer is likely to raise given the terms of the bond issue. This is the 'indicative bid'.
3. **Mandate announcement**. Once the issuer has decided upon the bank(s) to raise the finance on its behalf, it will announce the names of the banks that have been given the mandate to arrange the issue on its behalf.
4. **Credit rating**. Vital to the amount of finance that can be raised will be a credit rating from one of the credit rating agencies. The details of the proposed terms and conditions of the bond will have to be provided to the agency to get a credit rating, and there may be a need for credit enhancements, such as insurance, to enable a higher rating to be achieved.
5. **Roadshow**. Once the bank running the issue has been appointed, the bank will arrange and run a series of visits to the potential buyers of the bonds. This is commonly described as the 'roadshow', because it involves travelling around a number of major financial centres to see the key investors.
6. **Listing**. As mentioned above, if the bond is to be listed it will need a prospectus to submit to the relevant listing authority.
7. **Syndication**. For larger bond issues there will be a number of banks acting for the issuer, described as a lead manager (the primary contact with the issuer) and the other co-managers that will sell into their particular client base, perhaps based on geographical regions. The total of all the banks involved is the 'syndicate'.

6.6 TAKEOVER FINANCINGS

LEARNING OBJECTIVE

2.6.6 Understand methods of raising new capital to finance takeovers: follow-on offerings; rights issues; convertible bond offerings

When financing the takeover of another company, the predator can choose between raising equity - perhaps by way of a follow-on offering or a rights issue - or raising debt. A hybrid between debt and equity is also a possibility in the form of a convertible bond issue.

The mechanics of each of these possibilities are discussed in the following sections of this chapter:

- Follow on offerings are discussed in Section 5.6.
- Rights issues are covered in Section s 5.8 and 8.1.
- Convertible bond offerings are discussed in Section 5.11.

7. SHARE CAPITAL AND CHANGES TO SHARE OWNERSHIP

7.1 SHARE BUYBACKS

LEARNING OBJECTIVE

2.7.1 Understand why share buybacks are undertaken: governing regulation: resolution at AGM, limits on percentage of shares and price, use of company's own money; key aspects of share buybacks – criteria to comply with; different structures regarding block trades; accelerated bookbuild – best efforts basis; accelerated bookbuild – back stop price; bought deal

Share buybacks are where a company decides to use its own money to buy back shares from existing investors. There are two obvious situations where share buybacks might be considered:

1. Where the company has reduced its activities (perhaps having sold a major part of its business) and has surplus cash to return to shareholders.
2. Where the company wants to reorganise its capital structure to include more debt and less equity. In these circumstances the company can borrow money (by issuing bonds or from banks), and use it to buy back and therefore reduce the number of shares it has in issue.

There will inevitably be restrictions on company's ability to buy back its own shares, partly to prevent shareholders from being unfairly preferred to creditors, and partly to make sure that the company has gained approval to buy back from its own shareholders. To prevent unfair prejudice against the creditors, regulation limits the amount that can be used to repurchase shares. In the UK, there are various accounting tests that need to be satisfied to prevent erosion of what is referred to as the 'creditors' buffer'. In simple terms, the creditors' buffer is the money originally paid into the company as capital.

Approval from shareholders generally requires a resolution at the AGM to grant permission to buy shares back. Such permissions inevitably place limits on the percentage of shares to be purchased and the price paid to those shareholders that sell.

The actual mechanics of undertaking a share buyback once regulatory and shareholder approval has been gained can be done in a variety of ways, such as:

- **Block trades** – where an investment bank acting for the company will seek to do a small number of large trades with investors, perhaps through an exchange.
- **Accelerated bookbuild** – where the investment bank will contact a number of institutions, investors in the company, seeking their willingness to sell at particular price points. If the buyback is sufficiently large to require a syndicate, some of the more junior members may only be willing to be involved on a best efforts basis, and the whole syndicate will have a price which it cannot go above (the '**back stop price**').
- **Bought deal** – this is where the buyback is achieved by agreeing the terms with the investment bank(s) at the outset. The investment bank guarantees to buy back the particular number of shares, potentially for more than the company is paying, if necessary.

7.2 STAKE BUILDING

LEARNING OBJECTIVE

2.7.2 Understand how and why stake building is used: strategic versus acquisition; direct versus indirect: direct – outright purchase, indirect – CFDs; disclosure thresholds, including mandatory takeover threshold

A stake is simply a shareholding, and many investors buy stakes in companies simply for the investment potential. Sometimes stakes are built in companies for reasons over and above the simple investment potential. **Strategic stakes** may be accumulated in order to prevent a company being taken over by a competitor and to influence the company concerned. This may be in order to protect supplies – the company may be a key supplier of raw materials to the strategic stakeholder, without which the strategic stakeholder may have difficulty obtaining the quantity and quality of raw materials it seeks.

A stake may be accumulated in the hope of bringing about an **acquisition**. An acquisition of another company is achieved by purchasing more than 50% of the shares, and thereby gaining 'control' of the votes and the company. It is usual to talk in terms of the acquiring company being the 'predator' or 'offeror' and the company being acquired as the 'target' or 'offeree'.

For a potential predator building a stake in order to eventually acquire a target company, there are certain regulatory restrictions.

Firstly, as a stake becomes more significant, there are **disclosure requirements**. In the UK these disclosure requirements are contained within the FSA's **Disclosure and Transparency Rules**. An investor is judged to have a **notifiable interest** in a public company if he holds 3% or more of its shares. At this point he is obliged to inform the company of his holding.

Once the investor's holding is above 3%, he must also inform the company if it rises or falls through a whole percentage point.

- A stake of 3.7% rising to 4.1% would need to be reported, but a stake of 3.7% rising to 3.9% would not.
- A stake of 5.4% falling to 4.9% would need to be reported, but a stake of 5.4% falling to 5.1% would not.

An investor must also inform the company if his stake falls back to below 3%.

Why is this disclosure deemed necessary, when the company maintains a register of its shareholders? The notifiable interest rules not only include those shares held directly by the investor, but also those shares held indirectly by parties connected to them, known as **connected parties**. These would include shares held by the following:

- the investor's spouse;
- the investor's infant children (less than 18 years old);
- companies controlled by the investor. For these purposes, control is assumed if the investor holds at least one third of the voting rights of the company;
- concert parties. This is simply an agreement between two or more persons to influence the company together, such as voting together. If the combined holding reached 3% or more it would become notifiable, as if it were a single holding.

As seen above, 3% is the level at which notification starts and this information must be reported in writing to the company and the FSA within two business days.

Fund managers and operators of regulated collective investment schemes (such as authorised unit trusts and open-ended investment companies) are deemed to be non-beneficial holders and are exempt from reporting at 3%. Interests held by investment managers and OEICs, and in general non-beneficial owners, are under the Disclosure and Transparency Rules (DTR 5) subject to disclosure at 5% and 10% (but not at the percentages in between 5% and 10%) and then at every percentage above 10% (DTR 5.1.5). Also, under DTR 5, market makers have an exemption only for holdings below 10% (DTR 5.1.3 and 5.1.4).

Some shareholders are completely exempted from the disclosure rules, eg, if the shares are held by:

- a market maker, or dealer in shares, for the purposes of that business;
- a custodian (which is not able to control the voting rights of the shares concerned).

The company is required to maintain a **register** of notifications of interests in shares and make this available at its registered office.

At the time of writing, shares acquired under contracts for differences (CFDs) are not subject to these disclosure requirements, although the FSA continues to analyse how best to deal with CFDs.

Secondly, and in addition to the rules relating to notification and disclosure of significant shareholdings, there are also rules laid down by the **Panel on Takeovers and Mergers** (**POTAM** or **PTM**) in the UK that apply to stakebuilding during the course of a takeover bid. Under PTM rules, a **mandatory offer** is required if any person either:

1. acquires shares that take their holding to 30% or more of the voting rights of the target company; or
2. increases their holding from a starting point of 30% or more, but less than 50%.

If a mandatory bid is required, the consideration offered must be in the form of cash, or there must be a cash alternative. The cash offer must not be less than the highest price paid by the offeror in the previous 12 months.

There are some exceptions to this rule, the main one being for additions to the offeror's stake during the course of a formal offer. In any other instances the Panel's permission would be required to acquire shares that breach the rule.

During the course of an offer, dealings in relevant securities by the offeror or the offeree company, or any associates, for their own account must be publicly disclosed. The requirement is that disclosure must be made to the Panel and a Regulatory Information Service (such as the London Stock Exchange's Regulatory News Service, or 'RNS') by noon on the business day following the transaction.

Relevant securities are the shares of the offeror and offeree, and any derivatives such as options on these shares.

Additionally, PTM rules require that anyone holding more than 1% (before or after the transaction) of the offeree or offeror company shares must disclose any further transactions (excluding acceptance of the offer itself) to the Panel and a Regulatory Information Service by noon on the next business day.

8. CORPORATE ACTIONS

8.1 RIGHTS ISSUES

LEARNING OBJECTIVE

2.8.1 Understand the use of rights issues: reasons for a rights issue; structure of rights issue; stages of rights issue; pre-emptive rights; ability to sell nil paid

A rights issue is an issue by a company of new shares (a secondary issue) for cash to the existing shareholders in proportion to their existing holding. It is usually at a discount to the current market price. A rights issue is an attractive way for a company to raise new finance for the following reasons:

- There is no dilution of shareholders' interest, ie, someone who held 20% of the shares before the issue will hold 20% after (assuming they take up their rights).
- The issue is at a discount to the current market price to make it attractive.

- A shareholder who does not want to subscribe more cash and take up his rights can sell them, receiving cash as payment for the dilution of interest that he will suffer.
- Such issues are generally underwritten to cater for those individuals who do not want to exercise their rights, thus the company can be sure of raising all the finance it requires.

In essence, a rights issue is a way of avoiding the negative effects of dilution on shareholders. Dilution occurs when new shares in a company are issued, diluting the influence and value of the existing shares.

8.1.1 Mechanics of a Rights Issue

New shares are offered in proportion to each shareholder's existing shareholding, usually at a price deeply discounted to that prevailing in the market to ensure that the issue will be fully subscribed and sometimes to reduce, or even avoid, the cost of underwriting the shares. The number of new shares issued and the price of these shares will be determined by the amount of capital to be raised.

The right to participate in such an issue is only conferred upon those shareholders who hold the issuing company's shares cum-rights – that is, those who hold the company's shares before trading in the shares is conducted on an ex-rights, or without rights, basis. The ex-rights period begins on, or shortly after, the day on which the rights issue announcement is made and runs for a further 21 days through to the acceptance date, the date by which the shareholder should have decided whether or not to take up these new shares.

Those entitled to participate in the rights issues are advised of their entitlement by means of a Provisional Allotment Letter. The Provisional Allotment Letter is renounceable and transferable and it sets out the shareholder's existing shareholding, the rights allotted over the new shares and the acceptance date. The ex-rights period begins on the day after the allotment letter is posted.

As these new shares rank equally, or *pari passu*, with the existing shares in issue, once the existing shares are declared ex-rights, the market price should fall to reflect the dilution effect that the new shares will have on the prevailing share price. The price to which the shares should fall is termed the **theoretical ex-rights price**, and its method of calculation is shown below.

The formula for the theoretical ex-rights price is as follows:

$$\frac{\left[\left(\begin{array}{c}\text{No. shares held cum-rights}\\ \text{x}\\ \text{cum-rights share price}\end{array}\right) + \left(\begin{array}{c}\text{No. rights allocated}\\ \text{x}\\ \text{rights issue price}\end{array}\right)\right]}{\text{Total no. shares held assuming rights exercised}}$$

The difference between the theoretical ex-rights price and the rights issue price is known as the **nil paid value**, and the calculation and significance of this will be illustrated in the following sections.

As noted above, shareholders have 21 days to decide how to react to the announcement following receipt of the provisional allotment letter and must choose between one of the four following courses of action:

- **Option One – Take up the rights nil paid in full**
  Take up the rights in full by purchasing all of the shares offered. To take up the rights in full, the shareholder simply sends the company the Provisional Allotment Letter with a cheque by the due date.

- **Option Two – Sell the rights nil paid in full**
  Sell the rights nil paid in full. If a shareholder entitled to take up the rights issue decides not to, then they can sell the rights to these new shares nil paid. The purchaser of the nil paid rights will be able to take up the shares at the discounted price. Essentially they have a short-dated option on these new shares that can only be exercised, or traded, during the three-week, ex-rights period. To sell the rights nil paid in full the shareholder must sign the form of renunciation on the reverse of the Provisional Allotment Letter and send it to their broker by the due date.

- **Option Three – Sell part of rights nil paid to preserve current stake without dilution**
  Sell sufficient rights nil paid to finance the take up of the remaining rights. This course of action would be taken by a shareholder wishing to retain their shareholding in the company but without any desire to invest any further capital at this stage. When selling the rights nil paid in part, the shareholder does exactly the same as when selling them in full but requests that their broker split the allotment letter in accordance with the number of rights sold and those to be taken up. One of the split allotment letters will go to the purchaser of the rights and the other to the original shareholder.

- **Option Four – Take no action**
  Any shareholder not taking any action by the acceptance date stipulated in the provisional allotment letter will automatically have their rights sold nil paid. The proceeds, less any expenses incurred by the company, are then distributed to all such shareholders on a pro rata basis. For the smaller shareholder not wishing to increase their shareholding in the company, this is often the most economic way to proceed.

8.1.2 Pre-Emption Rights

Legally, the current shareholders of a company have prior rights to subscribe for any new issues of shares for cash before they can be offered to anyone else. These are called their pre-emption rights and their purpose is to ensure that the level of influence or control that a shareholder has is not diluted by any issue without his prior knowledge and agreement.

The existence of pre-emption rights means that listed companies cannot issue equity shares, convertibles or warrants for cash other than to the current equity shareholders of the company, except with their prior approval in general meeting.

It is quite common to see the waiving of pre-emption rights as a proposed special resolution at the AGM of public companies. Shareholders can vote to forgo their pre-emption rights for a period of up to five years, though the stock exchange's rules for listed companies are stricter, requiring such a resolution to be passed at each AGM.

EXAMPLE OF DILUTION

Suppose an investor holds 400 shares out of a total of 10,000 shares in XYZ plc, a 4% stake in the company. XYZ plc then decides to issue 10,000 further shares. That means that there are now 20,000 shares in issue. The investor's original 400 shares now represents a 2% stake rather than a 4% stake. That is dilution.

UK company law offers some protection against dilution, with most companies requiring a special resolution from shareholders for new shares to be allotted in cash to anyone other than the existing shareholders in proportion to their existing holding. This is known as the shareholders' pre-emptive right.

In the above example, the investor's pre-emptive right would be to be offered 400 of the further issue of 10,000 shares.

8.1.3 Ability to Sell Nil Paid

As seen in the mechanics of a rights issue, existing shareholders do not have to participate in the rights issue but can sell the rights nil paid, either in part or in full. A fuller discussion of the method of calculating the nil paid value is discussed below, but the essential feature is that the issuer provides the current shareholders with a transferable 'security' which can be sold to other investors and which protects them from dilution as defined above.

8.1.4 Impact of a Rights Issue on the Share Price

LEARNING OBJECTIVE

2.8.2 Be able to calculate the impact of a rights issue on the share price

To illustrate the impact on the share price for a company which undertakes a rights issue, the following are the key variables in the example discussed below.

- Prior to the rights issue the company has issued one million shares with a nominal value of £1.00 each. The par value is the nominal value which has been determined by an issuing company as a minimum price.
- The share premium account shows a balance of £0.5 million. The share premium account of a company is the capital that a company raises upon issuing shares that is in excess of the nominal value of the shares.
- The company wishes to raise new capital for expansion and undertakes a one for four rights issue at a price of £1.50 in order to raise £400,000.
- The company's accounts before the rights issue show that net assets are £2 million and retained profits of £0.5 million
- The market price of the shares prior to the rights offering is £3.00 per share.

What is the impact on the accounts and the theoretical market price per share of this issue?

A one for four rights issue means that for every four shares previously in existence, one new share will be issued. In our example, one million shares were previously in issue, and 250,000 new shares will be issued at a price of £1.50 in order to raise the £400,000 cash required.

In terms of the accounts the 250,000 new share issue will increase the share capital to 1.25 million shares, the profit and loss will remain unchanged but the share premium account will need to be adjusted. The reason for this adjustment is that for the £400,000 raised, each of the 250,000 new shares can be issued at the nominal value of £1 but the additional £150,000 raised in excess of the nominal or face value of the shares is allocated to the share premium account as indicated in the simple balance sheet perspective in the table below.

The total capitalisation of the company will have increased to £2.4 million and can be broken down according to the upper part of the table which reflects the rights issue from an accounting perspective.

The impact on the share price can be seen from the calculation of the theoretical market price in the lower part of the table. The price for the shares should have fallen from £3.00 per share before the rights issue to £2.70 after the issue to reflect the new capitalisation divided by the greater number of shares now outstanding.

Rights Issue			
Impact on the Accounts (All amounts in £'000)			
	Before	Issue	After
Net assets	2,000	400	2,400
Share capital			
1m £1 Ordinary shares	1,000	250	1,250
Share premium	500	150	650
Profit and loss	500		500
Totals	2,000	400	2,400
Impact on the share price			
	Shares ('000)	Price £	Value (£'000)
Before	1,000	3.00	3,000
Rights Issue	250	1.50	375
After	1,250		3,375
Market Price for shares	£2.70		

Another perspective on this can be seen simply by looking at the following formula which only requires knowledge of the share price before the rights issue and the actual terms of the rights issue.

As noted earlier, the formula for the theoretical ex-rights price is as follows:

$$\frac{\left[\begin{pmatrix}\text{No. shares held cum-rights}\\ \text{x}\\ \text{cum-rights share price}\end{pmatrix} + \begin{pmatrix}\text{No. rights allocated}\\ \text{x}\\ \text{rights issue price}\end{pmatrix}\right]}{\text{Total no. shares held assuming rights exercised}}$$

Description	**Number of shares**	**Price per share (pence)**	**Total Value of Holdings (pence)**
Shares held cum-rights	4	300	1,200
Rights allocated – new share entitlement	1	150	150
Post rights issue assuming rights taken up	5		1,350
Theoretical ex-rights price = 1,350/5		270	

8.2 SCRIP OR BONUS ISSUES

LEARNING OBJECTIVE

2.8.3 Understand the use of scrip (also known as bonus or capitalisation) issues and why a company will undertake a scrip issue

A company may issue new shares to its shareholders for no consideration or *pro bono*, raising no further capital. The reasons for this are varied; sometimes as a public relations exercise to accompany news of a recent success or as a means of reducing the current market price to make its shares more marketable.

It can also be used to tidy up shareholders' funds by converting undistributable capital reserves into share capital. A company simply converts its reserves, which may have arisen from issuing new shares in the past at a premium to their nominal value and/or from the accumulation of undistributed past profits, into new ordinary shares. These shares rank *pari passu* with those already in issue and are distributed to the company's ordinary shareholders in proportion to their existing shareholdings free of charge.

Although as a result of the bonus issue the nominal value of the company's share capital will increase proportionately to the number of new shares issued, the net worth or intrinsic value of the business should remain the same. However, given that the company's earnings, or profits, and dividends will now be spread over a wider share capital base, the company's earnings per share (EPS) and dividends per share (DPS) should fall proportionately with the number of new shares in issue. This should result in the market price of the shares reducing by this same proportion, thereby leaving the company's market capitalisation unchanged.

Traditionally, once a UK company's share price starts trading well into double figures in £s, or in the US once its market price exceeds $200, its marketability starts to suffer as investors shy away from the shares. Therefore, a reduction in a company's share price as a result of a bonus issue usually has the effect of increasing the marketability of its shares. It can also raises expectations of higher future dividends. This in turn usually results in the share price settling above its new theoretical level and the company's market capitalisation increasing slightly.

8.2.1 Impact of a Scrip Issue on the Share Price

LEARNING OBJECTIVE

2.8.4 Be able to calculate the impact of a scrip issue on the share price

In the table below, the one million ordinary shares which were only partly paid for are, as a result of the scrip issue or capitalisation, now fully paid for, which has required a transfer of £0.25 million from retained profits to the share capital account. This has resulted in the bonus issue of 250,000 shares, and when the market capitalisation is divided by this enlarged number of shares the share price falls from £3.00 to £2.25.

Bonus, Scrip or Capitalisation			
Impact on the Accounts (all amounts in £000)			
	Before	Issue	After
Net assets	2,250		2,250
Issued Share capital			
1m £1 Ordinary shares partly paid	750		750
1m £1 Ordinary shares fully paid		250	250
Share premium	1,000		1,000
Retained Profit	500	(250)	250
Totals	2,250	0	2,250
Impact on the Share Price			
	Shares (000)	Price £	Value (£000)
Before	750	3.00	2,250
Scrip issue	250		
After	1,000		2,250
Market Price for Shares	£2.25		

EXAMPLE

XYZ plc makes a bonus issue to its shareholders on a one for four basis to coincide with the launch of a new product. Prior to the announcement of the issue, the company's ordinary shares traded at 200p per share. If the company had one million ordinary shares, each with a nominal value of 25p in issue prior to the announcement, calculate:

- **The nominal value of the company's share capital immediately before and immediately after the announcement**
- **The new theoretical market price for the shares**
- **The market capitalisation of the company immediately before and immediately after the announcement based on the pre-existing share price and the new theoretical market price.**

Solution

Nominal value of the company's share capital

- **Immediately before = 1m x 25p = £250,000**
- **Immediately after = 1m x (5 / 4) x 25p = £312,500**

Theoretical market price

The theoretical market price will be 200p x (4 / 5) = 160p

Market capitalisation

- **Immediately before = 1m x 200p = £2m**
- **Immediately after = 1m x (5 / 4) x 160p = £2m**

8.3 MAXIMUM NIL PAID RIGHTS

LEARNING OBJECTIVE

2.8.5 Be able to calculate the maximum nil paid rights to be sold to take up the balance at nil cost

From the discussion in 8.2, option three is the situation where investors can choose to sell some of their entitlement and use the cash raised to take up the rest of the offer. In effect they can buy a sufficient number of shares in the offering to preserve their position without dilution but without having to invest additional funds into the business.

The number of nil paid rights to be sold to take up the balance at nil cost is given by the equation:

$$\frac{\text{Issue price of new shares x number of shares allocated}}{\text{Theoretical ex-rights price}}$$

As nil paid rights cannot be sold in fractions, the number must be rounded up to nearest integer or whole number value.

The actual process of preserving one's position without suffering any dilution but without having to invest new proceeds is sometimes known as 'swallowing the tail' and can be demonstrated in the table below which is expanded from the one given earlier. The table assumes the position of an investor whose current holdings, cum-rights, is 2,000 shares, and all of the same information is the same as contained in the rights issue case study discussed in 8.1.4.

Description	Number of shares	Price per share (pence)	Total Value of Holdings (pence)
Shares held cum-rights	2,000	300	600,000
Rights allocated – new share entitlement	500	150	75,000
Post rights issue assuming rights taken up	2,500		675,000
Theoretical ex-rights price = 1,350/5		270	
Nil paid rights value		120	
Number of nil paid rights to be sold	278		
Amount raised from selling nil rights			33,360
Number of nil paid rights required to avoid dilution	222		
Cost of purchasing rights to avoid dilution			33,300
Gain/Loss from financing to preserve current stake			60
Total value of shares post rights = 2,000+222 x £2.70	599,940		
Total value of position post rights	600,000		
Net Change in Position			0

As can be seen from the bottom row the net change in the investor's position is zero, ignoring transaction costs. By selling 278 nil paid rights and using the proceeds to purchase 222 new shares, accompanied by the tiny cash gain on the proceeds, the investor is in exactly the same position as before the rights issue.

8.4 VALUE OF NIL PAID RIGHTS

LEARNING OBJECTIVE

2.8.6 Be able to calculate the value of nil paid rights

The formula for calculating the theoretical ex-rights price =

$$\frac{\left[\left(\begin{array}{c}\text{No. shares held cum-rights}\\ \times\\ \text{cum-rights share price}\end{array}\right) + \left(\begin{array}{c}\text{No. rights allocated}\\ \times\\ \text{rights issue price}\end{array}\right)\right]}{\text{Total no. shares held assuming rights exercised}}$$

As can be seen, it is straightforward to substitute the following values from the company provided above

Number shares held cum-rights	=	4
Cum rights share price	=	£3.00
Number of rights allocated	=	1
Rights issue price	=	£1.50
Total shares assuming rights exercised	=	5
Solving	=	{[4 x £3.00] + [1 x £1.50]}/5 = £13.50/5 = £2.70

Given this example, the price of each nil paid right should be calculated from the ex-rights share price – price of the new shares = 270p – 150p = 120p.

Obviously, it would not be rational to pay more than 120p for the right to purchase a new share for 150p when the ex-rights price of the existing shares in issue is 270p.

8.5 STOCK SPLIT AND SCRIP ISSUE

LEARNING OBJECTIVE

2.8.7 Understand the difference between a stock split and a scrip issue

The reduction in the share price as a result of a bonus issue may have its advantages, but it also has disadvantages. If share prices are falling, it may result in the price dropping below the nominal value which would prevent a company from raising finance by issuing more shares.

An alternative way of lowering the price per share but avoiding this problem is to undertake a split. A share split is achieved by dividing the existing share capital into a larger number of shares with a lower nominal value per share, though the overall nominal value of all the shares will remain the same.

Let us consider the company discussed in relation to the rights issue again.

The company has issued one million ordinary shares at £1 nominal or par value but wishes now to reduce the price of its shares by replacing that issue with a new issue of 2.5 million shares at a nominal value of £0.20p. The results can be seen on the simplified section of the balance sheet as follows. In effect the company is engaging in a 2.5:1 stock split. Before the split issue the shares are trading at £3 each.

Share Split			
Impact on the Accounts (all amounts in £000)			
	Before	Issue	After
Net assets	2,000		2,000
Share capital			
1m £1 Ordinary shares	1,000	(1,000)	
2.5m £0.20 Ordinary shares		1,000	1,000
Share premium	500		500
Profit and loss	500		500
Totals	2,000	0	2,000
Impact on the Share Price			
	Shares (000)	Price £	Value (£000)
Before	1,000	3.00	3,000
Split issue	1,500		
After	2,500		3,000
Market Price for Shares	£1.20		

In terms of market capitalisation it can be seen that the price per share will drop to £1.20 per share. The prior market capitalisation was £3 million based on 1 million shares but there are now 2.5 million shares issued and the market price for the shares is therefore £3 million/2.5 million shares. The new share price of £1.20 is below the original nominal value of £1.00 per share, but is still considerably above the new nominal value of £0.20 per share. Hence, this will not cause any problems in issuing new shares.

EXERCISE 1

A company has a one for one bonus issue. What is the ex-bonus price (the price after the issue) if the cum-bonus price (the price before the issue) is £10? Here is a blank table to help:

	Number of shares	Price per share	Total value of holding
Before			
Bonus			
After			

The answer to this exercise can be found on the following page.

EXERCISE ANSWERS

Exercise 1:

	Number of shares	Price per share	Total value of holding
Before	1	£10.00	£10.00
Bonus	1	£0.00	£0.00
After	2		£10.00

CHAPTER THREE

PRIMARY AND SECONDARY MARKETS

This syllabus area will provide approximately 22 of the 100 examination questions

1. METHODS OF TRADING AND PARTICIPANTS

1.1 QUOTE-DRIVEN VERSUS ORDER-DRIVEN SYSTEMS

LEARNING OBJECTIVE

3.1.1 Understand the differences between quote-driven and order-driven markets and how they operate

Stock exchanges exist throughout the world as centralised forums for dealing in investments.

For companies offering shares and bonds, these exchanges provide a means of raising money in order to develop and expand. For investors, they provide a safe marketplace for buying and selling their investments.

The major example of a stock exchange in the UK is the London Stock Exchange (LSE). The LSE is like a club whose members are able to take advantage of the club's facilities. In the case of the LSE, the members are investment banks and stockbroking firms. The facilities that the exchange offers are its trading systems.

Trading systems provided by exchanges around the world can be classified on the basis of the type of trading they offer. Broadly, systems are either quote-driven or order-driven:

- **Quote-Driven Systems**. On quote-driven systems, market makers agree to buy and sell at least a set minimum number of shares at quoted prices. The buying price is the 'bid' and the selling price is the 'offer'. The prime example of a quote-driven equity trading system is NASDAQ in the US.
- **Order-Driven Systems**. On order-driven systems, the investors (or agents acting on their behalf) indicate how many securities they want to buy or sell, and at what price. The system then simply brings together the buyers and sellers. Order-driven systems are very common in the equity markets, where the New York Stock Exchange, the Tokyo Stock Exchange and the LSE's Stock Exchange Electronic Trading Service (SETS) are all examples of order-driven equity markets.

The presence of market makers on quote-driven systems provides liquidity that might be lacking on an order-driven system. Market makers are required to quote two-way prices, resulting in an ability for trades to be executed. In contrast, an order-driven system could lack liquidity, since transactions can only be matched against other orders – if there are insufficient orders, trades cannot be matched.

The orders that await matching are included in the so called 'order book'. The buy side of the order book lists orders to buy, and the sell side of the order book lists orders to sell. New sell orders entered into the system potentially match existing orders on the buy side. New buy orders potentially match existing sell side orders in the order book.

Increasingly trading systems are run electronically, allowing participants to trade via computer screens. However, there are notable exceptions: the New York Stock Exchange still retains a physical trading floor where buyers and sellers gather to trade.

As we will see later in this chapter, some trading systems combine features of both order-driven and quote-driven systems – these are referred to as 'hybrid' systems and include the LSE's SETSqx (considered later in this chapter).

1.2 PARTICIPANTS

LEARNING OBJECTIVE

3.1.2 Know the functions and obligations of: market makers; broker/dealers; inter-dealer brokers; stock lending and borrowing intermediaries

There are two roles that firms can play on exchanges like the LSE.

Member firms of an exchange like the LSE can act in two different capacities or roles – one role is to act as a principal and the other is to act as an agent. This does not preclude the fact that individual firms cannot act in both capacities, at some times it may be acting as an agent and at others it may be acting as a principal.

When a firm is acting as a **principal** it is essentially buying shares for its own account, in the hope of the shares increasing in value before it sells them, or in the case of a short transaction selling borrowed shares at a higher price at the time of borrowing than the price it has to pay when it wishes to replace or cover the borrowed shares. Firms acting in this way are can also be described as performing their function as dealers and in more specialised cases, as outlined below, as **market makers**.

When a firm is acting as an **agent** they are essentially arranging and making deals on behalf of other third parties and they make money when acting in this capacity by charging a commission on the deal. This agency role is commonly described as acting as a **broker**.

For instance, when acting as an agent or broker a firm will receive orders to buy and sell equities on behalf of their clients, and find matches for the trades that their clients want to make. In return for these services, brokers charge commission.

If a firm decides to focus only on acting as a principal it is known simply as a dealer and some LSE member firms have chosen simply to buy and sell equities for their own account.

Most exchange's members are **broker/dealers**. This means they have the dual capacity to either arrange deals (acting as a broker), or to buy and sell shares for themselves (acting as a dealer).

Some of an exchange's member firms have chosen to take on the special responsibilities of a **market maker**. When a firm acts as a market maker it stands ready to provide a source of liquidity to certain sections of the market such as the SETSqx system considered later in this chapter. By being prepared to provide a bid for shares that third parties want to sell and an ask for parties that want to buys shares at any time, the market maker smoothes-out the more erratic price movements that can occur without this additional source of market liquidity.

To become a market maker a member firm must **apply** to the stock exchange, giving details of the securities in which they have chosen to deal. They must provide prices at which they are willing to buy and sell a minimum number of their chosen shares throughout the course of the trading day.

Because some of the exchange systems rely on market makers to honour their commitments, the exchange closely vets firms before allowing them to quote prices to investors. In return for agreeing to take on these extra responsibilities, market makers hope to enjoy the benefits of a steady stream of business, from broker dealers and from other investors.

An **inter-dealer broker (IDB)** is an exchange member firm that has registered with the exchange to act as an agent between dealers (such as market makers). When one dealer trades with another dealer, it prefers its identity to remain a secret. This is the key benefit of using an IDB. The IDB is acting as agent for the dealer, but settles any transactions as if it were principal, in order to preserve the anonymity of the dealer. An IDB is not allowed to take principal positions, and an IDB has to be a separate firm, not a division of another broker dealer.

Some firms specialise by acting as **stock borrowing and lending intermediaries (SBLIs)**. These are firms that arrange for one party (perhaps a market making member firm) to borrow shares from another party (perhaps a long-term holder of shares, like a pension fund). This may arise because the market maker has sold shares it does not own – known as 'selling short'. By borrowing shares, the market maker can satisfy the need to deliver the shares. After an agreed period, the borrower will return an equivalent number of the same shares to the lender. The borrower is charged a fee for arranging the transaction (paid to the SBLI), and for borrowing the shares (paid to the lender). During the period of the loan, the lender retains all the benefits of owning the shares (such as dividends) except the voting rights.

2. TRANSACTION REPORTING

2.1 REPORTABLE TRANSACTIONS

LEARNING OBJECTIVE

3.2.1 Understand the definition of a reportable transaction

In order to keep track of what the various firms are doing, the regulator needs to collect data on the deals that have been done. For example, the FSA requires transactions to be reported where they involve authorised firms and involve certain designated investments that include shares, bonds and certain derivatives. They specifically do not include stock lending or borrowing transactions, repo or reverse repo transactions, asset trading transactions or syndications.

Special requirements were issued by the FSA during turbulent equity market conditions in September 2008 requiring institutions and traders to report transactions, for a limited time period, that fall under the heading of 'short selling'. Short selling is the practice of borrowing a security from its owner and selling that security with a view to purchasing and replacing it at a lower price. The FSA, in line with similar directives issued by the SEC in the US and regulators in Australia, took the view that the practice of short selling was disruptive to markets and that requiring institutions to report any such transactions may act as a disincentive to this kind of trading. In October 2008, there was an extension to the time period covered under the SEC directive which prohibits the naked short selling of a list of almost 800 securities in the US equity market.

2.2 ROLE AND PURPOSE OF TRADE AND TRANSACTION REPORTING

LEARNING OBJECTIVE

3.2.2 Understand the role and purpose of transaction reporting for the firm and the regulator

Transaction reporting or settlement reporting is done to facilitate settlement of the transaction and provide information to the regulator, enabling review of transactions after the fact – a measure of market completeness.

Trade reporting is a mechanism to feedback to the marketplace on market depth and liquidity – a measure of market transparency. Trade reports must include a variety of details, including the identity of the reporting member firm, the date and time of the transaction, the security traded and the type of trade. The type of trade is detailed by using a trade type indicator. Trade type indicators include the following:

B	for a broker to broker transaction
M	for a market maker to market maker transaction
X	for an agency cross trade, arranged by a member firm
K	for a block trade
PN	for a worked principal portfolio trade notification
WN	for a worked principal single security trade notification
NM	for a transaction that is 'not to mark' – used where there is permission not to publish the trade

2.3 RESPONSIBLE PARTY

LEARNING OBJECTIVE

3.2.3 Know which party to a transaction is responsible for reporting including transactions carried out by overseas branches

For domestic transactions on systems run by the London Stock Exchange, both parties to a transaction should report to CREST by 8.00pm on the day of the trade. For international equities the Thomson Report, an online trade confirmation service provided by an organisation called Omgeo, can be used for settlement reporting, with transactions reported by both participants by 9.00pm on the day of the trade.

2.4 REPORTING CHANNELS AND SYSTEMS

LEARNING OBJECTIVE

3.2.4 Know the reporting channels and systems

In this section, a number of systems run by the LSE are mentioned. They are:

- SETS – the Stock Exchange Electronic Trading Service;
- IOB – the International Order Book;
- ITBB – the International Bulletin Board;
- IRS – the International Retail Service;

All will be covered in more detail later in this chapter.

2.4.1 Order Book Transactions

Trade reporting is automatic for all those trades that are executed on the LSE's electronic order books – embracing UK equities traded on SETS, depository receipts traded on the IOB and international equities traded on the ITBB. Since the trades are executed automatically on the order books, they will generate automatic trade reports and there is no need for participants to manually report the trades.

2.4.2 Off Order Book Transactions on IOB and ITBB

'Off order book' transactions are trades executed by one or more member firms in IOB or ITBB securities away from the order book, often over the telephone. Such trades need to be reported by the member firm to the exchange within three minutes of execution.

On the IRS, only one party is required to trade report and the report is required within three minutes of the trade. The report should be submitted by the more senior party to the trade, ie, the committed principal that is acting as market maker. Note that committed principal seniority is established by being a committed principal in one or more shares, not necessarily the shares in which the trade is executed. If a deal was done between committed principals, it is the selling committed principal that is responsible for reporting the trade.

Trades in gilt-edged securities need to be reported into the LSE within the same timetable as trades in equity securities (normally within three minutes of the trade) by reference to the trade reporting period.

- The trade reporting period is the period when the LSE system is able to accept trade reports. It runs from 7:15am to 5:15pm.
- If a trade is executed between 7:15am and 8:00am, the report must be submitted before 8:00am or within three minutes, if later.
- If a trade is executed within the last three minutes of the trade reporting period, it should be submitted before 5:15pm.
- If a trade is executed outside the trade reporting period, it must be submitted before 7:45am in the next trade reporting period.

As with equities, the responsibility for trade reporting rests with the more senior party to the trade, ie, the market maker member firm, followed by the broker-dealer member firm, followed by the non-member. If the two parties to the trade are of the same seniority, it is the selling member firm that trade reports.

The main details that need to be included within the trade report are as follows:

- The identity of the reporting member and their counterparty;
- Date and time;
- Whether the trade is a buy or sale;
- Trade type (for example agency or principal);
- Security and quantity traded;
- Price;
- Settlement due date;
- Any special conditions (such as ex-dividend trades).

The Exchange is then free to publish trade details as it chooses. The trades will be published on a daily basis in the **Stock Exchange Daily Official List (SEDOL)**.

Transaction reports for settlement purposes are required via CREST by a deadline on each business day of 8.00pm.

2.4.3 TRAX

TRAX is the post-trade, pre-settlement, trade matching and regulatory confirmation system mainly used for bond trades in the OTC market. It was launched by ICMA (formerly known as ISMA) in 1989, initially to eliminate the costs and risks associated with paper-based trade confirmation. TRAX offered an electronic alternative, enabling counterparties to identify potential misunderstandings and problem trades early in the settlement cycle.

It operates as a reporting hub to multiple regulators (competent authorities) within the EU/EEA and is the primary approved reporting mechanism for bonds.

3. LONDON STOCK EXCHANGE (LSE) – UK EQUITIES

3.1 STOCK EXCHANGE ELECTRONIC TRADING SYSTEM (SETS)

LEARNING OBJECTIVE

3.3.1 Understand the rules, procedures and requirements applying to dealing through the Stock Exchange Electronic Trading System (SETS) in the following areas: order book features; order management; worked principal agreements; limitations and benefits of trading through SETS

SETS is the abbreviated name for the Stock Exchange Electronic Trading System.

Basically, SETS is a computer system that automatically matches orders to buy and orders to sell equities. It is formally described as an electronic order-driven system.

It operates an electronic order book into which LSE member firms submit their orders to buy and sell equities, and when there are orders that can be matched, SETS automatically brings them together. The SETS system is available to all LSE member firms and automatic trading takes place on it between 8.00am and 4.30pm each business day.

The shares traded on SETS include:

- Shares in companies within the FTSE All Share.
- Exchange-traded funds and commodities.
- The most traded AIM and Irish securities.

Example companies include BP, GlaxoSmithKline, HSBC and Marks & Spencer.

3.1.1 The SETS Order Book

In the order book, orders are given priority first by price and then by time.

The electronic screen reflecting the order book for the shares of the fictional company ABC plc might look something like this:

Company: ABC plc			
Orders to buy		**Orders to sell**	
Volume	**Price**	**Volume**	**Price**
10,000	**315**	**316**	**4,000**
2,000	**315**	**317**	**12,000**
4,000	**314**	**318**	**14,000**
8,000	**313**	**318**	**3,000**

The order priority adopted by SETS is by price, and then time. The best buy and sell prices are always at the top of the two columns of orders and will be executed first. In the case of the **buy orders** this is the **highest priced order** (315p in the above example, where the order to buy 10,000 shares must have been entered into the system before the order to buy 2,000 shares).

In the case of the sell orders this is the **lowest priced order** (316p in the above example). Below the best priced orders all of the other orders are displayed, giving an immediate picture of the depth of liquidity on the order book.

Essentially, the way that the SETS system works is that LSE members have access to the order book and can enter orders electronically. If a firm of brokers entered a sell order on behalf of a client for up to 12,000 shares in ABC plc at the best available price, the order would be executed by the system by matching with the best buy orders (10,000 and 2,000 shares). The matched order would proceed to settlement at 315p per share, and be immediately revealed to the market in terms of size (12,000 shares) and price (315p).

The minimum order size is a single share and there is no maximum order size.

3.1.2 SETS Auctions

At the start of automatic execution on SETS each day there is an opening auction. Leading up to the auction, the period between 7.50am and 8.00am is known as the **opening auction call period**. In this period no trading takes place however, three types of order (limit, iceberg and market orders) can be placed on the order book to take part in the opening auction.

The auction itself does not necessarily happen at 8.00am. Instead, it is subject to a **random start** and will occur at 8.00am plus a random number of seconds between 0 and 30. The **auction** uses an **uncrossing algorithm**, through which those orders that overlap on the order book are executed at the single price that maximises the number of shares traded. Simultaneously, the opening price for the security is calculated. During the course of the uncrossing, no further orders can be added and existing orders cannot be deleted or amended.

There is a possibility of the opening auction being delayed beyond its scheduled time. The delay can be caused by either market orders not being fully satisfied, or the price arrived at by the uncrossing algorithm being extreme, or a combination of both of these. The resultant delay is termed an 'extension'.

- A **market order extension** occurs if there are unexecuted market orders on the order book following the auction. This extension is two minutes plus an additional 0–30 second random end period;
- A **price monitoring extension** occurs if the opening price is more than the price tolerance level of 5% away from the price of the last automated trade, which took place on the previous business day. The price tolerance level is a predefined percentage threshold either side of a base price set by the LSE and currently standing at 5% for the opening auction. The price monitoring extension is five minutes long, again plus an additional 0–30 second random end period.

So, there is the potential for a seven to eight minute delay to the opening auction if both the market order and price monitoring extensions are applied.

Once the opening auction is complete, automatic execution commences. As orders are entered onto the system, SETS tries to match them. If SETS finds a buyer and seller with agreeable prices and volumes, the trade is automatically executed.

There is a possibility of an interruption to this automatic execution of orders. If the price of a trade is more than the price tolerance level away from the previous trade price, an **Automatic Execution Suspension Period (AESP)** occurs to allow investors time to react to large price changes. The price tolerance level during the continuous trading period varies from 5% to 25%, depending upon the share.

The AESP lasts for five minutes (plus a period of 0–30 seconds) and during this time no trades are executed (although orders can be entered, deleted and amended). Automatic execution then recommences after the uncrossing auction program is run.

If a SETS security is suspended from trading by the Exchange, as with an AESP, no execution takes place, although orders can be entered, deleted or amended.

After 4.30pm, when automatic execution is completed, the trading day ends with another auction. The auction call period runs from 4.30pm to 4.35pm, and at 4.35pm (plus a period of 0–30 seconds) the auction uncrossing algorithm is run.

If auction matching occurs in the closing auction, then the day's closing price will be based on the closing auction price. If no execution occurs, the Volume Weighted Average Price (VWAP) of the last ten minutes of continuous trading will be used. In the event of no automatic trades in the VWAP period, the last automatically executed trade price will be used.

For the last 25 minutes until 5.00pm, SETS allows participants to delete orders. No execution takes place during this period.

3.1.3 Worked Principal Agreements (WPA)

A worked principal agreement is where a firm agrees to buy or sell a large number of shares for a client. Because of the size of the transaction, the LSE allows the trade to remain secret for a time.

Typically, an institutional investor, like a pension fund wishing to buy (or sell) a large quantity of shares, contacts an LSE member firm. The two parties enter into a provisional agreement – the LSE member firm agrees a limit price and size upon which the pension fund hopes the actual execution will achieve some improvement. This agreement is the Worked Principal Agreement (WPA) between the LSE member firm acting as principal and the institutional client. The terms are reported to the exchange in the form of a Worked Principal Notification (WPN), but not published.

The LSE member firm then attempts to find counterparties with whom to execute the trade at prices better than the limit agreed. If the LSE member firm is unable to find sufficient counterparties, the deal will go ahead, with the LSE member meeting the remainder of the client's requirement.

A WPA is only allowed if the number of shares involved is at least **eight times the Normal Market Size** of the shares in question (normal market size is covered in section 3.5 of this chapter), or it is a **portfolio transaction of 20 or more stocks** which includes at least one SETS security. The parties must execute and report the trade by whichever of the following occurs first the completion of the trade, or:

- the firm managing to complete 80% of the deal (for a single stock WPA), or 100% (for a portfolio WPA); or
- the market close on that business day (in relation to SETS securities, this is the end of the closing auction at 4.35pm).

3.1.4 Viewing the SETS Order Book

Any market participant can view the SETS order book for a particular security (by looking at a Bloomberg screen, for example). However, membership of the LSE is required to interact with the order book. It is for brokers and dealers only.

3.2 SETS ORDER TYPES

LEARNING OBJECTIVE

3.3.2 Understand the following order types and their differences: limit; at best; fill or kill; execute and eliminate; iceberg; multiple fills

There are six types of order that can be entered into SETS, each will be treated slightly differently by the system.

1. **Limit orders** have a price limit and a time limit, eg, a limit order may state 'sell 1000 shares at 360p by next Tuesday'. SETS will attempt to sell these shares at a price no worse than 360p by next Tuesday. Any time limit up to a maximum of 90 days can be put on these orders. If no time limit is placed on the order, it will expire at the end of the day that it is entered. Limit orders can be partially filled, and it is only limit orders that are displayed on the SETS order book.

2. **Iceberg orders** are a particular type of limit order. They enable a market participant with a particularly large order to partially hide the size of their order from the market and reduce the market impact that the large order might otherwise have. The term 'iceberg' comes from the fact that just the top part of the order is on view (the peak of the iceberg), the rest is hidden (the bulk of the iceberg is below the water). Once the top part of the order is executed, the system automatically brings the next tranche of the iceberg order onto the order book. This process continues until the whole of the iceberg order has been executed, or the time limit for the order expires.
3. **At best orders** can only be input during automatic execution (explained in more detail below) and have no specified price. The order will fill as much as possible at any available price and the remainder will be cancelled (ie, it does not wait on the order book to match against later orders).
4. **Execute and eliminate orders** can only be entered during automatic execution. As with the at best order, this type will execute as much of the trade as possible and cancel the rest. However, unlike an at best order, this order type has a specified price and will not execute at a price worse than that specified.
5. **Fill or kill orders** can only be entered during automatic execution. They normally have a specified price (although they can be entered without one) and either the entire order will be immediately filled at a price at least as good as that specified, or the entire order will be cancelled (ie, if there are not enough orders at the price specified or better).
6. A **market order** can only be entered during auction call periods (explained in more detail below). This is an unpriced order with highest priority for execution. This order would be used if you wish to maximise your chance of trading during the auctions.

3.3 CENTRAL COUNTERPARTY

LEARNING OBJECTIVE

3.3.3 Understand the operation and purpose of the LSE's Central Counterparty: LCH.Clearnet Limited; x-clear; benefits and any limitations

SETS transactions utilise a central counterparty. The central counterparty is either the **London Clearing House (LCH.Clearnet)** or **SIS x-clear (x-clear)**. The impact of the central counterparty is best illustrated by way of a simple example:

EXAMPLE

A trade is executed on SETS that involves A agreeing to sell some shares to B. One of the central counterparties, say LCH.Clearnet, steps in between the two parties and two new obligations replace the initial obligation of A to sell to B. The two obligations are for A to sell to LCH.Clearnet and then for LCH.Clearnet to sell to B. This transfer of obligation is known as novation.

If either of the two parties to this transaction (A or B) were to default, it would no longer affect the other party, as they no longer have a contract with each other. It would only impact LCH.Clearnet.

The use of a central counterparty provides certain benefits to market participants, particularly:

- **Reduced counterparty risk**. The risk that the other side of the transaction will default is reduced because they are replaced by one of the central counterparties, both of which are well capitalised and have insurance policies in place lessening the risk of default. This reduces the risk of systemic collapse of the financial system;
- **Providing total anonymity**. Both sides of the trade do not discover who the original counterparty was.
- **Reduced administration**. All trades are settled with one of the two central counterparties, rather than a variety of counterparties improving operational efficiency.
- **Facilitating netting of transactions**. Because all the trades are with a central counterparty, receipts and payments for transactions in the same share that settle on the same day can be netted against each other;
- **Improved prices**. Because more participants are willing to transact anonymously, it is argued that a central counterparty results in improvements in price.

The central counterparty charges a flat fee to both parties for fulfilling its role and also requires margin payments (similar to derivatives margin) to reduce their potential loss, should one party default. CREST is the settlement system that is used to settle the transactions between the central counterparty and the member firms. CREST will be covered in more detail in Chapter 4.

3.4 TRADING HALTS

LEARNING OBJECTIVE

3.3.4 Know the LSE's right to call for a halt in trading in any listed security: for any reason; length of trading halt

The London Stock Exchange reserves the right to prohibit any transaction from being dealt on exchange for any reason. This is referred to as a trading halt, and typically arises from the suspension of a security's listing.

If a security is suspended, permission is required from the exchange before a member firm can effect a transaction in that security. The length of the trading halt is at the discretion of the exchange. Trades that have occurred, but have not yet settled at the time of suspension, are settled as normal.

3.5 SETSqx

LEARNING OBJECTIVE

3.3.5 Know the features and requirements of SETSqx dealing: SETSqx as an order-driven trading system; relative illiquidity; securities covered; Normal Market Size; minimum number of market makers

SETSqx (Stock Exchange Electronic Trading Service – quotes and crosses) is the London Stock Exchange's trading service for less liquid securities. Less liquid securities are those domestic listed securities that are not traded on SETS or SETSmm (SETSmm is used for trading medium sized companies and is not included within the current syllabus).

SETSqx is a hybrid system, combining some of the order-driven features of SETS with the potential for two-way quotes from market makers. Functionally it is similar to the SETS order book, with buy and sell orders displayed in a central order book. However, it is supplemented by one or more market makers also displaying two-way prices. Furthermore, unlike SETS, execution on the central order book is only at periodic auctions (uncrossings) that occur four times per day – at 8.00am, 11.00am, 3.00pm and 4.35pm. Like SETS, these auctions can be subject to 'price monitoring extensions'.

The order types that are accepted into the SETSqx central order book are anonymous limit orders and named orders, which detail the firm as well as the order. Any member firm has the option to phone the counterparty behind a named order and fill the order before the next uncrossing if the two parties agree.

The minimum number of market makers for securities traded on SETSqx is zero, but if there are one or more market makers they must provide continuous liquidity throughout the trading day. They must quote prices to buy or sell at least one times the normal market size (NMS).

3.5.1 Normal Market Size

Something used on both SETS and SETSqx is a share classification system based on a company's Normal Market Size (NMS). The London Stock Exchange sets this figure quarterly for each listed security. It is an indication of liquidity and represents the number of shares traded in an average deal for this company.

The NMS figure for each company is assigned to one of 15 bands – based on the number of shares. They are:

100
200
500
1,000
2,000
3,000
5,000
10,000
15,000
25,000
50,000
75,000
100,000
150,000
200,000

Although you are unlikely to be required to remember all of the bands for the exam, they give you an idea of the variability of liquidity of listed company shares, and the smallest and largest levels should be remembered.

The NMS is used to derive levels for **Worked Principal Agreements** on SETS and the NMS is also the minimum quantity that market makers must be willing to buy or sell on SETSqx. It is alternatively referred to as the **Minimum Quote Size (MQS)**.

4. LONDON STOCK EXCHANGE INTERNATIONAL EQUITY MARKET

As well as providing trading mechanisms for domestic shares, the LSE is also an important centre for trading international equities. There are three trading services for international equities provided by the LSE that are included in the examination syllabus: the International Order Book (IOB), the International Bulletin Board (ITBB) and the International Retail Service (IRS).

4.1 THE INTERNATIONAL ORDER BOOK (IOB)

LEARNING OBJECTIVE

3.4.1 Understand the rules, procedures and requirements applying to dealing through The International Order Book (IOB) in the following areas: securities covered; minimum and maximum trading sizes; who can access the IOB

The International Order Book (IOB) is an order-driven trading service primarily for depository receipts of international securities. It operates in the same way as the SETS order book with one additional feature – the facility for inputting orders that are not anonymous. Such orders are commonly referred to as 'named orders' and are placed by LSE member firms dealing in a principal capacity and wanting to display their willingness to deal on the order book. The acronym that identifies the firm appears next to their order on the IOB.

Both Global Depository Receipts (GDRs) and American Depository Receipts (ADRs) are traded on the IOB, mostly from companies in developing countries in Central and Eastern Europe and Asia. Orders are required to be for at least 50 shares, with no restriction on the maximum order size. The IOB is accessible to all LSE member firms. The depository receipts are either traded on the IOB as a 'continuous trading day' security, or as an 'auction only' security.

4.1.1 Continuous Trading

The more liquid, actively traded depository receipts are continuously traded with the market opening with an auction at 9:00am, followed by continuous trading of matched orders until 3:30pm, with a closing auction approximately 10 minutes later. The IOB follows a similar process to SETS, with the opening and closing auctions subject to random starts and a pre-opening 10 minute period for orders to be input.

IOB: Continuous Trading Day

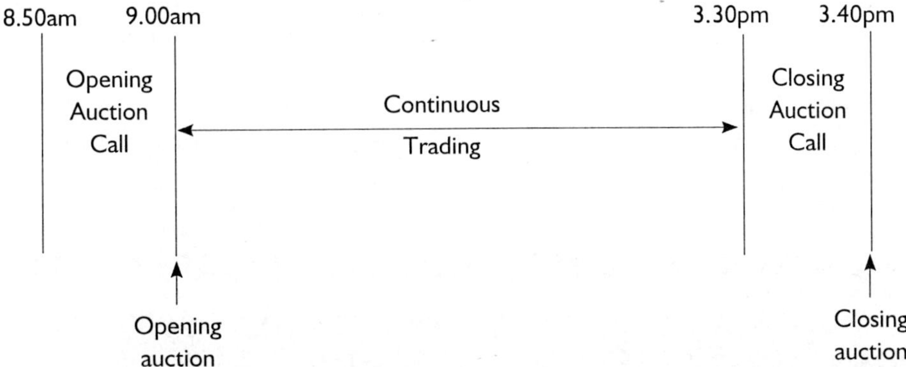

Between 8.50am and 9.00am member firms are able to enter and delete limit orders, iceberg orders, named orders and market orders. The match for these orders will not occur until a random start of between 9.00am and 30 seconds later, when the auction uncrossing algorithm is run. However, like SETS, before the trades are actually executed a price monitoring check is run. If the auction price is above or below 5% either side of the previous day's closing price, the auction call period is extended by a further five minutes. There is also the possibility of a two minute market order extension if there are any unexecuted market orders at the time the auction uncrossing is run.

During the continuous trading period there are price monitoring checks before execution takes place. If the price exceeds set thresholds from the previous trade, then the automatic execution will be suspended for five minutes and restarted with an auction match.

The closing auction call period starts at 3.30pm and 3.40pm with a random end. The closing auction match has the possibility of two price monitoring extensions, lasting five minutes each.

4.1.2 Auction Only Trading

The 'auction only' model is for the less liquid depository receipts. Trades can be input in a lengthy pre-auction period, and are then only traded at one of three auctions each day.

IOB: Auction Only Trading Day

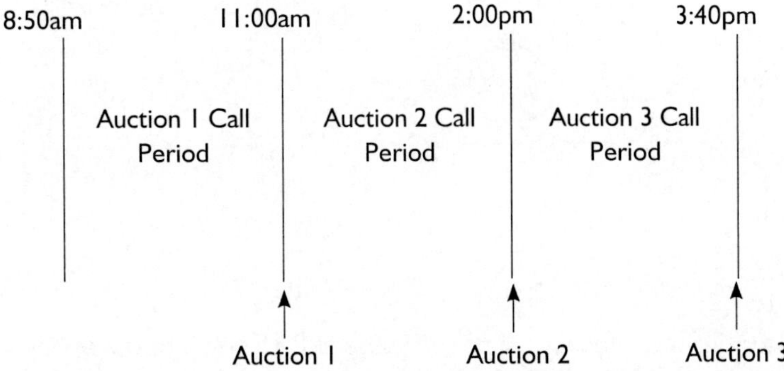

The first auction occurs with a random start of up to 60 seconds after 11.00 am, with the call period for orders starting at 8.50am and ending at 11.00am. As with the continuous trading model, there is a possibility of a market order extension of 2 minutes and a price monitoring extension of five minutes.

The second and third auctions occur at 2.00pm and 3.40pm, again with a random start of up to 60 seconds and the possibility of a market order extension (2 minutes) and a price monitoring extension of five minutes.

4.2 THE INTERNATIONAL BULLETIN BOARD (ITBB)

LEARNING OBJECTIVE

3.4.2 Understand the rules, procedures and requirements applying to dealing through the International Bulletin Board (ITBB) in the following areas: market makers' obligations; when to enter two way prices; price quotes during and outside the mandatory quote period; who can access the ITBB

The International Bulletin Board (ITBB) is similar to the domestic SETSqx system. It is an order-driven trading service provided by the LSE for a range of international equities – example companies include Sony Corporation from Japan, Colgate-Palmolive from the US and Euro Disney from France. It combines an order book with electronically-executable market maker quotes, although there is no requirement for a set number of market makers for each security. Indeed, if a security attracts no market makers, the method of trading simply collapses to that of a continuous order book or auction only model as applied on the International Order Book.

The individual equities are each quoted in the currency of their home market and assigned a default place of settlement that members will use to settle order book trades. The standard trading day for the continuous order book is as follows:

ITBB: Continuous Trading Day

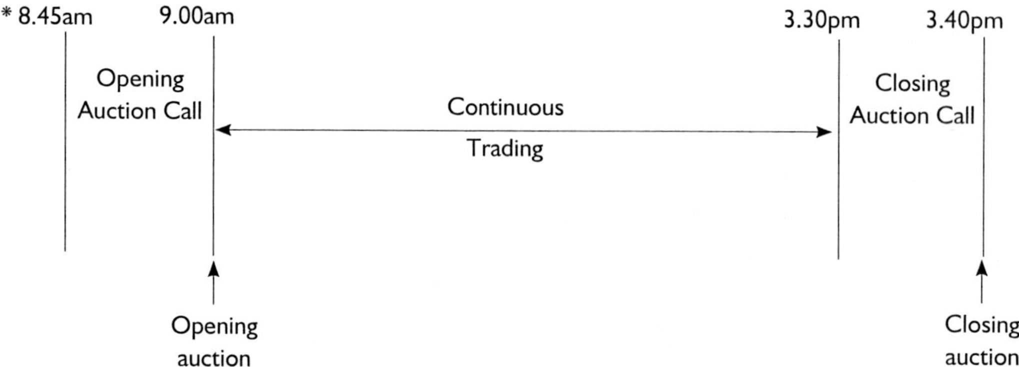

- Note for Japanese Securities the opening call period starts at 8:15 am with the opening auction at 8:30am.

The standard trading day for the auction-only equities is as follows:

ITBB: Auction Only Trading Day

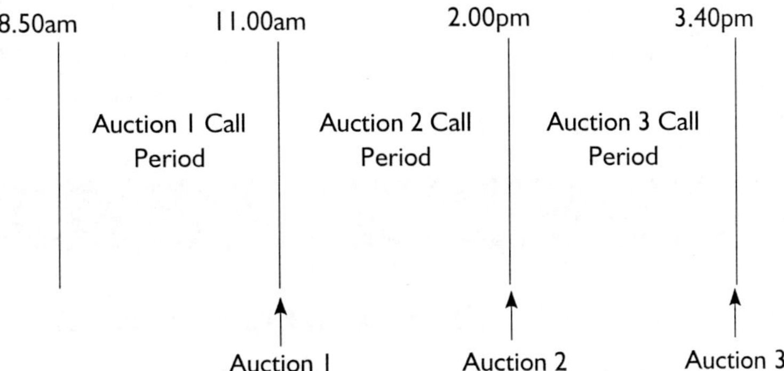

For the equities that attract one or more market makers, the market makers are obliged to quote two-way prices by entering 'committed principal' orders on each side of the order book with the quantity of securities being at least one half of the normal market size. The LSE does specify a maximum spread that the market makers are allowed to have between their buy and sell prices.

The market makers are required to post their orders within 60 seconds of the uncrossing of the opening auction, replenish their orders within 60 seconds of their execution, deletion or expiry and maintain the two orders throughout the mandatory period that starts at the uncrossing of the opening auction and ends at the end of the closing auction.

The market makers are not obliged to post orders outside the period of automatic execution, during automatic execution suspension periods nor the five minutes after the end of such auctions.

Transactions undertaken by LSE member firms in securities traded on the International Bulletin Board are defined as 'on-exchange' and need to be reported into the exchange. There are a variety of systems that can be used to transaction report international equity trades, including the LSE's Exchange Reporting System, the Thomson Report and TRAX. The transaction reporting requirement exists regardless of whether the deal is undertaken via the order book or away from the order book.

4.3 INTERNATIONAL RETAIL SERVICE (IRS)

LEARNING OBJECTIVE

3.4.3 Understand the purpose of and firms' obligations towards the International Retail Service (IRS): purpose of the IRS; 'Committed Principals'; Mandatory Quote Period for most European stocks; Currency of quotation

This service is aimed at UK private client brokers and their clients. It provides access to major European and US blue chip stocks, priced in £s.

Committed principals (CPs) provide two-way prices throughout a mandatory committed principal period for those securities in which they have registered. For the majority of European securities this period is 8:15am–4:00pm, and for US securities 2:45pm–5:00pm.

The two-way prices appear on the screen as buy and sell orders and the brokers can submit orders to execute against committed principal orders. If there is a single committed principal in any security, then the exchange specifies the maximum spread between bid and offer prices that they can apply.

5. OTHER EQUITY MARKETS

5.1 TRADING ON THE NYSE AND ON THE LSE

LEARNING OBJECTIVE

3.5.1 Know how trading on the NYSE compares with trading on the LSE: specialists

Many traditional distinctions that have been made regarding the *modus operandi* or manner in which markets operate, especially the distinction between OTC markets and exchange traded markets, are far less easy to make than previously. The increasing adoption of electronic trading platforms as well as regulatory change resulting from MiFID, for example, which has led to the proliferation of alternative trading venues and electronic communications networks (ECNs), means that electronic order matching systems have become the de facto mode of operation for most trading activities.

Partly as a result of this and especially with the innovations which will result from the introduction of the new Millennium and Turquoise systems which are scheduled to be in operation by September 2010, many of the distinctions between the NYSE and the LSE are becoming a part of market folklore.

Perhaps the only key difference today is that the NYSE still has designated market makers, sometimes known as 'specialists', for the stocks which are traded on the exchange whereas the LSE has a more heterogeneous structure which includes specific market makers in certain securities but no 'specialists' as that term is traditionally understood.

Let us begin by describing the role of a 'market maker'. A market maker is financial intermediary, often an investment bank or specialist dealer, that quotes both a buy and a sell price in a financial instrument or commodity held in inventory, hoping to make a profit on the bid-offer spread, or turn. The key point is that according to this precise definition of the market maker function, the market maker maintains an inventory of positions and stands ready to buy or sell the securities for which it makes a market on demand from other market participants.

As with a lot of financial terminology, some imprecision has entered the discussion of the role of market makers, but in fairness with the advent of sophisticated high frequency trading platforms, where 'taking a position into inventory' could mean holding it for a nano-second, it becomes harder to separate out the different kinds of 'liquidity' providers in contemporary capital markets.

5.1.1 Designated Market Makers or Specialists

The New York Stock Exchange (NYSE) has designated market makers, formerly known as 'specialists', who act as the official market maker for a given security. The market makers provide a required amount of liquidity to the security's market, and take the other side of trades when there are short-term buy-and-sell-side imbalances in customer orders. This helps prevent excess volatility, and in return, the specialist is granted various informational and trade execution advantages.

To return to the more traditional notion of the 'specialists' working on the NYSE floor, they have been described as fulfilling three main roles to ensure a fair and orderly market:

5.1.2 Auctioneer

The NYSE is an auction market where bids and asks are continuously published to all investors. It is the job of the specialist to ensure that all bids and asks are reported in an accurate and timely manner, that all marketable trades are executed and that order is maintained on the floor. Along with posting the daily bid and ask prices, the specialist must also set the opening price for the stock every morning. This price can greatly differ from the previous day's closing price based on after-hours news and events. The role of the specialist is to find the correct market price based on supply and demand.

5.1.3 Catalyst

In addition to the notion that a market maker acts as a facilitator, the role of the specialist has been seen as one of encouraging enough market interest in the particular stocks for which they are designated market makers. This is carried out by specialists seeking out recently active investors in cases where the bids and asks can't be matched. This aspect of the specialist's job helps to induce trades that may not have arisen within the context of a more passive and automated notion of the role of the market maker.

5.1.4 Principal

One of the key differentiators which distinguishes the designated market maker role rather than the light weight version of the market maker role is that the specialist is expected to hold inventory in the stocks which they 'represent'. In other words, they act not only as agent and facilitator of liquidity but also as a principal and hold stocks in their own accounts. In cases where there's a demand-supply imbalance of a particular security, the specialist must make adjustments by purchasing and selling out of his/her own inventory to equalise the market. For example, a specialist is required to buy shares for their own inventory in the event of a large sell-off. They will also buy shares for their inventory in the event of a large sell-off.

On the London Stock Exchange (LSE) there are no equivalents of designated market makers as just described, however, there are market makers but their role is less formally defined and even that more loosely defined role is becoming more indistinct as the changes in the underlying technology more closely resemble an electronic order matching system.

At present on the LSE, there are official market makers for many securities (but not for shares in the largest and most heavily traded companies, which instead use an automated system called TradElect). Some of the LSE's member firms take on the obligation of always making a two-way price in each of the stocks in which they make markets. Their prices are the ones displayed on the Stock Exchange Automated Quotation (SEAQ) system and it is they who generally deal with brokers buying or selling stock on behalf of clients.

5.1.5 Liquidity Rebates

Exchanges are having to fight much harder to retain their role within a decentralised market system where investors have many 'off-exchange' choices as to where to conduct business. There is also a lot of competition amongst exchanges as transnational trading and settlement has meant that the actual place or geographical location of an exchange becomes fairly meaningless in a virtual world of electronic trading.

One area of competition amongst exchanges is to encourage market makers to use their platforms over others by providing liquidity rebates for each share that is sold to or purchased from each posted bid or offer. In this respect, the ARCA facility which is becoming a very significant division of the NYSE/ Euronext platform, and hosts the trading of most exchange traded funds (ETF's), has been one of the most aggressive in providing liquidity rebates as a way of promoting business.

5.2 PLUS

LEARNING OBJECTIVE

3.5.2 Know the rules, procedures and requirements of trading securities on PLUS: Recognised Investment Exchange; securities covered: PLUS listed; PLUS quoted; PLUS traded – listed or unlisted

PLUS Markets plc (PLUS) is another stock exchange in London in addition to the London Stock Exchange (LSE). Like the LSE, it is a recognised investment exchange in the UK and provides a trading platform for securities that are on the full list, on the LSE's AIM market and other securities that are traded on its own PLUS market.

PLUS provides both a primary listing facility for those securities seeking access to the full list (referred to as PLUS listed), and has a primary listing facility for smaller, growing companies like the LSE's AIM market (referred to as PLUS quoted).

In the secondary market, so-called 'PLUS traded' securities can be purchased or sold on the trading platform and these securities embrace both listed and unlisted securities, including those that are PLUS listed and those that are PLUS quoted.

6. GOVERNMENT BONDS

LEARNING OBJECTIVE

3.6.1 Understand the basic characteristics and purpose of government bond markets in the US, UK, Japan and the Eurozone: ratings and the concept of 'risk-free'; currency, credit and inflation risks; inflation indexed bonds

The government bond markets are the facilities that enable investors to buy and sell bonds issued by the relevant government – such as UK gilts, issued on behalf of the UK government and US Treasury notes and bonds issued on behalf of the US government. They are important since they are the benchmark bonds on which the return provided by other bonds is based.

For example, the yield available on UK gilts is considered the risk-free rate for sterling denominated bonds – after all, it is the UK government that ultimately controls the printing of sterling, so the UK gilts are effectively credit risk-free. If a 15-year gilt was trading at a price to produce a 5% yield, a 15-year sterling denominated corporate bond would be expected to yield 5%, plus a margin to cover the increased credit risk that the corporate borrower presents.

A conventional government bond still displays two particular risks to investors: inflation risk to all investors, and currency risk if it is an overseas investor. To counter currency risks, governments can, and occasionally do, issue bonds denominated in currencies other than their home currency, for example the US government issuing a euro-denominated bond. This type of bond would remove the currency risk for a Eurozone investor, but would lose an element of the risk-free status, since the US government cannot print euros.

To counter inflation risks, government bonds can be issued that pay a coupon that is linked to an inflation index – if the inflation rate increases, the investors will get a larger coupon to compensate. These bonds also link the redemption amount to an inflation index – like the coupon, the investor will get a greater amount on redemption, if inflation has been significant over the life of the bond.

6.1 PARTICIPANTS IN THE GOVERNMENT BOND MARKETS

LEARNING OBJECTIVE

3.6.2 Know the functions, obligations and benefits of the following in relation to government bonds: with respect to the UK, US, Japan and the Eurozone: primary dealers; broker dealers; inter-dealer brokers; Government issuing authority such as the UK Debt Management Office

In addition to the government itself, there are three major groups of participants that facilitate deals in the government bond markets:

- Primary dealers – such as gilt-edged market makers (GEMMs) in the UK.
- Broker dealers.
- Inter-dealer brokers.

These three participants will be illustrated using the UK government bond market as an example.

6.1.1 Issuing Agency

The Debt Management Office (DMO) is the issuing agency for the UK government. It is an executive agency of the Treasury, making new issues of UK government securities (gilt-edged securities or gilts). Once issued, the secondary market for dealing in gilts is overseen by two bodies, the DMO and the LSE.

The DMO is the body that enables certain LSE member firms to act as primary dealers, known as gilt-edged market makers (GEMMs). It then leaves it to the LSE to prescribe rules that apply when dealing takes place.

6.1.2 Gilt-Edged Market Makers (GEMMs)

The GEMM, once vetted by the DMO and registered as a GEMM with the LSE, becomes a primary dealer and is required to provide two-way quotes to customers (clients known directly to them) and other member firms of the LSE throughout the normal trading day. There is no requirement to use a particular system like SEAQ for making those quotes available to clients, and GEMMs are free to choose how to disseminate their prices.

The obligations of a GEMM can be summarised as follows:

- To make effective two-way prices to customers on demand, up to a size agreed with the DMO, thereby providing liquidity for customers wishing to trade.
- To participate actively in the DMO's gilt issuance programme, broadly by bidding competitively in all auctions and achieving allocations commensurate with their secondary market share – effectively informally agreeing to underwrite gilt auctions.
- To provide information to the DMO on closing prices, market conditions and the GEMM's positions and turnover.

The privileges of GEMM status include:

- executive rights to competitive telephone bidding at gilt auctions and other DMO operations, either for the GEMM's own account or on behalf of clients;
- an exclusive facility to trade as a counterparty of the DMO in any of its secondary market operations;
- exclusive access to gilt inter-dealer broker (IDB) screens.

A firm can register as a GEMM to provide quotes in either:

- all gilt-edged securities; or
- gilt-edged securities excluding index linked gilts; or
- index-linked gilts only.

There are exceptions to the requirement to customers, including the members of the LSE. The obligation does not include quoting to other GEMMs, fixed interest market makers or gilt inter-dealer brokers.

6.1.3 Broker-Dealers

These are non-GEMM LSE member firms that are able to buy or sell gilts as principal (dealer) or as agent (broker). When acting as a broker, the broker dealer will be bound by the LSE's best execution rule, ie, to get the best available price at the time.

When seeking a quote from a GEMM, the broker-dealer must identify at the outset if the deal is a small one, defined as less than £1 million nominal.

6.1.4 Gilt Inter-Dealer Brokers

Gilt inter-dealer brokers arrange deals between gilt-edged market makers anonymously. They are not allowed to take principal positions and the identity of the market makers using the service remains anonymous at all times. The IDB will act as agent, but settle the transaction as if it were the principal. The IDB is only allowed to act as a broker between GEMMs, and has to be a separate company and not a division of a broker/dealer.

6.1.5 Government Issues in the US

The Federal Reserve is the coordinator of the issuance of US government securities. As with the UK, it conducts auctions on a regular basis and appoints primary dealers which include the major investment banks as conduits in the auction process to place bids and to buy the issue on behalf of their clients or for their own account.

Regular weekly T-Bills are commonly issued with maturity dates of 28 days (or 4 weeks, about a month), 91 days (or 13 weeks, about 3 months), 182 days (or 26 weeks, about 6 months), and 364 days (or 52 weeks, about 1 year). Treasury bills are sold by single price auctions held weekly.

Like other securities, individual issues of T-bills are identified with a unique CUSIP number. The 13-week bill issued three months after a 26-week bill is considered a re-opening of the 26-week bill and is given the same CUSIP number.

During periods when Treasury cash balances are particularly low, the Treasury may sell cash management bills (or CMBs). These are sold at a discount and by auction just like weekly Treasury bills. They differ in that they are irregular in amount, term (often less than 21 days), and day of the week for auction, issuance, and maturity. When CMBs mature on the same day as a regular weekly bill, usually Thursday, they are said to be on-cycle. The CMB is considered another reopening of the bill and has the same CUSIP. When CMBs mature on any other day, they are off-cycle and have a different CUSIP number.

With the advent of TreasuryDirect, individuals can now purchase T-Bills online and have funds withdrawn from and deposited directly to their personal bank account and earn higher interest rates on their savings.

Treasury bonds (T-Bonds, or the long bond) have the longest maturity, from twenty years to 30 years. They have a coupon payment every six months like T-Notes, and are commonly issued with maturity of 30 years.

The US Federal government suspended issuing the well-known 30-year Treasury bonds (often called long-bonds) for a four and a half year period between 2001 and 2006, but now issues about as many 30-year bonds as ten-year notes.

6.1.6 Government Issues in Japan

Japanese Government Bonds (JGB's) are issued by the Bank of Japan and as the name implies, government bonds are the bonds issued by the government, which is responsible for interest and principal payments. Interest is paid every six months, and principal payments are secured at maturity.

JGB's are available with various maturity periods. Coupon-bearing bonds, which feature semiannual interest payment and principal payment at maturity, have maturities of two, five, five (for retail investors), ten, ten (inflation-indexed), ten (for retail investors), 15 (floating-rate), 20, 30 and 40 years.

The Japanese government also offers a separate strips program as discussed in the next section.

6.1.7 Government Issues in the Eurozone

The Eurozone consists of the 16 states which have adopted the euro as their currency and for whom their monetary policy is determined by monthly meetings of the European Central Bank (ECB). Each of the member states issues government bonds which have the credit rating associated with the country of issue rather than the Eurozone as a whole. The German government will issue bunds denominated in euros and the French government will issue OATs.

European laws prevent the ECB from buying debt directly from governments on the so-called primary market in the way the US and British central banks have done during the financial crisis, but not on the secondary market.

For the first time in the institution's history, the European Central Bank will buy Eurozone government bonds to help support fractured markets, abandoning its firm resistance to full-scale asset purchases in light of Greece's debt crisis.

The ECB announced in May 2010 that the move, dubbed the 'nuclear option' by many economists, was justified because of government promises to meet strict budget targets and step up consolidation efforts.

The announcement was part of a decision reached by the European Union and the International Monetary Fund to pledge nearly $1 trillion in loans to defend the euro after it had fallen approximately 20% against the US dollar during 2010.

Under the plan, the ECB will buy and sell both Eurozone government and private bonds on the secondary market. The main activities undertaken by the ECB have been the purchases of large quantities of Greek, Portuguese and Spanish bonds from private sector banks throughout the Eurozone. There has been considerable criticism of this move by certain sections of the more conservative financial community within the EZ states, especially from German bankers.

Unlike the decisions to introduce 'quantitative easing' taken by the Bank of England in the UK and the Federal Reserve System in the US, the fact that the bond purchases will be offset by liquidity absorbing operations means they will not expand the reserves to the banking system.

6.2 STRIPS

LEARNING OBJECTIVE

3.6.3 Know the basic purpose and characteristics of the strip market: result of stripping a bond; number of securities possible from a strippable bond; zero coupon securities

STRIPS is an acronym of Separate Trading of Registered Interest and Principal of Securities. Stripping a bond involves trading the interest (each individual coupon) and the principal (the nominal value) separately. Each strip forms the equivalent of a zero-coupon bond. It will trade at a discount to its face value, with the size of the discount being determined by prevailing interest rates and time.

To illustrate how STRIPS work , a ten year gilt can be stripped to make 21 separate securities: 20 strips based on the coupons, which are entitled to just one of the half-yearly interest payments; and one strip entitled to the redemption payment at the end of the ten years.

EXAMPLE

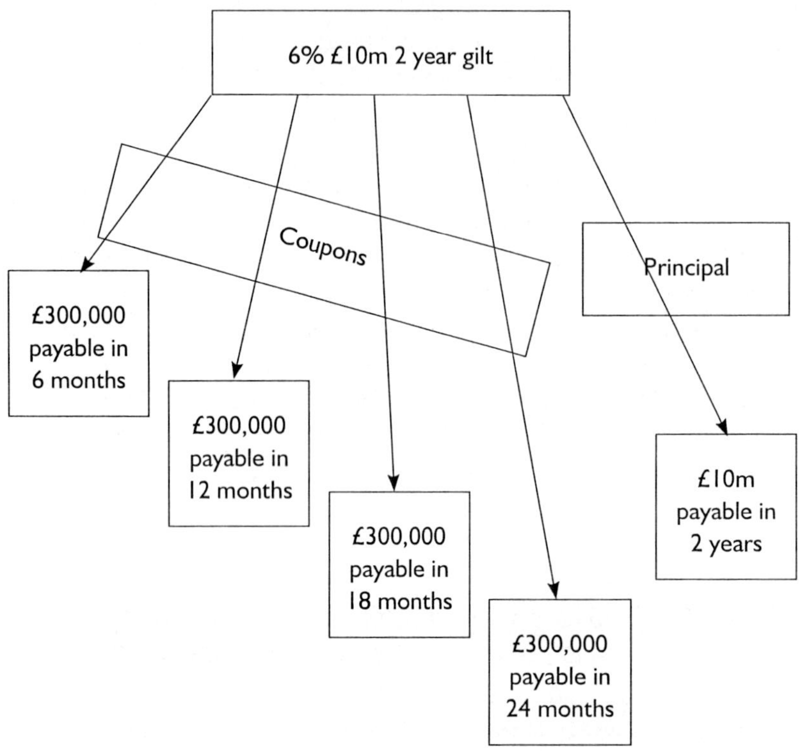

A STRIPS market has been developed in the UK within the gilts market. Only those gilts that have been designated by the DMO as 'strippable' are eligible for the STRIPS market, not all gilts. Those gilts that are stripped have separate registered entries for each of the individual cash flows that enable different owners to hold each individual strip, and facilitates the trading of the individual strips. Only GEMMs, the Bank of England or the Treasury are able to 'strip' gilts.

The key benefits of strips are that investors can precisely match their liabilities, removing any reinvestment risk.

EXAMPLE

An investor wants to fund the repayment of the principal on a £5m mortgage, due to be paid in five years' time. Using gilts, there are three major choices:

1) **He could buy a £5m nominal coupon paying gilt, but the coupons on this would mean that it would generate more than £5m.**

2) **He could buy less than £5m nominal, attempting to arrive at £5m in 5 years. However, he would have to estimate how the coupons over the life of the bond could be reinvested and what rate of return they would provide – his estimate could well be wrong.**

3) **He could buy a £5m strip. This would precisely meet his need.**

As seen in the example, strips can precisely meet the liabilities of the investor, removing any 'reinvestment risk' that is normally faced when covering liabilities with coupon paying bonds. Furthermore, investors in gilt strips need not worry about the risk that the issuer of the bonds will default – gilt edged securities are considered to be free of any default risk (also known as credit risk).

6.3 BOND PRICES AND BOND FUTURES

LEARNING OBJECTIVE

3.6.4 Understand the broad mechanisms by which bond prices are driven by bond future prices

We have seen how the price of a bond is driven by a number of factors, such as credit rating and required yields. Clearly, the required yield will itself be driven by expected future interest rates. A key indicator of the markets collective expectation of **future** interest rates is implicit within derivatives of bonds, such as bond futures. As a result, the prevailing price of bonds are to an extent, driven by the price at which derivatives of those bonds are trading, such as bond futures.

One of the most actively traded global futures contracts is the US Thirty-Year Treasury Bond contract which trades on the Chicago Board of Trade. This contract has excellent liquidity and provides a vehicle for hedging one's exposure to a broad variety of fixed income instruments as well as an opportunity for speculating on the future direction of interest rates and specifically as one component in a speculation about interest rate spreads, between, for example, corporate investment grade bonds or high yield bonds versus US Treasuries.

The futures contracts can be settled by a cash payment at the time of the contract's maturity or by the owner of a contract delivering certain bonds which are subject to a standardised definition or conversion factor. This gives rise to the practice amongst participants in the futures and cash markets for bonds of making continuous and precise calculations as to which particular bonds are the 'cheapest to deliver' at the time of settlement of a futures position.

The relationship between the cash market for bonds and the futures markets in government bonds exemplifies the manner in which all cash and derivative markets are driven by a relatively simple arbitrage mechanism. The concept of cheapest to deliver is a vital component in this arbitrage strategy which will tend to eliminate discrepancies arising in price between the trading of actual bonds in the cash market and the trading of, for example, US Treasury Bond futures. If pricing discrepancies should arise on a temporary basis these will tend to be eliminated as in any arbitrage by selling the relatively more expensive item (ie, the cash bond or the derivative depending on the particular circumstances) and buying an offsetting position in the corresponding alternate position of either the underlying asset or the futures contract.

The interaction between the cash price of bonds and the futures prices is a dynamic two-way process in which prices are constantly being adjusted through arbitrage and through the activities of 'hedgers' as well as speculators.

7. CORPORATE BOND MARKETS

7.1 CHARACTERISTICS

LEARNING OBJECTIVE

3.7.1 Understand the characteristics of corporate bond markets: decentralised dealer markets and dealer provision of liquidity; the impact of default risk on prices; the differences between bond and equity markets; dealers rather than market makers; bond pools of liquidity versus centralised equity exchange

As we have seen, the price of a corporate bond is based on the equivalent government bond, less a discount to represent the risk that the corporate may default compared to the default risk-free nature of the government bond. Unlike the market for equities, the method of dealing in corporate bonds tends to be away from the major exchanges in what is commonly described as a **decentralised dealer market**. The dealers provide liquidity by being willing to buy or sell the bonds. As we will see below, the systems that the dealers use to display their willingness to deal are numerous, with each being described as a separate 'pool' of liquidity.

7.1.1 Default

In the corporate bond market, unlike the government bond markets where it is assumed that no sovereign borrower will default, the determination of the likelihood that a corporate borrower may default is a vital part in the pricing mechanism for corporate bonds.

7.1.2 Ratings Agencies

Organisations such as Standard & Poor's, Moody's and Fitch are credit rating agencies who provide a rating system for corporate bonds. The highest grade corporate bonds are known as AAA or Aaa and these are bonds that these agencies have deemed the least likely to fail. Companies like General Electric (GE) have been given this status, although there is always the possibility of a downgrade when the perceived riskiness of the borrower changes.

Lower grade corporate bonds are perceived as more likely to default, where the borrower will have to entice lenders with a higher coupon payment and higher yield to maturity. Indeed, bonds with a rating below BBB– (in the case of Standard & Poor's and Fitch), or Baa3 (in the case of Moody's) are often referred to as junk bonds or speculative bonds which are non-investment grade.

The primary difference between the corporate bond market and the equity market relates to the nature of the security being traded. A corporate bond usually has a specified income stream in the form of coupon payments which will be paid to the holder of the bond, and a bondholder has a more senior claim against the assets of the issuer in the case of a bankruptcy or restructuring.

Investors in equities may receive a dividend payment from the corporation but this is less certain and can fluctuate. Indeed, less mature companies may not even pay a dividend. The equity holder also has a greater risk that if the corporation which has issued the shares becomes insolvent or undergoes a re-structuring there may be insufficient assets to be liquidated or reorganised and then distributed to shareholders. In such instances shareholders may find that their equity stakes in a corporation have little or no residual value.

The primary function and role of market makers in corporate bonds is to provide liquidity to the marketplace and to act as a facilitator or agent in trades between the principals. Dealers are those that have been appointed by the corporate issuer to act as distributors on their behalf in the issuance and underwriting of bond issues. There is often a combination of such roles by large financial institutions.

A decentralised dealer market structure is one that enables investors to buy and sell without a centralised location. In a decentralised market, the technical infrastructure provides traders and investors with access to various bids/ask prices and allows them to deal directly with other traders/dealers rather than through a central exchange.

The foreign exchange market is an example of a decentralised market because there is no single exchange or physical location where traders/investors have to conduct their buying and selling activities, trades can be conducted via an inter bank/dealer network that is geographically distributed. The trading in corporate bonds is also conducted through a decentralised dealer network that can provide pools of liquidity for the conduct of trade between buyers and sellers without the requirement of all trades to be cleared through an exchange.

8. DEALING METHODS

8.1 TRADING METHODS FOR BONDS

LEARNING OBJECTIVE

3.8.1 Know the different trading methods for bonds: bond trading has moved from voice trading (ie, by telephone) to e-trading using systems such as: OTC inter-dealer voice trading (eg, direct dealer to dealer, dealer to dealer via voice broker); inter-dealer (B2B) electronic market (eg, electronic trading platforms (ETPs) such as MTS, Brokertec); OTC customer to dealer voice trading; customer to dealer (B2C) electronic market (eg, ETPs such as TradeWeb, BondVision, proprietary Single Dealer Platform (SDP); on exchange trading

Bond trading including both corporate and government bonds is either conducted between dealers, some of which is arranged by inter-dealer brokers, or between dealers and their customers, like asset managers.

Dealer-to-dealer trading can occur in three ways:

- Direct telephone contact.
- Indirect via an inter-dealer broker voice broking the deal.

- Via an electronic market, known as an electronic trading platform, such as MTS or Brokertec.

Dealer-to-customer trading is done either by voice trading between the two parties, or via an electronic platform, such as TradeWeb, BondVision or proprietary single dealer systems developed by some of the larger banks.

A relatively small proportion of corporate bond dealing takes place via the exchanges, like the London Stock Exchange.

8.2 TRENDS IN TRADING METHODS

LEARNING OBJECTIVE

3.8.2 Understand the different trends between trading methods (see the syllabus learning map at the back of the book for the full learning objective)

Investors can trade marketable bonds among themselves in principal to principal deals and this can be done at any time. However, most trading is done through the network of bond dealers, and more specifically, the bond trading desks of major investment dealers. The dealers occupy the pivotal position in the vast network of telephone and electronic platforms that connect the interested players. Bond dealers usually 'make a market' for bonds. What this means is that the dealer has traders whose responsibility is to know all about a group of bonds and to be prepared to quote a price to buy or sell them.

Dealers provide 'liquidity' for bond investors, thereby allowing investors to buy and sell bonds more easily (B2C) and with a limited concession on the price. Dealers also buy and sell amongst themselves (B2B) either directly or anonymously via bond brokers, an exercise which is known as proprietary trading as the profit and loss for such trades are taken on to the dealer's books rather than its customers or clients.

The primary incentive for trading bonds amongst dealers is to take a spread between the price the bonds are bought at and the price they are sold at. This is the main way that bond dealers make (or lose) money. Dealers often have bond traders located in the major financial centres and are able to trade bonds 24 hours a day (although not usually on weekends).

According to a research study entitled *Electronic Bond Trading: Reaching the Tipping Point*, published by Celent: 'the fixed income market has undergone dramatic changes over the past several years and become increasingly electronic. Currently, electronic trading represents 57% of the US fixed income market's average daily volume (ADV) and is projected to reach 62% of ADV by 2010'.

The development of electronic trading has advanced furthest in the most liquid US fixed income segments — US treasury and mortgage-based securities (MBS). Currently, electronic trading represents nearly 80% of treasury segment volume and 32% of MBS. US corporate bonds are notoriously illiquid and less likely to be traded electronically. Overall, standardisation of the fixed income product and the resultant liquidity is the key deciding factor whether a bond will be traded electronically or not.

The development of fixed income electronic platforms has led to a change in market structure and a diversification of product offerings. Major platforms have expanded their product coverage either geographically in Europe and Asia or by entering other markets such as derivatives products.

In order to offer differentiation and create competitive advantage, some electronic trading platforms are including and enhancing value-added services such as STP solutions, expansion into OTC derivatives, and multi-asset trading platforms.

8.2.1 OTC Platforms

To illustrate the highly specialised manner in which the trading of most bonds is presently conducted, the following material from research note entitled Transparency Proposals for European Sovereign Bond Markets, by Peter Dunne at Queens University in Belfast is very helpful. The paper explains the current system and electronic trading facilities in the two segments of the euro-denominated sovereign bond market:

Two kinds of trading interfaces are provided one for dealer to dealer trading (B2B) and one for dealer to buy side clients such as asset managers and pension funds (B2C):

1. Business to Business (B2B) electronic trading platforms include BrokerTec, Euronext and MTS (the MTS platforms combine country-specific and euro-benchmark markets).
2. The Business to Client (B2C) segment mainly consists of request-for-quote (RFQ) platforms, including BondVision (a subsidiary of euro-MTS), TradeWeb and Bloomberg-Bond-Trader (BBT).

Request for quote (RFQ) systems allow investors to request quotes from a number of dealers simultaneously. Dealers can respond to such requests very quickly and trades can be executed electronically.

There are no significant B2C electronic orderbooks, so pre-trade transparency of the B2B market must suffice as the best guide to prices that investors can expect to obtain in potential B2C trades. Investors can request quotes simply to gain pre-trade information but investors can't be sure that they are receiving the same information as other investors. It should also be noted that dealers do not generally know what prices are being quoted by other dealers (although on most RFQ platforms the under-bidder is informed that they quoted closest to the accepted price).

Despite its limited transparency, RFQ systems are a significant improvement over voice communication in terms of ease and speed of trading. RFQ systems also bring dealers into direct competition with each other and this would be expected to deliver price improvement for investors.

Since the RFQ system doesn't provide pre-trade transparency, except on request, the information provided by the B2B segment must substitute. Thus, while the success of an RFQ trading system is at odds with the smooth running of the B2B electronic platform, the RFQ system itself cannot function very well without B2B transparency.

A 'catch-22' for transparency regulators is therefore, that imposing increased transparency on B2C activity increases the risks and reduces the incentives for dealers to provide continuous liquidity in the inter-dealer market. Indeed, any form of transparent trading in the B2C segment (such as the introduction of a parallel electronic orderbook) could represent a large threat to the efficient working of the B2B electronic trading system and this might in-turn alter the entire structure and approach to primary issuance.

8.2.2 Summary of OTC Trading and Current Regulatory Issues

Innovations in the technology used in both OTC markets and in more traditional exchange based markets are converging and it is becoming harder to distinguish between them. Price transparency, issues related to fees and perhaps most importantly the risk of counterparty default are also attracting a lot of attention from policy makers and regulators following the collapse of major players such as Bear Stearns and Lehman Brothers who were some of the early adopters and principal players in the development of OTC trading methods for bonds and derivatives.

- The activities of these quasi-exchanges have drawn the ire of politicians, who regard the lack of transparency in over-the-counter markets as a threat to the stability of the financial system. In November, the G20 group of nations issued a declaration that dealt specifically with the need for greater transparency in OTC derivatives markets. Charlie McCreevy, European Commissioner for internal market and services, said: 'We need to take urgent steps to bring OTC derivative trading out from the shadows'.
- In addition to regulatory pressure, inter-dealer brokers are also facing the prospect of lower revenues, according to analysts. Investment banks use OTC instruments to hedge risk associated with their other operations, so OTC trading is likely to fall as banks shrink their balance sheets and trade less.
- Futures exchanges have long coveted the high margins of OTC products and are seeking to benefit from the heightened regulatory scrutiny of inter-dealer brokers. NYSE Euronext's Liffe, the London-based derivatives market, has launched a clearing house for credit derivatives. The Chicago Mercantile Exchange, Deutsche Börse-owned derivatives market Eurex and Atlanta-based IntercontinentalExchange are also now beginning operations in this area.
- Revenues from electronic brokerage will account for 65% of total revenues over the next two years, up from 5% in 2004, according to Celent. The industry has also consolidated around four or five large groups. Celent estimated the top three brokers command 70% of total industry revenue, up from less than 50% in 2001.
- Consolidation of the inter-dealer broker market has been going on for some time. The largest brokers are unlikely to merge with one another, but will continue to identify and buy niche players. Such evolution has reduced the differences between inter-dealer brokers and exchanges.
- Inter-dealer brokers (IDBs) are increasingly implementing trading platforms that are similar to the exchange model. Indeed it could just as easily be argued that the exchange model is morphing more into a similar electronic matching network that has been a characteristic of the OTC market for man years. In essence, the difference between OTC trading and exchange based trading is blurring.
- Despite this growing similarity, inter-dealer brokers seem able to avoid much of the pressure banks put on exchanges to cut fees. That may be because they deal in less transparent products, making it difficult to compare tariffs.
- Another explanation is that fees are less of an issue in OTC markets because volumes are smaller than in their public counterparts.

- Inter-dealer brokers play a useful role in locating liquidity in the European options market, which is fairly illiquid. That usefulness may be most pronounced when market conditions are volatile, as banks tap the expansive knowledge of voice brokers to locate products.
- Inter-dealer brokers are increasingly being contacted by the buy-side directly due to the risk involved when dealing with prime brokers following the collapse of Lehman Brothers. IDBs were already serving that market, and that has accelerated since September 2008 due to the concern over sell-side providers.
- IDBs are also expanding into new geographical regions as they seek crucial local relationships.
- Electronic trading of OTC derivatives as opposed to voice based trading specifically, has improved price transparency and supervision of trading. About 80% of all credit default swap indices and 50% of single-name credit default swaps are traded electronically, compared with none two years ago.
- Some parts of the swap market are now being cleared by clearing houses. A substantial share of interest rate swap trades are cleared through SwapClear, the oil derivatives market is cleared through Nymex Clearport or Ice Clear and the EU emissions market is cleared through LCH. Clearnet.

8.3 FACTORS THAT INFLUENCE BOND PRICING

LEARNING OBJECTIVE

3.8.3 Know the factors that influence bond pricing: issuer factors: yield to maturity, seniority, structure, technical factors, credit rating, specific issuer prospects, default risk, liquidity, benchmark bonds; market factors; benchmark bonds; liquidity premiums for highly-traded bond issues; indicative pricing versus firm two way quotes; bid/offer spreads; availability of a liquid repo market and the difficulty in offering illiquid bonds; inability to borrow or cover shorts; impact of interest rates

Broadly, the factors that influence the prices of bonds can be sub-divided into two: issuer factors, and market factors. As seen in earlier chapters, the characteristics of a particular issue and the quality of the issuer encompass the following:

- Issuer's current credit rating (which itself will reflect the issuer's specific prospects) and highlight the issuer's default risk.
- The structure and seniority of the particular issue, for example, the bonds may be high or low priority in the event of default by the issuer and may be structured in a way that gives the bonds particular priority in relation to particular assets (such as mortgage-backed bonds).
- The above aspects, combined with prevailing yields available on other benchmark bonds (such as government issues in the same currency, with similar redemption dates), will determine the required yield to maturity and, therefore, the appropriate price.

Additionally, market factors will include the following:

- Liquidity – the more liquid bonds tend to be more expensive, encompassing a liquidity premium and having lower bid/offer spreads.
- Method of trading – some bonds attract firm quotes while others are traded with indicative quotes only, the precise price will only be arrived at by negotiation.
- Ability to borrow – bonds with active repo markets, and the ability to short positions relatively easily, will inevitably react more quickly to underlying interest rate changes and, therefore, yield changes.

The difficulties that can arise in the trading and pricing of bonds were especially acute during the 1998 crisis which began with the default by Russia on its bonds and led to the collapse of Long Term Capital Management – a major fund that specialised in the trading of fixed income instruments and various arbitrage strategies. One of the difficulties that arose during this crisis was the mis-pricing in the US Treasury market where the most recently issued long term bond, which is known as the 'on the run' bond, trades at a premium to those bonds which had been issued previously and which are known as 'off the run.' If investors have a preference, during a crisis, for the most liquid instruments, and they may hoard the 'on the run' bonds and force their price to be out of normal alignment with similar bonds which have a slightly different maturity date.

This can result in a breakdown in complex strategies designed to exploit the spreads or price differences across the yield spectrum.

8.4 QUOTATION METHODS

LEARNING OBJECTIVE

3.8.4 Know the different quotation methods (ie, yield, spread, price) and the circumstances in which they are used

There are two major elements of a quote for a bond – the **price** and, as a result of the price, the **yield**. Most traders will be looking for particular yields and then adjust the price to achieve that yield.

When dealing in corporate bonds, or across different bond markets (such as different countries' government bonds), traders and researchers will also be looking at the yield **spreads** that are available and anticipating changes in those spreads – eg, assessing whether the additional yield that is currently available for a BBB-rated sterling-denominated corporate bond over a gilt with similar maturity is likely to increase or decrease.

9. MARKET DATA

9.1 INFLATION AND INTEREST RATE EXPECTATIONS

LEARNING OBJECTIVE

3.9.1 Understand the relationship between inflation and interest rate expectations

A major driver of bond prices is the prevailing interest rate and expectations of interest rates to come. Yields required by bond investors are a reflection of their interest rate expectations, eg, if interest rates were expected to rise, bond prices would fall to bring the yields up to appropriate levels to reflect the interest rate increases and vice versa. To remain competitive, equities prices would also suffer.

The interest rate itself is heavily impacted by inflationary expectations. Simplistically, if inflation was expected to be at 4% per annum, the interest rate would have to be greater than this in order to provide the investor with any real return. The interest rate might stand at 7% per annum.

If economic news suggested that inflation was likely to increase further, to say 6%, then the interest rate would increase too, perhaps up to 9%.

The reverse would be true if inflation was expected to fall.

Technically, the interest rate referred to in the preceding paragraphs is the **nominal interest rate**. The nominal rate is the interest rate including inflation. The interest rate excluding inflation is generally referred to as the **real interest rate**.

9.2 INTEREST RATES AND SECURITIES PRICES

LEARNING OBJECTIVE

3.9.2 Understand how interest rates impact securities pricing

As explained above, when interest rates rise, or are expected to rise, securities prices tend to fall. Bonds fall in price to bring about a more competitive yield and equity prices fall to remain competitive with bonds and because companies may now face increased costs on their borrowing, reducing profits. Consumers are also likely to reduce expenditure because of increased costs on their borrowing (such as mortgages) which will adversely impact company sales.

In contrast, when interest rates fall, or are expected to fall, securities prices tend to rise. Bonds rise in price to reduce the yield in line with the fall in interest rates that is expected. Other investments, such as equities, will also rise in price since cheaper interest rates will reduce the costs of borrowing for companies and, therefore, likely increase their profits.

10. REGULATORY INFORMATION AND FINANCIAL COMMUNICATIONS

10.1 MAIN SOURCES

LEARNING OBJECTIVE

3.10.1 Know the main sources of regulatory information and financial communications within UK equity: RNS, PIPS & SIPS; Bloomberg, Reuters; analyst research; websites: FSA, LSE, EU (Europa, CESR)

As we have seen, companies that have their shares traded on the LSE need to keep market participants posted on any price sensitive information that might have arisen. For example, if a company has won a new, significant contract or simply announced its most recent set of results, it needs to inform the market participants in an orderly manner. This is achieved by notifying one of the FSA's 'Regulatory Information Services'.

Regulatory Information Services are also referred to as Primary Information Providers or PIPs. PIPs simply offer a service that receives regulatory information from listed companies, process that information and disseminate it by circulating it to Secondary Information Providers (or SIPs).

The SIPs then disseminate the information to the wider financial community such as stockbrokers and research analysts.

The PIPs include the LSE's own Regulatory News Service (RNS) as well as others such as PR Newswire and Newslink. The SIPs include well known information providers like Reuters, Bloomberg and Thomson Financial. The information that reaches the financial community via the PIPs and SIPs is used to inform and update research reports written by research analysts that comment on the likely future movements in the companies' share prices.

Obviously, this is not the only source of information that may impact securities' prices and trading generally. Regulatory websites, such as the FSA, LSE and European Union sites like Europa and CESR (the Committee of Securities Regulators), will be of interest to financial services firms and investors alike.

CHAPTER FOUR

SETTLEMENT

This syllabus area will provide approximately 6 of the 100 examination questions

1. INTRODUCTION TO SETTLEMENT SYSTEMS

LEARNING OBJECTIVE

4.1.1 Know the principal details of settlement in UK, EU, US and Japan: DVP; free delivery; trade confirmation; settlement periods; instruments settled; settlement systems: Euroclear UK & Ireland; LCH.Clearnet; Clearstream; DTCC; Jasdec

Settlement occurs after a deal has been executed. It is simply the transfer of ownership from the seller of the investment to the buyer, combined with the transfer of the cash consideration from the buyer to the seller. However, the process actually consists of several key stages, collectively described as **clearing and settlement**:

- **Confirmation** of the terms of the deal by the participants.
- **Clearance** – the calculation of the obligations of the deal participants, the money to be paid and the securities to be transferred.
- **Settlement** – the final transfer of the securities **(delivery)** in exchange for the final transfer of funds **(payment)**.

In any situation, the seller is unlikely to be willing to hand over legal title unless he is sure that the cash is flowing in the opposite direction, known as delivery versus payment (DVP). Similarly, the buyer is unlikely to be willing to hand over the cash without being sure that the legal ownership is passing in the other direction, known as cash against delivery (CAD).

There are two basic elements to the settlement of trades that can differ across different instruments and/or markets.

- **Timing of settlement:** this is normally based on a set number of business days after the trade is executed, known as **rolling settlement**.
- **Settlement system:** there are a variety of settlement systems that are used in particular markets, for example, the majority of transactions in UK equities are settled via an electronic settlement facility called CREST.

CREST is a computer system that settles transactions in shares, gilts and corporate bonds, primarily on behalf of the LSE. It is owned and operated by a company that is part of the Euroclear group of companies, called **Euroclear UK & Ireland**. CREST has the status of a Recognised Clearing House (RCH) and, as such, it is regulated by the FSA.

The financial instruments settled by CREST are **dematerialised**. Paper share certificates are replaced by an electronic entry in the underlying company's register of members. This allows shares transactions to be settled electronically.

CREST **clears** the trade by matching the settlement details provided by the buyer and the seller. The transaction is then **settled** when CREST updates the register of the relevant company to transfer the shares to the buyer, and at the same time CREST instructs the buyer's bank to transfer the appropriate amount of money to the seller's bank account.

In summary, to complete the settlement of a trade, CREST simultaneously:

- **updates the register of shareholders:** CREST maintains the so-called 'operator register' for UK companies' dematerialised shareholdings;
- **issues a payment obligation:** CREST sends an instruction to the buyer's payment bank to pay for the shares;
- **issues a receipt notification:** CREST notifies the seller's payment bank to expect payment.

If a trading system provides a central counterparty to the trades (such as LCH.Clearnet for trades on SETS), it is the central counterparty that assumes responsibility for settling the transaction with each counterparty. The buyer and seller remain anonymous to each other.

For SETS trades, CREST gives the option to LSE member firms to settle with LCH.Clearnet on a gross basis or on a net basis. If a firm has 20 orders executed in the same security through SETS, they can either settle 20 trades with LCH.Clearnet (settling gross), or choose to have all 20 trades netted so that the firm just settles a single transaction with LCH.Clearnet.

The settlement period (the time between the trade and the transfer of money and registration) for UK equities is **normally on a T+3 basis**, where T is the trade date and 3 is the number of business days after the trade date that the cash changes hands and the shares' registered title changes. In other words, if a trade is executed on a Tuesday, the cash and registered title will change three business days later, on the Friday. So, if the trade is executed on a Wednesday, it will be the following Monday that settlement will occur. This is referred to by the LSE as **standard settlement**. Standard settlement applies to all deals automatically executed on an LSE trading system, such as SETS.

The following table provides an overview of the settlement systems in the UK, EU, the US and Japan:

Country/Region	Instruments settled	Settlement period	System name
UK	Listed equities and corporate bonds	T+3	CREST
	Government bonds (gilts)	T+1 (cash settlement)	CREST
EU (particularly Germany)	Listed German equities	T+2	Clearstream
	International bonds	T+3	Clearstream/Euroclear
US	Listed equities	T+3	Depository Trust Clearing Corporation (DTCC)
	Government bonds	T+1	DTCC
Japan	Listed equities and convertible bonds	T+3	Japan Securities Depositary Center (JASDEC)

2. CUSTODIANSHIP

LEARNING OBJECTIVE

4.1.2 Know the concept of custody and the roles of the different types of custodian; Global; Regional; Local

2.1 SERVICES PROVIDED BY CUSTODIANS

When an institutional investor invests in securities, it will commonly employ the services of a custodian to administer these securities by:

- Providing safe keeping of the investor's assets in the local market;
- Making appropriate arrangements for delivery and receipt of cash and securities to support settlement of the investor's trading activities in that market;
- Providing market information to the investor on developments and reforms within that market;
- Collecting dividend income, interest paid on debt securities and other income payments in the local market;
- Managing the client's cash flows;
- Monitoring and managing entitlements through corporate actions and voting rights held by the investor in the local market;
- Managing tax reclaims and other tax services in the local market;
- Ensuring that securities are registered and that transfer of legal title on securities transactions proceeds effectively;
- Ensuring that reporting obligations to the regulatory authorities, and to other relevant bodies, are discharged effectively.

2.2 ROLE AND RESPONSIBILITY OF A CUSTODIAN

The primary responsibility of the custodian is to ensure that the client's assets are fully protected at all times. Hence, it must provide robust safekeeping facilities for all valuables and documentation, ensuring that investments are only released from the custodian's care in accordance with authorised instructions from the client.

Importantly, the client's assets must be properly segregated from those of the custodian and appropriate legal arrangements must be in place to ensure that financial or external shock to the custodian does not expose the client's assets to claims from creditors or any other party.

An investor faces choices in selecting custody arrangements in regard to a portfolio of global assets. The possible paths can be summarised as follows:

- Appointing a local custodian in each market in which he/she invests (often referred to as direct custody arrangements).
- Appointing a global custodian to manage custody arrangements across the full range of foreign markets in which he/she has invested assets.
- Making arrangements to settle trades and hold securities and cash with a Central Securities Depository (CSDs) within each market, or to go via an International Central Securities Depository (ICSD).

2.3 GLOBAL CUSTODY

A global custodian provides investment administration for investor clients, including processing cross-border securities trades and keeping financial assets secure (ie, providing safe custody) outside of the country where the investor is located.

The term global custody came into common usage in the financial services world in the mid-1970s, when the Employee Retirement Income Security Act (ERISA) was passed in the US. This legislation was designed to increase the protection given to US pension fund investors. The Act specified that US pension funds could not act as custodians of the assets held in their own funds. Instead, these assets had to be held in the safekeeping of another bank. ERISA went further to specify that only a US bank could provide custody services for a US pension fund.

Subsequently, use of the term global custody has evolved to refer to a broader set of responsibilities, encompassing settlement, safekeeping, cash management, record keeping and asset servicing (eg, collecting dividend payments on shares and interest on bonds, reclaiming withholding tax, advising investor clients on their electing on corporate actions entitlements), and providing market information. Some investors may also use their global custodians to provide a wider suite of services, including investment accounting, treasury and FX, securities lending and borrowing, collateral management, and performance and risk analysis on the investor's portfolio.

Some global custodians maintain an extensive network of branches globally and can meet the local custody needs of their investor clients by employing their own branches as local custody providers. Citi, for example, maintains a proprietary branch network covering 48 markets. Consequently, Citi, acting as global custodian for an investor client, may opt to use its own branch to provide local custody in many locations where the investor holds assets.

2.4 SUB-CUSTODY

A sub-custodian is employed by a global custodian as its local agent to provide settlement and custody services for assets that it holds on behalf of investor clients in a foreign market. A sub-custodian effectively serves as the eyes and ears of the global custodian in the local market, providing a range of clearing, settlement and asset servicing duties. It will also typically provide market information relating to developments in the local market, and will lobby the market authorities for reforms that will make the market more appealing and an efficient target for foreign investment.

In selecting a sub-custodian, a global custodian may:

- appoint one of its own branches, in cases where this option is available;
- appoint a local agent bank that specialises in providing sub-custody in the market concerned;
- appoint a regional provider that can offer sub-custody to the global custodian across a range of markets in a region or globally.

2.5 LOCAL CUSTODIAN

Agent banks that specialise in providing sub-custody in their home market are sometimes known as single-market providers. Stiff competition from larger regional or global competitors has meant that these are becoming a dying breed. However, some continue to win business in their local markets, often combining this service with offering global custody or master custody for institutional investors in their home markets. Examples include Bank Tokyo Mitsubishi, Mizuho Corporate Bank and Sumitomo Bank in Japan, Maybank in Malaysia and United Overseas Bank in Singapore.

A principal selling point is that they are local market specialists and that is what they do – hence they can remain focused on their local business without spreading their attentions broadly across a wide range of markets. A local specialist bank may be attractive in a market in which local practices tend to differ markedly from global standards, or where a provider's long standing relationship with the local regulatory authorities and/or political elite leaves it particularly well placed to lobby for reforms on behalf of its cross-border clients.

Reciprocal arrangements may be influential in shaping the appointment of a local provider in some instances. Under such an arrangement, a global custodian (A) may appoint the local provider (B) to deliver sub-custody in its local market (market B). In return, the custodian (A) may offer sub-custody in its own home market (market A) for pension and insurance funds in market B that use provider B as their global custodian.

In summary, the strengths of a local custodian may include:

- They are country specialists.
- They can be the 'eyes and ears' of global custodian or broker/dealer in local market.
- They will have regular dealings with financial authorities and local politicians – may be well placed to lobby for reforms that will improve the efficiency of the local market.
- They have expert knowledge of local market practice, language and culture.
- They may offer opportunities for reciprocal business.

A local custody bank may be perceived to have the following disadvantages when compared with a regional custodian:

- Their credit rating may not match up to requirements laid down by some global custodians or global broker/dealers.
- They cannot leverage developments in technology and client service across multiple markets (unlike a regional custodian) – hence product and technology development may lag behind the regional custodians that it competes with.
- They may not be able to offer the price discounts that can be extended by regional custodians offering custody services across multiple markets.

2.6 REGIONAL CUSTODIAN

A regional custodian is able to provide agent bank services across multiple markets in a region.

For example, Standard Chartered Bank and HSBC have both been offering regional custody and clearing in the Asia-Pacific and South Asian region for many years, competing with Citi and some strong single market providers for business in this region. In Central and Eastern Europe, Bank Austria Creditanstalt/Unicredit Group, Deutsche Bank, ING Group, Raiffeisen Zentralbank Osterreich and Citi each offer a regional clearing and custody service. In Central and South America, Citi and Bank Itau (the Brazilian bank that purchased Bank Boston's established regional custody service) offer regional custody, in competition in selected markets, with HSBC, Bank Santander and Deutsche Bank.

Employing a regional custodian may offer a range of advantages to global custodian or global broker/dealer clients:

- Its credit rating may be higher than for single-market custodian.
- It can cross-fertilise good practice across multiple markets – lessons learned in one market may be applied, where appropriate, across other markets in its regional offering.
- It can leverage innovation in technology, product development and client service across multiple markets – delivering economies of scale benefits.
- It can offer standardised reporting, management information systems and market information across multiple markets in its regional offering.
- Economies of scale may support delivery of some or all product lines from a regional processing centre – offering potential cost savings and efficiency benefits.
- Its size and regional importance, plus the strength of its global client base, may allow a regional custodian to exert considerable leverage on local regulators, political authorities and infrastructure providers. This may be important in lobbying for reforms that support greater efficiency and security for foreign investors in that market.
- A global client may be able to secure price discounts by using a regional custodian across multiple markets.

In some situations, a regional provider may be perceived to have certain disadvantages when compared with a local custody bank:

- A regional custodian's product offering may be less well attuned to local market practice, service culture and investor needs than a well-established local provider.
- A regional custodian may spread its focus across a wider range of clients and a wider range of markets than a single market provider. Hence, a cross-border client may not receive the same level of attention, and the same degree of individualised service, as may be extended by a local custodian.
- Some regional custodians may lack the long track record, customer base and goodwill held by some local custodians in their own market.

3. REGISTERED TITLE

LEARNING OBJECTIVE

4.1.3 Understand the implications of registered title: registered title versus unregistered (bearer); legal title; beneficial interest; voting rights; right to participate in corporate actions

When settling a trade involving UK shares, settlement must involve communicating the change in ownership to the company registrar. This is because the issuing company maintains a register listing all of its shareholders. Whenever shares are bought or sold, a mechanism is required to make the company registrar aware of the change required to the register.

If there were no register, the shares would be described as unregistered or **bearer shares** and physically handing over the shares would be a valid transfer of ownership.

So, **registered title** simply means ownership that is backed by registration. In terms of share ownership, registered title gives shareholders the right to vote on important company matters, to claim dividends on their shares and to participate in other corporate actions such as rights issues.

When shares are bought and sold, it is the **company registrar** who is responsible for updating the **register of members** and giving the new owner registered title.

Busy shareholders often want to avoid the administrative tasks connected with registered title, so they choose to appoint their stockbroker, or another professional, to act as a **nominee**.

The nominee takes the registered title to the shares and all the responsibilities that go with it, but the nominee's client retains **beneficial ownership** – it is the client that ultimately receives all of the cashflows generated by the shares. The nominee is referred to as the **legal owner** of the shares and the client retaining the benefits of ownership, mainly the dividends and capital growth, is known as the **beneficial owner**.

4. DESIGNATED AND POOLED NOMINEES

LEARNING OBJECTIVE

4.1.4 Understand the basics of designated and pooled nominee accounts and their uses, and the concept of corporate nominees: designated nominee accounts; pooled nominee accounts; details in share register; function of corporate nominees; legal ownership; effect on shareholder rights of using a nominee

UK company law prevents registrars and companies from recognising anyone other than the **name on register** or in the case of a corporation, their duly appointed attorney.

Institutional investors employing professional investment management firms to manage their assets are highly unlikely to hold these securities in their own name ('name on register'). The reason for this is simple: the person whose name appears on the share register receives every piece of documentation sent out by the company and would be obliged to sign all share transfers and other relevant forms such as instructions for rights issues and other corporate events. To ensure safe custody of assets and remove this administrative burden from the investor thus allowing the speedy processing of transfers, institutional (and, increasingly, private client) shareholdings are held in the names of 'nominee' companies.

Nominee companies have long been established as the mechanism by which asset managers and custodians can process transactions on behalf of their clients. Given that many investment management firms have outsourced some or all of their investment administration activities to the specialist custodians, the vast majority of institutional shareholdings in fact now reside in nominee accounts overseen by the specialist custodians.

As far as the company is concerned, the nominee name appearing on its share register is the **legal** owner of the shares for the purposes of benefits and for voting. However, **beneficial** ownership continues to reside with the underlying client.

It is this separation of ownership which allows the custodians, under proper client authorities, to transfer shares to meet market transactions and to conduct other functions without the registrar requiring sight of the signature or seal of the underlying client.

Registrars cannot recognise a trust as the beneficial owner of shares, so in order to look beyond the legal ownership of any holding, the registrar can issue at any time a notice under section 793 of the Companies Acts. This will require the nominee company to disclose the name of the beneficial owner of the shares, so that at least the company may be aware for whom the nominee is acting. A notice issued under section 793 of the Companies Act (which came into force on 20 January 2007 and replaced the section 212 notice under the Companies Act 1985), allows a public company to issue a notice requiring a person it knows, or has reasonable cause to believe, has an interest in its shares (or to have had an interest in the previous three years) to confirm or deny the fact, and, if the former, to disclose certain information about the interest, including information about any other person with an interest in the shares.

4.1 TYPES OF NOMINEE COMPANIES

Nominees can be classified into three types:

- **Pooled** (or 'Omnibus'), whereby individual clients are grouped together within a single nominee registration;
- **Designated**, where the nominee name includes unique identifiers for each individual client, eg, XYZ Nominees Account 1, Account 2, Account 3 etc;
- **Sole**, where a single nominee name is used for a specific client, eg, ABC Pension Fund Nominees ltd.

How the shareholdings are registered is of vital importance when it comes to voting.

It is now generally accepted that there are no real advantages from a security point of view as to which type of nominee arrangement is used to register the shares. However, clients brought together with others in a pooled nominee have no visibility to the company: it is the single nominee name, covering multiple clients, which the company recognises. Importantly, from a voting perspective, it is only the single bulk nominee which is entitled to vote; no separate entitlement accrues from the registrar's standpoint to each individual client making up the total holding.

Some companies offer their shareholders certain perks, such as discounts on their products. By using a nominee (either a designated or a pooled structure), the shareholder perks may not be available to the individual investor. This is simply because the stockbrokers may be unwilling to undertake the necessary administration to facilitate the provision of these perks.

One reason for registering shares in a designated or sole nominee name would be if the underlying investor requires dividends to be mandated to a particular bank account, rather than being collected by the custodian, registration in an omnibus account is not practicable.

Designation or individual registration can also help some aspects of auditing and it affords a good control mechanism where identical bargains may have been executed for different clients (for example on the same date, for the same number of shares and for the same settlement consideration).

4.2 CORPORATE NOMINEE

A corporate nominee (alternatively referred to as a **corporate sponsored nominee**) is where the issuing company itself provides a facility for its smaller shareholders to hold their shares within a single **corporate nominee**.

The corporate nominee is a halfway house between the pooled and the designated nominee structures offered by stockbrokers. It will result in a single entry for all the shareholders together in the company's register (like the pooled nominee) but beneath this the issuing company (or its registrar) will be aware of the individual holdings that make up the nominee. In a similar way to the designated nominee structure, the company will be able to forward separate dividend payments to each of the individual shareholders, as well as voting rights and other potential shareholder perks. Shares held within a corporate nominee in dematerialised form enable quick and easy transfer through CREST.

4.3 LEGAL OWNERSHIP STATUS

A person or company established to hold shares on behalf of the investor. The nominee is the legal owner of the shares. The original investor becomes the 'beneficial owner' entitled to receive dividends and the capital growth of the shares, but not the automatic right to attend company meetings etc.

4.4 SHARE REGISTER

Shares in the UK are held in registered form. This means that the certificate is simply evidence of ownership. The proof that counts is the name and address held on the company's share register.

There is a statutory requirement for a minimum of one shareholder and for the details of shareholders to be put on public record.

Upon incorporating a company (be it a new or ready-made, shelf company or a tailor made company), one can either act as a shareholder in one's own name, or a financial services firm equipped to handle incorporations or a custodian can provide you with a nominee shareholder with a view to securing your corporate privacy. For the purpose of privacy, some clients do not wish to be identified as shareholders of the companies that they have set up and will, therefore, wish to appoint nominee shareholders. These nominee shareholders will hold the shares on trust for the beneficial owners and only they will be identified on the register of shareholders.

Each nominee shareholder appointed will sign a declaration of trust to the beneficial owner that they are holding the shares on behalf of the beneficial owner and will return the shares into the name of the beneficial owner or will transfer them to another party as requested. A nominee shareholder is normally a company created for the purpose of holding shares and other securities on behalf of investors.

One reason frequently cited by custodians for insisting on pooled nominee arrangements is the vexed question of 'costs'. Operating a designated nominee account should give rise to few additional costs from the custodian's point of view, as the existing nominee name can easily be used with the addition of a unique designation. Whilst there may be a slight increase in the receipt of Section 793 requests and a small amount of extra work involved, eg, in the receipt of separate income payments, the actual procedures are identical and should be capable of being easily absorbed into the existing administration and processing routines.

If the client insists on using a sole nominee name to register the shareholdings, this might involve some costs for the custodian connected with the establishment of a nameplate nominee company and the requisite appointment of directors, the completion of annual returns, etc. The custodian may seek to pass these comparatively meagre costs on to the client, but more usually they will be absorbed within the standard custody tariff.

Neither of these two nominee approaches are likely to give rise to additional transaction charges imposed on the custodian by CREST, the UK's electronic share settlement system, as individual sales and purchases are relayed across the system regardless of how the assets are registered.

One area where additional transactions may occur, giving rise to additional costs, is in respect of securities lending. However, the CREST charges for such transactions are as low as 50p each and a client would need to undertake an inordinate amount of loans and recalls for these transaction charges to become a significant amount.

Such small additional amounts need to be seen against the typical custody tariff for UK securities of around 1 basis point (0.01%) of the value of assets under custody and a further charge of approximately £20 for each trade settled. Also, in the case of securities lending, the custodian usually retains a share of the extra income generated. This is often around 30%, again drawing any additional transaction costs in respect of loan movements created by a separately registered or designated nominee account.

4.5 SUMMARY

Custodians and their nominees now control the majority of share registrations for institutional investors, even for clients who may not have directly appointed custodians but whose asset management firms have outsourced their investment administration to these providers.

Custodians uniquely identify their clients' holdings by segregating these in their computer systems, as it is largely these systems which drive the calculation and application of dividends and other entitlements. However, this segregation is not the same as having an individually identifiable holding for a particular client on company share registers.

It is largely impractical for an institutional investor to achieve 'name on register', so the recognised practice is to use nominee names whereby the custodian, or other duly authorised agent, is legally entitled to perform the transfer and administration of the assets on behalf of, and under the authority of, the underlying beneficial owner.

Many custodians prefer to pool all their clients into one single nominee registration but this does remove the visibility of the underlying investor and makes individual client voting much more cumbersome.

Clients can request their custodian to adopt an individual registration solely for their particular shareholdings. Typically this takes the form of a standard nominee name with a unique designation for each client. The costs of such separate registration and its ongoing maintenance are minimal relative to overall custody and securities lending charges and are often absorbed by the custodians.

5. STAMP DUTY AND STAMP DUTY RESERVE TAX (SDRT)

LEARNING OBJECTIVE

4.1.5 Know which securities may be subject to UK stamp duty/SDRT

Stamp duty is a tax payable on documents that transfer certain kinds of property by the purchaser of that property. If property can be handed over, eg, furniture, there is no charge to stamp duty, because there is no document executed on which to charge the duty. Some property, such as houses, land and shares in a company, can only be transferred in a prescribed legal form and the legislation requires that documents liable to stamp duty may not be registered or used unless they have been duly stamped. Since owners want to be able to demonstrate their title to property, they are effectively required to have their document stamped if they want it to be recognised as their own.

There are different rates of stamp duty for shares and for other property. Stamp duty on share transfers is **charged to the purchaser at 0.5%** of the price (excluding any commissions payable to the stockbroker), with no threshold. Normally there is no charge on the issue, as distinct from the transfer of shares. The duty is rounded to the next £5, so that a transfer of shares priced at £800 would be charged at £5, and a transfer priced at £1,240 would be charged at £10.

However, there is a charge of **1.5% made on the creation of a bearer share, or the transfer of shares into a depositary receipt** (eg, ADR), because subsequent transfers will not attract stamp duty.

In summary:

Rate:	0.5% of the consideration value of the purchase (rounded up to the next £5)
Paid by:	the buyer
Trigger:	transfer to new ownership (not primary issue)
Example:	UK equity transfers

Stamp duty depends upon there being a document to stamp. It cannot be used for paperless transactions. Stamp Duty Reserve Tax (SDRT) was, therefore, introduced to cater for the paperless transfer of shares through CREST. The SDRT regulations impose an obligation on the operator of CREST (Euroclear UK & Ireland) to collect SDRT on transfers going through the system.

SDRT applies in place of stamp duty in cases where the agreement is not completed by an instrument of transfer (ie, a document, the stock transfer form). The tax is **charged at 0.5% on the consideration** given for the transfer, payable by the purchaser. Unlike stamp duty, there is no rounding to the next £5, and it is charged to the penny.

The following is a summary of the major instances where SDRT is charged:

Situation	Why can't we charge stamp duty?	Rate of SDRT	Levied When?
Transfer of nominee holdings	No change of name on certificate but beneficial owner has changed	½%	On each transfer
CREST transactions	No paper certificate to stamp	½%	On each transfer

6. SECURITIES EXEMPT FROM STAMP DUTY

LEARNING OBJECTIVE

4.1.6 Know which transactions are exempt UK stamp duty

Gilts and bonds are not liable to stamp duty unless they are equity-related, for example, convertible into equity. Gifts are not liable to stamp duty since there is no consideration paid on the transactions.

Securities that are exempt from stamp duty, such as gilts and non-convertible bonds, are also exempt from SDRT. For both stamp duty and SDRT there are also exemptions for purchases by registered charities, on-exchange stock lending transactions, gifts and purchases by LSE member firms (who are granted 'intermediary' status) and the clearing house.

According to Schedule 15 of the Finance Act of 1999 which relates to the application of the duty for bearer instruments the following are relevant exemptions from stamp duty.

Stamp duty is not chargeable under this Schedule on renounceable letters of allotment, letters of rights or other similar instruments where the rights under the letter or other instrument are renounceable not later than six months after its issue.

6.1 INSTRUMENTS RELATING TO NON-STERLING STOCK

Stamp duty is also not chargeable under Schedule 15 on the issue of an instrument which relates to stock expressed:

- in a currency other than sterling, or
- in units of account defined by reference to more than one currency (whether or not including sterling), or
- on the transfer of the stock constituted by or transferable by means of any such instrument.

Further definitions of instruments which are exempt also include:

A unit under a unit trust scheme or a share in a foreign mutual fund shall be treated as capital stock of a company formed or established in the territory by the law of which the scheme or fund is governed.

A 'foreign mutual fund' means a fund administered under arrangements governed by the law of a territory outside the UK under which subscribers to the fund are entitled to participate in, or receive payments by reference to, profits or income arising to the fund from the acquisition, holding, management or disposal of investments.

In relation to a foreign mutual fund 'share' means the right of a subscriber, or of another in his right, to participate in or receive payments by reference to profits or income so arising.

7. CUM- AND EX-DIVIDEND

LEARNING OBJECTIVE

4.1.7 Understand the concepts, requirements, benefits and disadvantages of deals executed cum, ex, special cum and special ex: timetable; effect of deals on the underlying right; effect on the share price before and after a dividend; the meaning of 'books closed', 'ex-div' and 'cum div', cum and ex rights; effect of late registration; benefits that may be achieved; disadvantages/risks; when dealing is permitted

Normally, a company's shares are quoted **cum-dividend**. This means that buyers of the shares have the right to the next dividend paid by the company. However, there are brief periods when the share becomes **ex-dividend**, meaning that it is sold without the right to receive the next dividend payment. The **ex-dividend** period occurs around the time of a dividend payment.

The sequence of events leading up to the dividend payment is as follows.

1. Dividend declared:
   On this date the company announces its intention to pay a specified dividend on a specified future date. The declaration must occur at least three clear business days before the ex-dividend date.

2. Ex-dividend date:
   The ex-dividend date is invariably a Wednesday, the first Wednesday that falls at least three clear business days after the day that the dividend was declared.

3. Record or books-closed date:
   The record, or **books-closed** date is the date on which a copy of the shareholders' register is taken. The people on the share register at the end of this day will be paid the next dividend. The books-closed date is the second business day after the ex-dividend date. Because the ex-dividend date is a Wednesday, the books-closed date is usually a Friday, except where the Friday is a public holiday, in which case the books-closed date is the next available business day.

4. Dividend paid:
   The dividend is paid to those shareholders who were on the register on the record/books-closed date.

5. Ex-dividend period:
   The period from the ex-dividend date up to the dividend payment date is the ex-dividend period. Throughout this period the shares trade **without** entitlement to the next dividend.

The relationship between the ex-dividend date and the books-closed date is easily explained. Since the equity settlement process takes three business days, for a new shareholder to appear on the register on the Friday they would have to buy the shares by Tuesday at the latest. Tuesday is the last day when the shares trade cum-dividend, because new shareholders will be reflected in the register before the end of the books-closed date. A new shareholder buying their shares on the Wednesday will not be entered into the register until the following week – too late for the books-closed date and therefore ex-dividend.

On the Wednesday when the shares first trade without the dividend (ex-dividend), the share price will fall to reflect the fact that if an investor buys the share he will not be entitled to the impending dividend.

At all times other than during ex-dividend periods, shares trade cum-dividend, ie, if an investor purchases shares at this time, he will be entitled to all of the future dividends paid by the company for as long as he keeps the share.

During the ex-dividend period, it is possible to arrange a **special cum-trade**. That is where, by special arrangement, the buyer of the share during the ex-dividend period **does** receive the next dividend. These trades can be done up to and including the day before the dividend payment date, but not on or after the dividend payment date.

In a similar manner to a special cum-trade, an investor can also arrange a special ex-trade. This is only possible in the 10 business days before the ex-date. If an investor buys a share during the cum-dividend period, but buys it special ex, he will not receive the next dividend.

Using special cum or special ex transactions enables the sellers or buyers to avoid the receipt of a dividend – essentially deciding whether or not they want to collect their right to the dividend. During the period when the LSE allows such trading, it effectively allows the right to the dividend to be traded. The motivation for investors buying or selling with or without the dividend entitlement tends to be related to tax. Dividend income is normally subject to income tax, so selling the right to the dividend might avoid some income tax.

The inherent disadvantage of special cum trades and **special ex trades** is that they will, potentially, result in dividends from the company being paid to the wrong person. Equally a trade that settles later than usual could mean that the correct owner is not reflected in the shareholders' register on the books-closed date – and the dividend is paid by the company to the wrong person. In such situations, it is the broker acting for the buyers (or seller, as appropriate) that will need to make a claim for the dividend.

8. CONTINUOUS LINKED SETTLEMENT

LEARNING OBJECTIVE

4.1.8 Understand what Continuous Linked Settlement (CLS) is and its purpose: the settlement of currencies across time zones; receiving and matching instructions; advantages; how it reduces settlement risk

As international trade and investment has increased, so has the foreign exchange market. The average daily volume in the global forex and related markets is continously growing and was last reported to be over US$4 trillion in April 2007 by the Bank for International Settlement.

Continuous Linked Settlement is a process by which most of the world's largest banks, manage settlement of foreign exchange among themselves (and their customers and other third-parties). The process is managed by CLS Group Holdings and regulated by the Federal Reserve Board of New York. Since it began operations, CLS has rapidly become the market-standard for foreign exchange settlement between major banks, and as of September 2007 it settles about 325,000 instructions a day in 17 currencies (which represent some 98% of global foreign exchange trading) and with an average daily value exceeding US$3.3 trillion.

CLS settles transactions on a PVP basis which in its long form means 'Payment versus Payment'. The two parties to a foreign exchange transaction will buy and sell the respective currencies exchanged and the payments made will occur simultaneously. Unless such simultaneity in payments is ensured there is a possibility of settlement risk which is also often referred to as Herstatt risk.

Before the establishment of the CLS foreign exchange transactions were settled by each side of a trade making separate payments. The risks implicit in this approach became clear in 1974, when the German banking regulators withdrew the banking licence of Bankhaus Herstatt, putting it into liquidation at the close of business on 26 June.

Bankhaus Herstatt had been active in the foreign exchange markets and had received currency from counterparties during the day, but had not yet made any payments when its licence was withdrawn and it was declared bankrupt. Several banks had irrevocably paid over deutschmarks to Herstatt during the day, but had not received the anticipated currency in exchange. In addition, banks had entered into forward trades that were not yet due for settlement, and some lost money replacing the contracts. In short, there were serious repercussions in the foreign exchange market after the Bankhaus Herstatt default and the intra-day settlement risk highlighted has subsequently been termed 'Herstatt risk'.

The result was the impetus to set up a more robust and reliable system that ensured payment from one party was only made where there was a payment coming in the opposite direction to fulfil the other side of the foreign exchange deal – payment versus payment or PVP. Continuous linked settlement, or CLS, was the result that solved the PVP problem, despite the counterparties potentially being in different parts of the world and time zones.

The CLS settlement process is focused on a five-hour window each business day from 7.00am to 12 midday in Central European Time (CET). This window was created to provide an overlap across the business days in all parts of the world and facilitate global trading.

By 6.30am CET the settlement members must submit their settlement instructions for transactions to settle that day. At 6.30am each settlement member receives a schedule of what monies need to be paid in that day. From 7.00am the settlement members pay in the net funds that are due to settle in each currency to their central banks, and CLS will then begin to attempt to settle deals. In the event that CLS Bank's strict settlement criteria are not met for each side of a trade, then no funds are exchanged. This achieves the payment versus payment system that removes the so-called Herstatt risk. Those trades that can be settled are settled and money is paid out via the central banks.

As outlined above, the payments made to CLS Bank are made via the central banks. In the UK, both sterling and euro payments are made via CHAPS (the Clearing House Automated Payment System). CHAPS is the electronic transfer system for sending payments between banks that operates in partnership with the Bank of England.

In Europe, the Trans-european Automated Real-time Gross settlement Express Transfer system (TARGET) is used. TARGET is an electronic transfer system for sending euro-denominated payments between banks, operating in partnership with the European Central Bank (ECB). UK banks link to TARGET via CHAPS euro payments.

CHAPTER FIVE

SPECIAL REGULATORY REQUIREMENTS

This syllabus area will provide approximately 4 of the 100 examination questions

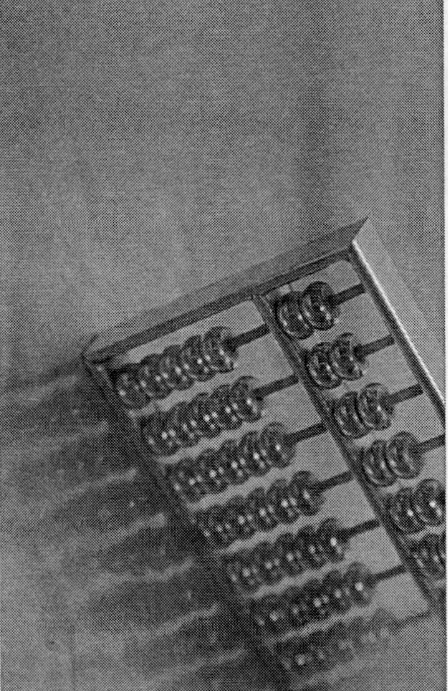

1. EU TAKEOVER DIRECTIVE

LEARNING OBJECTIVE

5.1.1 Know the implications of the EU Takeover Directive: that some countries continue with own rules as minimum standards directive and that takeover rules vary between states; application to all EU companies trading on an EU regulated market; requirements for a designated supervisory authority and scope for shared supervision; general principles of the Directive (Art. 3); consequences of a mandatory bid and different mandatory bid thresholds; publication of information on the bid (Articles 6 and 10)

A **takeover** occurs if one company buys a majority of the shares of another company; it gains control over the other company and is, therefore, termed the parent company, while the other company is its subsidiary. A **merger** is the term used when the two companies are of a similar size and come together to form a larger, merged entity.

The Takeover Directive is (like MiFID) one of the measures adopted under the European Union's Financial Services Action Plan. It aims to contribute to the creation of a single market in financial services by facilitating cross-border mergers and acquisitions and standardising protections for minority shareholders. The way that the Directive has been constructed is to require member states to implement certain minimum requirements, but to allow the member states to incorporate more stringent requirements if they wish.

The Takeover Directive applies to takeover bids for the securities of an EU company, where all or some of those securities are admitted to trading on a regulated market, such as a stock exchange, in one or more member states.

Under the Directive, member states are required to designate the authority (or authorities) competent for the purpose of supervising any bids, to ensure they meet the appropriate rules. Since the precise rules can vary across member states because of the minimum requirements approach taken by the Directive, there are requirements to determine which member state's rules apply and, therefore, the designated supervisory authority. It is the designated supervisory authority of the:

- member state in which the company subject to the offer (the offeree) has its registered office, where the offeree's securities are traded on a regulated market in that member state;
- member state in which the offeree's securities are traded, where the offeree's securities are traded on a regulated market in an EU country that is not the country in which it has its registered office.

Due to the possibility of cross-border takeovers involving an offeror in one member state and an offeree in another, the Directive also includes a requirement that supervisory authorities co-operate and supply each other with information when necessary.

The Takeover Directive's minimum requirements include six general principles that are covered in Section 2 below, and the requirement to launch a mandatory bid in certain circumstances. The mandatory bid provision states that where a natural or legal person, as a result of an acquisition by him or in concert with him, reaches a specified percentage to gain control, he is required to make a mandatory bid for the remaining shares at an equitable price. The equitable price is the highest price paid by the offeror for the same securities over a period of between six and twelve months prior to the bid.

The Directive also requires information about any takeover bid to be made public. The Directive states that the decision to make a bid is made public without delay, and that the supervisory authority is informed of the bid. Furthermore, the offeror is required to draw up and make public, in good time, an offer document containing the information necessary to enable the holders of securities in the offeree to reach a properly informed decision on the bid.

2. UK TAKEOVER CODE

LEARNING OBJECTIVE

5.1.2 Know the legal nature and purpose of the UK Takeover Code (Section 2 of the Introduction); the six General Principles; the definitions of 'acting in concert', 'dealings', 'interest in shares' and 'relevant securities'

The UK supervisory authority that carries out the regulatory functions required under the EU Takeover Directive is the **Panel on Takeovers and Mergers** (the **Panel** or **POTAM**). The Panel's requirements are set out in a Code that consists of six General Principles, and a number of detailed rules.

The Code is designed principally to ensure that shareholders are treated fairly and are not denied an opportunity to decide on the merits of a takeover. Furthermore, the Code ensures that shareholders of the same class are afforded equivalent treatment by an offeror. In short, the Code provides an orderly framework within which takeovers are conducted, and is designed to assist in promoting the integrity of the financial markets.

The Code is not concerned with the financial or commercial advantages or disadvantages of a takeover. These are matters for the company and its shareholders. Nor is the Code concerned with competition policy, which is the responsibility of government and other bodies.

Each of the six general principles are reproduced in full below. Although the detail of each principle is probably outside the syllabus, it is useful to be able to review the principles to fully appreciate the spirit of the Code. At its broadest, the Code simply requires fair play between all interested parties.

1. All holders of the securities of an offeree company of the same class must be afforded equivalent treatment; moreover, if a person acquires control of a company, the other holders of securities must be protected.

2. The holders of the securities of an offeree company must have sufficient time and information to enable them to reach a properly informed decision on the bid; where it advises the holders of securities, the board of the offeree company must give its views on the effects of implementation of the bid on employment, conditions of employment and the locations of the company's places of business.
3. The board of an offeree company must act in the best interests of the company as a whole and must not deny the holders of securities the opportunity to decide on the merits of the bid.
4. False markets must not be created in the securities of the offeree company, or the offeror company or of any other company concerned by the bid in such a way that the rise or fall of the prices of the securities becomes artificial and the normal functioning of the markets is distorted.
5. An offeror must announce a bid only after ensuring that he/she can fulfil in full any cash consideration, if such is offered, and after taking all reasonable measures to secure the implementation of any other type of consideration.
6. An offeree company must not be hindered in the conduct of its affairs for longer than is reasonable by a bid for its securities.

It is also important to be aware of the following terms that are used in the Code:

- Acting in concert – persons actively co-operating through the acquisition of shares to obtain or consolidate control of a company. The Code presumes that the following will be acting in concert:
  a. a company and other group companies (parent company, subsidiaries and associated companies);
  b. a company and its directors (including the directors' close relatives and related trusts);
  c. a company and its pension fund;
  d. a fund manager and investment vehicles which the manager manages with discretion;
  e. a client and its professional advisers.
- Dealings – these include the straightforward acquisition or disposal of securities, as well as involvement in derivative contracts on, or referenced to, the securities and any other action that may result in an increase or decrease in the number of securities a person is interested in.
- Interests in shares – a person is treated as having an interest in shares if he owns the shares, has a right to exercise or direct the voting rights on them, or is otherwise interested in those shares through derivatives. A person with only a short position does not have an interest in those shares.
- Relevant securities – these include the following:
  a. securities of the offeree company which are being offered for, or which carry, voting rights;
  b. equity share capital of the offeree company and an offeror;
  c. securities of an offeror which carry substantially the same rights as any to be issued as consideration for the offer; and
  d. securities of the offeree company and an offeror carrying conversion or subscription rights into any of the foregoing.

3. DISCLOSURE OF INTERESTS

3.1 PRINCIPLES BEHIND THE DISCLOSURE RULES

LEARNING OBJECTIVE

5.2.1 Understand the principles behind disclosure of interest rules and why they are required

In developed equity markets with a substantial number of listed companies, it is felt appropriate that when investors purchase (or sell) shares to bring about (or remove) a significant stake in a company, such information should be made available to the investing public. This will let others judge the likely impact on the price.

As we will see, the level at which a shareholding is deemed significant is set at 3% in the UK; for example, if a corporate raider built up a stake of 3% or more in a listed UK company, it would be disclosed to the market. This would enable other existing and potential investors to assess the company in full knowledge that there is a new significant shareholding.

3.2 DISCLOSURE RULES

LEARNING OBJECTIVE

5.2.2 Know the named disclosure of interest rules: EU under the Transparency Directive: the disclosure thresholds; to whom disclosure has to be made and within what time scale; differing implementation of the Transparency Directive across EEA countries; US Securities and Exchange Commission: the disclosure thresholds; to whom disclosure has to be made and within what time scales; UK under the Companies Act 2006, Section 793, in relation to company investigations

The disclosure rules vary in different jurisdictions. In this section we will consider three jurisdictions – the EU generally, more specifically the UK, and the US.

The EU has harmonised disclosure rules via the implementation of the **Transparency Directive**. The Transparency Directive establishes disclosure requirements on an ongoing basis for issuers who have securities admitted to trading on a regulated market situated or operated within the EU. Included within the Directive's requirements are notification requirements of both issuers and investors in relation to the acquisition and disposal of significant shareholdings in companies.

The notification requirement is triggered when the size of holdings reach, exceed, or move below certain thresholds. In the Directive these thresholds are set at 5%, 10%, 15%, 20%, 25%, 30%, 50% and 75%. The shareholder reaching or breaching the threshold is required to inform the issuer, and the issuer will then inform the market.

In the US, the Securities and Exchange Commission (SEC) requires disclosures by any person who directly or indirectly acquires a beneficial interest of 5% or more of any class of shares of a registered (and, therefore, listed) entity. The acquirer is required to issue a statement to both the SEC and the company within 10 days of acquisition.

Despite being an EU member state, the regulations relating to disclosure of shareholdings can (and do) vary from country to country. This is because, if they wish, EU member states are able to exceed the requirements of the Directive – a process known as 'super-equivalence'. On implementation of the Directive, the UK chose to retain its thresholds at 3% and each percentage point above that level.

So, under UK regulation, an investor is judged to have a **notifiable interest** in a public company if he holds 3% or more of its shares. At this point he is obliged to inform the company of his holding.

Due to recent changes in the UKLA's Disclosure and Transparency Rule 5 (DTR 5) an interest is now notifiable if the 3% interest is in the form of voting rights rather than simply holding the shares. Here for the purposes of clarification are some relevant excerpts from the DTR 5 section relating to voting rights.

"Voting rights attached to shares" are now disclosable, rather than "interests in shares". Voting rights may arise from holdings of financial instruments as well as shares.

Indirect holdings may result in a requirement for a notification to be made to the issuer, where a person may be able to control the exercise of voting rights (DTR 5.2.1R).

Appointing a proxy, for example, will (if the holding reaches the relevant threshold) require the shareholder and proxy holder to notify the issuer if, but only if, the appointment includes the power to vote in the discretion of the proxy holder.

Voting rights attached to shares are totally disregarded in six cases, that is:

1. shares acquired for clearing and settlement within a three trading day settlement cycle;
2. shares held by a custodian or bare nominee;
3. shares held (if less than 10%) by a declared market maker;
4. shares held (if not more than 5%) by an investment firm or credit institution;
5. shares held as collateral; and
6. shares acquired by a borrower under a stock lending agreement (DTR 5.1.3R).

Shareholders are deemed to have knowledge of the acquisition or disposal of voting rights (and hence time to notify starts to run from) no later than two trading days following the transaction in question or, if it was conditional upon an event outside the control of the parties to the transaction, when it becomes unconditional (DTR 5.8.3R).

Furthermore, once the investor's holding is above 3%, he must also inform the company if it rises or falls through a whole percentage point.

- A stake of 3.7% rising to 4.1% would need to be reported, but a stake of 3.7% rising to 3.9% would not.
- A stake of 5.4% falling to 4.9% would need to be reported, but a stake of 5.4% falling to 5.1% would not.

An investor must also inform the company if his stake falls back to below 3%.

The reason that this disclosure is deemed necessary, despite the fact that the company maintains a register of its shareholders, is that these notifiable interest rules not only include those shares held directly by the investor, but also those shares held by parties connected to them, known as **connected parties**. These would include shares held by the following:

- the investor's spouse;
- the investor's infant children (less than 18 years old);
- companies controlled by the investor. For these purposes, control is assumed if the investor holds at least one third of the voting rights of the company;
- concert parties. This is simply an agreement between two or more persons to influence the company together, such as voting together. If the combined holding reached 3% or more it would become notifiable, as if it were a single holding.

As seen above, 3% is the level at which notification starts and this information must be reported in writing to the company within **two business days**. If the company is listed, it must then report the same information to a primary information provider, such as the London Stock Exchange (LSE), by **the end of the following business day**.

Fund managers and operators of regulated collective investment schemes (such as authorised unit trusts and open-ended investment companies) are deemed to be non-beneficial holders and are exempt from reporting under the notifiable interest (3%) rule. Interests held by investment managers and OEICs, and in general non-beneficial owners, are under the Disclosure and Transparency Rules (DTR 5) subject to disclosure at 5% and 10% (but not at the percentages in between 5% and 10%) and then at every percentage above 10% (DTR 5.1.5). Also, under DTR 5, market makers have an exemption only for holdings below 10% (DTR 5.1.3 and 5.1.4).

Some shareholders are completely exempted from the disclosure rules, eg, if the shares are held by:

- a market maker, or dealer in shares, for the purposes of that business;
- a custodian (that is not able to control the voting rights of the shares concerned).

The company is required to maintain a register of notifications of interests in shares and make this available at its registered office.

Companies Act Section 793 Letter

Under Section 793 of the Companies Act 2006, a UK public company is able to send a written notice to any person that the company knows or suspects to be a shareholder and ask them to confirm whether they are holding any shares. The notice requests details of that shareholder's total interest in the company.

The notice can also request details of past shareholdings held at anytime in the last three years and, where the interest is a past interest, to give details of the identity of the person to whom the shares were sold if that is known.

However, it is rare for such a notice to be sent by the company registrar to an individual shareholder. These letters are usually sent to the **nominee companies** that appear on the register. A nominee company is the legal owner of shares on behalf of another beneficial owner.

The letter is sent to the **company secretary** of the **nominee company** requesting details of the true beneficial owner of the securities. This enables the registrar to identify when someone is using the nominee company to hide his identity and accumulate a substantial holding without anyone being aware of the fact.

Notices under Section 793 require a written response from the recipient within a reasonable time as may be specified in the letter. If requests are persistently ignored, the company could apply to court to have the shares held **frozen**. This would mean the shareholders would lose their rights to vote on those shares, lose their entitlement to dividends and be unable to sell them.

The company is required to keep a record of the Section 793 letters that have been sent, and the information received, in a separate part of its register of shareholders.

4. SPECIFIC REGULATIONS IN THE US, CANADA AND JAPAN

4.1 RESTRICTIONS

LEARNING OBJECTIVE

5.3.1 Know that these markets restrict the promotion and sale of foreign equity

The US, Canada and Japan all have rules and regulations in place to ensure that domestic investors do not have foreign equities sold and promoted to them, unless such equities have met, or exceeded, certain regulatory hurdles. Broadly, these regulatory hurdles aim to make sure that the company concerned is sufficiently well established and reputable to be held by domestic investors.

4.2 REGISTRATION

LEARNING OBJECTIVE

5.3.2 Know that foreign broker-dealers must be registered with the local regulator in these markets before they can disseminate research

For similar reasons to the restrictions outlined in the previous section, the US, Canada and Japan all have requirements relating to foreign broker-dealers. To ensure the regulatory standards of protection cannot be compromised, foreign broker-dealers are required to be registered with the local regulator before they are able to disseminate research to domestic investors.

CHAPTER SIX

ACCOUNTING ANALYSIS

This syllabus area will provide approximately 12 of the 100 examination questions

1. BASIC PRINCIPLES

1.1 THE PURPOSE OF FINANCIAL STATEMENTS

LEARNING OBJECTIVE

6.1.1 Understand the purpose of financial statements

Accounting can be defined as the recording, measuring and reporting of economic events, or activities, to interested parties in a useable form. It is about providing information relating to the financial and economic activities of a business in the form of a set of accounts. This set of accounts is alternatively referred to as the financial statements of the business. The need for accounting information in the form of financial statements was stimulated by the emergence of the limited liability company in the 19th century and the resulting separation of ownership and control. The financial statements provided information to the owners about the business that may have been managed by someone else.

However, although companies initially provided accounting information to satisfy the informational needs of their shareholders, the form this information now takes, and the way in which it is communicated, must also meet the disparate needs of other parties with a legitimate interest in the company's activities, performance and financial position. These other users include creditors, prospective investors, employees, financial analysts, institutional investors, as well as government, consumers and environmental groups.

The directors of a company are required to prepare financial statements and make other disclosures within an annual report and accounts. These set out the results of the company's activities during its most recent accounting period and its financial position as at the end of the period. The accounting period typically spans a 12-month period.

Broadly, these financial statements comprise three major statements:

1. **A balance sheet**. This provides a snapshot of the company's financial position as at the company's accounting year end by summarising the assets it owns and how they are financed at this one point in time. Under the Revised Accounting Standards (IAS 1) the balance sheet is now called the 'Statement of Financial Position' rather than a balance sheet although the new nomenclature is not mandatory.
2. **An income statement**. This statement summarises income (or revenue) that has been earned by the company over the accounting period. Broadly it is a summary of the trading activities of the company over the year – if income exceeds costs, the company has made a profit; if costs exceed income then the company has made a loss.

The income statement links the company's previous balance sheet with its current one. This relationship is depicted on the following page:

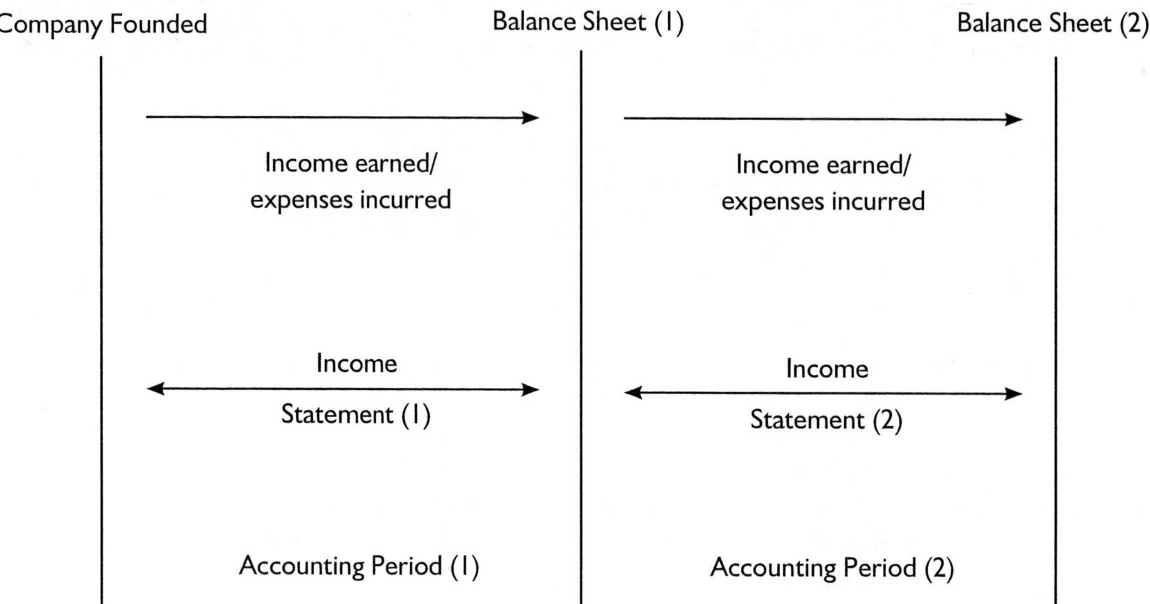

3. **A cash flow statement**. Companies must also publish a cash flow statement within their annual report and accounts. This financial statement identifies how much cash the company generated over the accounting period and how much cash has been spent. Under the Revised Accounting Standards (IAS 1) the cash flow statement is now called the 'Statement of Cash Flows' rather than a balance sheet although the new nomenclature is not mandatory.

The financial statements also include certain additional disclosures such as the comparative figures from the previous year's financial statements, explanatory notes to accompany certain individual balance sheet and profit and loss account items and disclosure of the company's accounting policies. The accounting policies are the basis on which the accounts have been prepared.

The information contained in the company's report and accounts is also required to be independently verified, or audited. An audit is an independent assessment of the company's accounts that have been prepared by the directors. This audit is concluded with an auditor's report to the members, or shareholders, of the company confirming whether or not the accounts give a true and fair view of the company's activities and financial position and whether they have been prepared in accordance with the law and other regulations. If so, then an unqualified audit report is issued. If not, then the auditor must issue a qualified report and state the reason for this qualification.

1.2 ACCOUNTING REGULATIONS

LEARNING OBJECTIVE

6.1.2 Understand the requirements for companies and groups to prepare accounts in accordance with applicable accounting standards: accounting principles; International Financial Reporting Standards (IFRS); IAS

The form and content of all company financial statements and their respective disclosures are prescribed by the law and mandatory accounting standards set by the accountancy profession. Accounting standards are authoritative statements of how particular types of transaction and other events should be reflected in financial statements. The combination of accounting regulations is often referred to as the 'generally accepted accounting principles' or GAAP. Each country's GAAP varies to a lesser or greater extent and there are efforts being made to harmonise GAAP throughout the world, spearheaded by the International Accounting Standards Board (IASB).

The IASB is an independent, privately-funded accounting standard-setter based in London. The Board members come from nine countries and have a variety of functional backgrounds. The IASB is committed to developing, in the public interest, a single set of high quality, understandable and enforceable global accounting standards that require transparent and comparable information in general purpose financial statements. In addition, the IASB co-operates with national accounting standard-setters to achieve convergence in accounting standards around the world.

Standards issued by the International Accounting Standards Board are designated International Financial Reporting Standards (IFRSs). There were standards issued by the IASB's predecessor (the International Accounting Standards Committee) that continue to be designated International Accounting Standards (IASs). The IASB has retained the IASs and also issues IFRSs.

The following is a list of recent amendments adopted by the International Accounting Standards Board.

- **Amendment A**
  All owner changes in equity are to be presented separately from non-owner changes in equity in a statement of changes in equity.

- **Amendment B**
  All non-owner changes in equity are to be presented in one or two statements of comprehensive income.

  Under the previous version of IAS 1, entities could present certain items of income and expense in the same accounting statement as the so called 'owner changes in equity' (for example increases in capital and capital distributions).

  Furthermore, the previous version of IAS 1 required certain items of income and expense to be presented in an income statement but permitted some flexibility as to where the other items of income and expense were presented: they could be presented either (as explained above) with all changes in equity (in a statement of changes in equity) or with other non-owner changes (in a statement of recognised income and expense (so-called 'SoRIE')).

IAS 1 (Revised) now requires: (a) all owner changes in equity to be presented separately from items of income and expense (so-called 'non-owner changes in equity'). It is therefore no longer possible to present non-owner changes in equity in the statement of changes in equity. The purpose of this revision is to distinguish items with different characteristics (ie, owner changes in equity from non-owners changes in equity) and therefore increase the clarity of the presentation; therefore all income and expenses are to be presented either in one statement (a statement of comprehensive income) or in two statements (an income statement and a statement of comprehensive income), separately from owner changes in equity.

- **Amendment C**
  Renaming the primary financial statements: statement of changes in equity, statement of cash flow, statement of comprehensive income and statement of financial position.

  The previous version of IAS 1 used the titles 'balance sheet' and 'cash flow statement' to describe two of the statements within a complete set of financial statements. IAS 1 (Revised) uses 'statement of financial position' and 'statement of cash flows' for those statements. The new titles are however not mandatory.

- **Amendment D**
  Entities are required to present a statement of financial position as at the beginning of the corresponding period where restatements have occurred. IAS 1 (Revised) requires an entity to disclose comparative information in respect of the previous period, ie, to disclose as a minimum two of each of the various accounting statements and related notes. IAS 1 (Revised) requires a third statement of financial position (ie, balance sheet) to be provided in certain circumstances (so that there are two opening balance sheets as well as two closing balance sheets). This third statement is required as at the beginning of the earliest comparative period whenever the entity retrospectively applies an accounting policy or makes a retrospective restatement of items in its financial statements, or when it reclassifies items in its financial statements. The purpose of this revision is to provide information that is useful in analysing an entity's financial statements.

- **Amendment E**
  Entities are required to disclose 'reclassification adjustments'.

  Under existing IFRS, some items of income and expense are recognised outside of the income statement initially and later, on the occurrence of a specified triggering event (such as, in some cases, realisation), moved from that statement and shown in the income statement. This process is known as 'recycling' and the entries involved are known as 'reclassification adjustments'. IAS 1 (Revised) requires an entity to disclose reclassification adjustments relating to each component of other comprehensive income. The purpose of this revision is to provide users with information to assess the effect of such reclassifications on profit or loss.

- **Amendment F**
  Entities are required to disclose income tax relating to each component of other comprehensive income IAS 1 (Revised) requires an entity to disclose income tax relating to each component of other comprehensive income. The previous version of IAS 1 did not include such a requirement. The purpose of this new requirement is to provide users with tax information relating to these components because the components often have tax rates different from those applied to profit or loss.

- **Amendment G**
  Entities are required to present dividends and related per-share amounts on the face of the statement of changes in equity or in the notes.

  The previous version of IAS 1 permitted a choice as to where entities disclosed the amount of dividends recognised as distributions to equity holders and the related per share amount: in the income statement, in the statement of changes in equity or in the notes. IAS 1 (Revised) allows dividends recognised as distributions to owners and related per share amount to be presented only in the statement of changes in equity or in the notes. The purpose of the revision is to ensure that owner changes in equity are presented separately from non-owner changes in equity (presented in the statement of comprehensive income).

1.3 GROUP VERSUS COMPANY ACCOUNTS

LEARNING OBJECTIVE

6.1.3 Understand the differences between group accounts and company accounts and why companies are required to prepare group accounts. (Candidates should understand the concept of goodwill and minority interests but will not be required to calculate these)

If a company invests in another company, all that appears in the accounts of the investing company is the original cost of the investment (in the balance sheet), and the dividends received (if there are any) appears in the investing company's income statement. This treatment is fine where the investment is a small, minority shareholding in another company. However, in instances where the investment is so significant that the investing company controls the other company, another accounting treatment is required – the preparation of **group** financial statements (known as group accounts). The investing company is described as the 'parent' and the company or companies that the parent company controls are described as subsidiaries. As long as a parent/subsidiary relationship exists, then the parent company should prepare and present a set of group accounts in addition to their individual company financial statements.

These group accounts present the financial statements as if the parent and the subsidiaries were a single entity, rather than distinct individual companies. This entails the addition of the assets of the parent plus all of the subsidiaries' assets to arrive at the group assets, and similar additions to arrive at the group's liabilities, revenues, expenses and cash flows.

Two particular issues can crop up when amalgamating the figures for the parent company and its subsidiaries:

1. **Goodwill**
   When presenting the group accounts as a single entity, the assets and liabilities of the subsidiaries are added to those of the parent company. This replaces the original cost of investment in the group balance sheet. If the cost of investment exceeded the net assets (assets less liabilities) of the subsidiary, the excess is described as 'goodwill' and appears as an asset in the group accounts.

2. **Minority interests**
   In circumstances where the parent company owns a majority of the shares in a subsidiary, but not all of the shares, there will be minority interests. For example, if a parent owned 75% of the shares of a subsidiary, the minority interest would be 25%; if it owned 51% of the shares the minority would be 49%. Because the presentation of the group accounts adds together all of the assets and liabilities of the subsidiaries, it includes some net assets that belong to the minority interests. These are reflected by including net assets and net income that belongs to the minority interests in the group balance sheet and income statement.

2. THE STATEMENT OF FINANCIAL POSITION

2.1 PURPOSE, FORMAT AND MAIN CONTENTS

LEARNING OBJECTIVE

6.2.1 Know the purpose of the Statement of Financial Position, formerly better known as the balance sheet and for the purpose of familiarity will be referred to that in the remainder of this section, its format and main contents

The balance sheet is a snapshot of a company's financial position at a particular moment. It is split into two halves that must always balance each other exactly, hence the name. The key information it provides to shareholders, customers and other interested parties is what the company owns (its assets), what the company owes others (its liabilities, or creditors) and the extent to which shareholders are providing finance to the company (the equity).

The balance sheet should reflect all of the reporting company's assets and liabilities, but over the years companies and their advisers often developed creative structures to enable items to remain 'off balance sheet' rather than 'on balance sheet'. The IASB and the adoption of its accounting standards should ensure that everything that should appear on the balance sheet is categorised as 'on balance sheet', and those items that are legitimately not assets or liabilities of the company should remain 'off balance sheet'.

The typical format of the balance sheet, with example figures, is provided below, followed by an explanation of each of the headings:

A plc Balance Sheet as at 31 December 2009	
£000	2009
Assets	
Non-current assets	
Property, plant and equipment	8900
Intangible assets	2100
Investments	300
	11300
Current assets	
Inventories	3600
Trade and other receivables	2600
Prepayments	120
Cash	860
	7180
Total assets	18480
Equity and liabilities	
Capital and reserves	
Share capital – 10m 50p ordinary shares	5000
Share capital – preference shares	100
Share premium account	120
Revaluation reserve	180
Retained earnings	6880
Total equity	12280
Non-current liabilities	
Bank loans	2000
Provisions	
	2000
Current liabilities	
Trade and other payables	4200
	4200
Total liabilities	6200
Total equity and liabilities	18480

2.2 ASSETS

An asset is anything that is owned and controlled by the company and confers the right to future economic benefits. Balance sheet assets are categorised as either non-current assets or current assets.

2.2.1 Non-Current Assets

Non-current assets are those in long-term, continuing use by the company. They represent the major investments from which the company hopes to make money. Non-current assets are categorised as:

- Tangible
- Intangible
- Investments

2.2.1.1 Tangible Non-Current Assets

A company's tangible non-current assets are those that have physical substance, such as land and buildings and plant and machinery. Tangible non-current assets are initially recorded in the balance sheet at their actual cost, or book value. However, in order to reflect the fact that the asset will generate benefits for the company over several accounting periods, not just in the accounting period in which it is purchased, all tangible non-current assets with a limited economic life are required to be depreciated. The concept of depreciation will be covered in more detail in the Section 2.2 below.

2.2.1.2 Intangible Non-Current Assets

Intangible non-current assets are those assets that, although without physical substance, can be separately identified and are capable of being sold. Ownership of an intangible non-current asset confers rights known as intellectual property. These rights give a company a competitive advantage over its peers and commonly include brand names, patents, trade marks, capitalised development costs and purchased goodwill.

As seen earlier, purchased goodwill arises when the consideration, or price, paid by the acquiring company for the target exceeds the fair value of the target's separable, or individually identifiable, net assets. This is not necessarily the same as the book, or balance sheet, value of these net assets:

purchased goodwill =

(price paid for company – fair value of separable net tangible and intangible assets)

Purchased goodwill is capitalised and included in the balance sheet and, once capitalised, cannot be revalued.

2.2.1.3 Investments

Non-current asset investments are long-term investments held in other companies. These investments might be equity investments or investments in debt instruments. They are recorded in the balance sheet at cost, less any impairment to their value.

2.2.2 Current Assets

Current assets are those assets purchased with the intention of resale or conversion into cash, usually within a 12 month period. They include stocks (or inventories) of finished goods and work in progress, the debtor balances that arise from the company providing its customers with credit (trade receivables) and any short term investments held. Current assets also include cash balances held by the company and prepayments. Prepayments are simply where the company has prepaid an expense, as illustrated by the following example:

EXAMPLE

XYZ plc draws up its balance sheet on 31 December each year. Just prior to the year end XYZ pays £25,000 to its landlord for the next three months' rental on its offices (to the end of March in the next calendar year).

This £25,000 is not an expense for the current year – it represents a prepayment towards the following year's expenses and is, therefore, shown as a prepayment within current assets in XYZ's balance sheet.

Current assets are listed in the balance sheet in ascending order of liquidity and appear in the balance sheet at the lower of cost or net realisable value (NRV).

2.3 DEPRECIATION AND AMORTISATION

LEARNING OBJECTIVE

6.2.2 Understand the concept of depreciation and amortisation

Depreciation is applied to tangible, non-current assets such as plant and machinery. An annual depreciation charge is made in the year's income statement. The depreciation charge allocates the fall in the book value of the asset over its useful economic life. This requirement does not, however, apply to freehold land and non-current asset investments which, by not having a limited economic life, are not usually depreciated.

To calculate the annual depreciation charge to be applied to a tangible asset, the difference between its cost and estimated disposal value, termed the depreciable amount, must first be established. This value is then written off over the asset's useful economic life by employing the most appropriate depreciation method. The most common depreciation method is the straight line method.

The straight line method simply spreads the depreciable amount equally over the economic life of the asset. The straight line method is given by the following formula:

$$\textbf{Straight line depreciation} = \frac{\textbf{(cost – disposal value)}}{\textbf{useful economic life in years}}$$

One thing to recognise about the annual depreciation charge is that it is an accounting book entry, or a non-cash charge. That is, no cash flows from the business as a result of making the charge: it is simply an accounting entry made against the income statement to reflect the estimated cost of resources used over an accounting period. The balance sheet value of the asset is given by its cost, less the accumulated depreciation to date, and is termed the net book value (NBV). This NBV does not necessarily equal the market value of the asset.

EXAMPLE

Depreciation

A machine purchased for £25,000 has an estimated useful economic life of six years and an estimated disposal value after six years of £1,000. Calculate the depreciation that should be charged to this asset and its NBV in years one to six, using the straight line depreciation method.

Solution

Straight depreciation

$$\text{Straight line depreciation} = \frac{\text{(cost – disposal value)}}{\text{useful economic life (years)}}$$

$$= \frac{(£25{,}000 - £1{,}000)}{6} = £4{,}000 \text{ per annum}$$

Year	Opening net book value	Depreciation	Closing net book value
1	25,000	4,000	21,000
2	21,000	4,000	17,000
3	17,000	4,000	13,000
4	13,000	4,000	9,000
5	9,000	4,000	5,000
6	5,000	4,000	1,000

By reducing the book value of tangible non-current assets over their useful economic lives, depreciation matches the cost of the asset against the periods from which the company benefits from its use.

On occasion, tangible assets, such as land, are not depreciated but periodically revalued. This is done on the basis of providing the user of the accounts with a truer and fairer view of the assets, or capital, employed by the company. To preserve the accounting equation, (total assets = equity and liabilities), the increase in the asset's value arising on revaluation is transferred to a revaluation reserve, which forms part of the equity.

Closely linked to the idea of depreciating the value of a tangible asset over its useful economic life is the potential need for intangible assets to be amortised over their useful economic lives. Amortisation, like depreciation, is simply a book entry whose impact is felt in the company's reported income and financial position but does not impact its cash position.

2.4 EQUITY

LEARNING OBJECTIVE

6.2.3 Understand the difference between authorised and issued share capital, capital reserves and revenue reserves

Equity is referred to in a number of ways, such as shareholders' funds, owners' equity or capital. Equity usually consists of three sub-elements: **share capital, capital reserves** and **revenue reserves**. Additionally, when group accounts are presented, there may be 'minority interests' within the group equity figure.

- **Share Capital**
  This is the nominal value of equity and preference share capital the company has in issue and has called up. This may differ from the amount of share capital the company is authorised to issue as contained in its constitutional documents – the company may have only called up some of its share capital and may not have issued all of the share capital that is authorised.

- **Capital Reserves**
  Capital reserves include revaluation reserves and the share premium account. The revaluation reserve arises from the upward revaluation of non-current assets, and the share premium reserve arises when the company issues shares at a price above their nominal value. Capital reserves are not distributable to the company's shareholders in the form of dividends as they form part of the company's capital base, although they can be converted into a bonus issue of ordinary shares.

- **Revenue Reserves**
  The major revenue reserve is the accumulated retained earnings of the company – this represents the accumulation of the company's distributable profits that have not been paid to the company's shareholders as dividends, but have been retained in the business. The retained earnings should not be confused with the amount of cash the company holds or with the income statement that shows how the retained, or undistributed, profit in a single accounting period was arrived at.

- **Minority Interests**
  As covered earlier in this chapter, minority interests arise when a parent company controls one or more subsidiary companies, but does not own all of the share capital. The equity attributable to the remaining shareholders is the minority interests and this is reflected in the balance sheet within the equity section.

In total, equity is the sum of the called up share capital, all of the capital reserves and the revenue reserves:

Equity = share capital + reserves

2.5 LIABILITIES

LEARNING OBJECTIVE

6.2.4 Know how loans and indebtedness are included within a balance sheet

A liability is an obligation to transfer future economic benefits as a result of past transactions or events; more simply, it could be described as money owed to someone else. Liabilities are categorised according to whether they are to be paid within, or after more than, one year:

- **Non-current liabilities**
  This comprises the company's borrowing not repayable within the next 12 months. This could include bond issues as well as longer term bank borrowing.

  In addition, there is a separate sub-heading for those liabilities that have resulted from past events or transactions and for which there is an obligation to make a payment, but the exact amount or timing of the expenditure has yet to be established. These are commonly referred to as 'provisions', as such provisions may arise as a result of the company undergoing a restructuring, for example. Given the uncertainty surrounding the extent of such liabilities, companies are required to create a realistic and prudent estimate of the monetary amount of the obligation once it is committed to taking a certain course of action.
- **Current liabilities**
  This includes the amount the company owes to its suppliers, or trade payables, as a result of buying goods and/or services on credit, any bank overdraft and any other payables such as tax, that are due within 12 months of the balance sheet date.

3. THE INCOME STATEMENT

3.1 PURPOSE AND CONTENTS

LEARNING OBJECTIVE

6.3.1 Know the purpose of the income statement, its format and main contents

The income statement summarises the company's income earned and expenditure incurred over the accounting period. The function of this financial statement is to detail how much profit has been earned and how the company's reported profit (or loss) was arrived at.

The amount of profit earned over the accounting period will impact the company's ability to pay dividends and how much can be retained to finance the growth of the business from internal resources.

Like the balance sheet, the format of the income statement is governed by the law and underpinned by the requirements of various accounting standards. The income statement of A plc is shown below. In reality, comparative numbers for the previous year and explanatory notes would be provided as well.

A plc Income Statement for the year end 31 December 2009			
	Notes	2008	2009
		£000	£000
Revenue		8,750	9500
Cost of sales		(6,600)	(7000)
Gross profit		2,150	2,500
Distribution costs		(90)	(110)
Administrative expenses		(20)	(30)
Loss on disposal of plant			(260)
Operating profit		2,040	2,100
Financial costs		(250)	(230)
Financial income		112	120
Profit before taxation		1,902	1,990
Taxation		(548)	(555)
Net income		1,354	1,435
Earnings per share (pence)		15.9p	16.1p

3.1.1 Revenue

The income statement starts with one of the most important things in any company's accounts: its sales revenues. In accounts, sales revenues are generally referred to as revenue, or sometimes turnover – it is simply everything that the company has sold during the year, regardless of whether it has received the cash or not. For a manufacturer, revenue would be the sales of the products that it has made. For a company in the service industry, it would be the consulting fees earned, or perhaps commissions earned on financial transactions.

3.1.2 Costs of Sales

The costs of sales are the costs to the company of generating the sales made in the financial year. These items are also sometimes known as the 'Cost of Goods Sold'. They typically include the costs of the raw materials used to make a product and the costs of converting those raw materials into their finished state, including the wages of the staff making the products.

3.1.3 Gross Profit

Total sales, less the costs of those sales, results in the gross profit for the year.

3.1.4 Operating Profit

Operating profit is also referred to as 'profit on operating activities'. It is the gross profit, less other operating expenses, that the company has incurred. These other operating expenses might include cost incurred distributing products (distribution costs) and administrative expenses such as management salaries, auditors' fees and legal fees. Administrative expenses would also include depreciation and amortisation charges. Additional items may be separately disclosed before arriving at operating profit, such as the profit or loss made on selling a non-current asset. When a non-current asset, such as an item of machinery, is disposed of at a price significantly different from its balance sheet value, the profit or loss when compared to this net book value (NBV) should be separately disclosed if material to the information conveyed by the accounts.

Operating profit is the profit before considering finance costs (interest) and any tax payable – so it can be described as **profit before interest and tax (pbit)**.

3.1.5 Finance Costs/Finance Income

Finance costs are generally the interest that the company has incurred on its borrowings – that may be in the form of bonds or may be bank loans and overdrafts. Finance income is typically the interest earned on surplus funds, such as from deposit accounts.

3.1.6 Profit before Tax

This is the profit made by the company in the period, before considering any tax that might be payable on that profit.

3.1.7 Corporation Tax Payable

This is simply the corporation tax charge that the company has incurred for the period.

3.1.8 Net Income

Now that tax and financing costs have been deducted we have a vital figure: net income. It reflects all the income earned during the period, less all of the expenditures incurred. This net income is also the profit attributable to the shareholders of the company because, in theory, it could all be distributed to shareholders as dividends.

3.1.9 Earnings per Share (EPS)

This is an important figure for readers of the financial statements and is always reflected at the bottom of the income statement, in pence. EPS is the amount of profit after tax that has been earned per ordinary share. EPS is calculated as follows:

$$\textbf{EPS} = \frac{\textbf{net income for the financial year}}{\textbf{number of ordinary shares in issue}}$$

3.1.10 Dividends

Some, or all, of the profit for the financial year can be distributed as dividends. Dividends to any preference shareholders are paid out first, followed by dividends to ordinary shareholders at an amount set by the board and expressed as a number of pence per share. The dividends for most listed companies are paid in two instalments: an interim dividend paid after the half-year stage, and a final proposed dividend to be paid after the accounts have been approved. The dividends are shown in the accounts in a note that reconciles the movement in equity from one balance sheet to another.

A plc statement of changes in equity for the year ended 31 December 2009						
	Ord Share Capital	Pref Share Capital	Share premium account	Revaluation Reserve	Retained earnings	Total
As at 1 January 2009	4,420	100		100	5,880	10,550
Gain on revaluation				80		80
Issue of shares	530		120			650
Net income for the year					1,435	1,435
Preference dividends paid					(5)	(5)
Ordinary dividends paid					(400)	(400)
As at 31 December 2008	5,000	100	120	180	6,880	12,280

3.2 CAPITAL VERSUS REVENUE EXPENDITURE

LEARNING OBJECTIVE

6.3.2 Understand the difference between capital and revenue expenditure

Money spent by a company will usually fall into one of two possible forms: **capital** expenditure or **revenue** expenditure.

Capital expenditure is money spent to buy non-current assets, such as plant, property and equipment. It is reflected on the balance sheet.

Revenue expenditure is money spent that immediately impacts the income statement. Examples of revenue expenditure include wages paid to staff, rent paid on property and professional fees, like audit fees.

4. THE STATEMENT OF CASH FLOWS

4.1 PURPOSE OF THE STATEMENT OF CASH FLOWS

LEARNING OBJECTIVE

6.4.1 Know the purpose of the Statement of Cash Flows, its format as set out in IAS 7

The statement of cash flows or as it was previously known, the cash flow statement, is basically a summary of all the payments and receipts that have occurred over the course of the year, the total reflecting the inflow (or outflow) of cash over the year.

A Statement of Cash Flows (as it is now known in accordance with the IAS 1 Revised) is required by accounting standard IAS 7.

In what follows the term cash flow statement will be used for familiarity and also to illustrate that the new title adopted by IAS 1 Revised is not mandatory.

The logic of adding a cash flow statement to a set of financial statements is that it enables the readers of the accounts to see clearly how cash has been generated and/or used over the course of the year. This is felt to provide easily understood information to the users of the accounts that supplements the performance figures provided by the income statement, and the statement of financial position given by the balance sheet.

IAS 7 Cash Flow Statements require a company's cash flows to be broken down into particular headings, as illustrated in the following example:

A plc Cash Flow Statement for the year ended 31 December 2009	
	2007
Operating activities	
Cash receipts from customers	4528
Cash paid to suppliers and employees	–2001
Cash generated from operations	2527
Tax paid	—
Interest paid	–150
Net cash from operating activities	4464
Investing activities	
Interest received	80
Dividends received	40
Purchase of fixed assets	–1890
Proceeds on sale of investments	120
Net cash used in investing activities	–1650
Financing activities	
Dividends paid	–435
Repayments of borrowings	–200
Proceeds on issue of shares	650
Net cash generated from financing activities	15
Net increase in cash and cash equivalents	2829
Cash and cash equivalents at the beginning of the year	425
Cash and cash equivalents at the end of the year	3254

Looking at the key cash flow statement headings in turn:

- **Operating activities** is the cash that has been generated from the trading activities of the company, excluding financing cost (interest).
- **Investing activities** details the investment income (dividends and interest) that has been received in the form of cash during the year and the cash paid to purchase new non-current assets, less the cash received from the sale of non-current assets during the year.
- **Financing activities** includes the cash spent during the year on paying dividends to shareholders, borrowing on a long-term basis or the cash raised from issuing shares, less the cash spent repaying debt or buying back shares.

The resultant total should explain the changes in cash (and cash equivalents) between the balance sheets. Many short-term investments are classified as cash equivalents, such as Treasury bills.

4.2 PROFIT VERSUS CASH

LEARNING OBJECTIVE

6.4.2 Understand the difference between profit and cash and their impact on the long term future of the business

Profit appears in the income statement and is the excess of revenues earned over the period, over the expenses incurred in that same period. Obviously, generating profits is necessary for the long-term survival of any business, although companies can (and many do) exhibit losses for a number of years. Without a profitable business, that business is unlikely to survive indefinitely.

The extent to which a company has generated (or used up) cash is detailed in the cash flow statement. Cash is generated when cash received exceeds cash paid out, and cash is used up when the cash paid out exceeds the cash received. Cash is often described as the 'lifeblood of the company' – without it the company will not survive. If a company does not have the cash to pay a liability when it is due, there is a possibility of the company being forced to close down.

When comparing profit against cash, there are some key differences. Because profit is based on revenues earned, not cash received, there is a possibility that the two figures for a company could be very different. For example, a company might make sales on credit and, therefore, recognise the revenues at the point of sale in the income statement. The cash received for those sales could be significantly later.

Similarly, profit is based on expenditure incurred, not cash paid and there can be significant differences between the two. A key example of the potential for difference is in the different treatments of the purchase of a non-current tangible asset, like a machine. In the income statement, the impact will be a gradual expense incurred each year for the depreciation of the machine. In the cash flow statement, the full cost will be paid in cash at the time of purchase.

Operating Cash Flow Statement for XYZ Limited for Year Ending 31 December 2009			
All figures are in £ Sterling			
Net income after tax		240,000.00	
Other additions to Cash			
Depreciation and Amortisation	35,000.00		Depreciation is not a cash expense; it is added back into net income for calculating cash flow
Decrease in Accounts Receivable	17,000.00		If accounts receivable decreases more cash has entered the company from customers paying off their accounts – the amount by which Accounts Receivable has decreased is an addition to cash
Decrease in Inventory			A decrease in inventory signals that a company has spent less money to purchase more raw materials. The decrease in the value of inventory is an addition to cash
Decrease in Other Current Assets	19,000.00		Similar reasoning to above for other current assets
Increase in Accounts Payable	26,000.00		If accounts payable increases it suggests more cash has been retained by the company through not paying some bills – the amount by which Accounts Payable has increased is an addition to cash
Increase in Accrued Expenses			For example deferring payment of some salaries will add to cash
Increase in Other Current Liabilities			Similar reasoning to above for increase in taxes payable
Total Additions to Cash From Operations			
Subtractions from Cash			
Increase in Accounts Receivable			If accounts receivable increases less cash has entered the company from customers paying their accounts – the amount by which Accounts Receivable has increased is a subtraction of cash
Increase in Inventory	–33,000.00		An increase in inventory signals that a company has spent more money to purchase more raw materials. If the inventory was paid with cash, the increase in the value of inventory is a subtraction of cash
Increase in Other Current Assets			Similar reasoning to above for other current assets
Decrease in Accounts Payable			If accounts payable decreases it suggests more cash has been used by the company to pay its bills – the amount by which Accounts Payable decreased is a subtraction from cash
Decrease in Accrued Expenses	–19,000.00		For example an increase in prepaid expenses results in a subtraction of cash
Decrease in Other Current Liabilities	–23,000.00		Similar reasoning to above for decrease in taxes payable
Total Subtractions from Cash from Operations		–75,000.00	
Total Operating Cash Flow		262,000.00	Equals Net Income After Tax + Total Additions to Cash From Operations + Total Subtractions From Cash from Operations

4.3 FREE CASH FLOW

LEARNING OBJECTIVE

6.4.3 Understand the purpose of Free Cash Flow and the difference between Enterprise Cash Flow and Equity Cash Flow

There is no single definition of 'free cash flow'. Logically, it perhaps should be drawn from the cash flow statement and represent the amount of cash that has been generated and that the company can choose what to do with. This might be the operating cash flow less the extent to which the company has to spend cash to maintain the operating capacity of the business. It is the latter figure that is difficult to isolate, and is likely to be a subjective judgement by the user of the accounts. The resultant figure might be adjusted further depending on whether the calculation is for free cash flow to the firm (enterprise cash flow), or just free cash flow to the shareholders (equity cash flow). This will be explored in more detail below.

Because of the difficulty in arriving at free cash flow from the cash flow statement, many users calculate a free cash flow figure from the income statement. This is generally arrived at by taking the net income from the income statement, adding back the charges for depreciation and amortisation and deducting capital expenditure. The capital expenditure will again be a judgement of the capital spend required to maintain the operating capacity of the business, with the use of income statement figures for operating cash flow presenting a smoother, potentially more representative figure for cash generation by removing the inconsistencies that payments in advance or in arrears can create.

As well as there being two potentially different sources for free cash flow (the cash flow statement or the income statement), there are further adjustments that might be made depending on whether the free cash flow is being calculated for the whole enterprise (the enterprise cash flow) or is being calculated for the equity holders only (the equity cash flow).

The enterprise cash flow is the free cash flow before considering payments made to any of the providers of finance to the firm. The providers of finance to the firm are both the lenders and the equity holders. The enterprise cash flow will, therefore, be the free cash flow before considering any financing costs.

In contrast the equity cash flow is the free cash flow to the shareholders, so it will be after any financing costs to the lenders, but before any dividend payments to the shareholders.

Cash Flow Statement for XYZ Limited for Year Ending 31 December 2009			
All figures are in £ Sterling			
Total Operating Cash Flow		262,000.00	Equals Net Income After Tax + Total Additions to Cash From Operations + Total Subtractions From Cash from Operations
Investment/Capital Expenditures			
Additions to Cash From Investments			
Decrease in Fixed Assets	150,000.00		Sale of a building will lead to an addition to cash
Decrease in Notes Receivable	12,000.00		A reduction in notes receivable indicates that cash will have been received
Decrease in securities, investments			Securities will have been sold thereby raising cash
Decrease in intangible, non-current assets			Sale of a patent or copyright will lead to an addition of cash
Total Additions to Cash From Investments		162,000.00	
Subtractions from Cash for Investments			
Increase in Fixed Assets			Purchase of a building will lead to a subtraction from cash
Increase in Notes Receivable			An increase in notes receivable indicates that cash has not been received
Increase in securities, investments	–64,000.00		Securities will have been purchased thereby reducing cash
Increase in tangible non-current assets	–250,000.00		Purchase of a copyright will lead to a reduction of cash
Total subtractions from Cash for Investments		–314,000.00	
Total Enterprise Cash Flow		110,000.00	Equals Total Operating Cash Flow + Additions to Cash from Capital Investments + Subtractions from Cash From Capital Investments
Financing Activities			
Additions to Cash From Financing			
Increase in Borrowings		50,000.00	Additional net borrowing will lead to an addition of cash
Increase Capital Stock			Additional net equity capital paid in will lead to an addition of cash
Total Additions to Cash From Financing		50,000.00	
Subtractions from Cash for Financing			
Increase in Borrowings			Net reduction in borrowing will lead to a subtraction of cash
Increase Capital Stock			Retirement of net equity capital paid in will lead to a subtraction of cash

(Continued on following page.)

Total Subtractions From Cash for Financing			
Total Equity Cash Flow		160,000.00	Equals Total Enterprise Cash Flow + Additions to Cash from Financing + Subtractions from Cash From Financing
Subtractions from Cash for Dividends			
Dividends Paid		–100,000.00	
Total Free Cash Flow		60,000.00	Equals Total Equity Cash Flow – Dividends Paid Out
Cash at beginning of period		450,000.00	
Cash at end of period		510,000.00	

5. FINANCIAL STATEMENT ANALYSIS

Overview of Financial Analysis

The three principal financial statements and associated explanatory notes published by companies in their report and accounts furnish the user with a considerable amount of information. However, the needs of the user can be met more precisely by employing ratio analysis as key relationships can be established and trends identified by consolidating this information into a more readily useable form. Ratios are commonly employed by analysts to assess the prospects for a particular company and, therefore, the investment potential of the shares of that company, as well as assisting other interested parties in assessing the company such as the Board, suppliers, competitors and employees.

The purpose of ratio analysis is three-fold:

1. To assist in assessing business performance by identifying meaningful relationships between numbers contained within company financial statements that may not be immediately apparent. Although there are no statutory rules as to how ratios should be calculated, there should be logic in the numbers being related to each other.
2. To summarise financial information into an easily understandable form.
3. To identify trends, strengths and weaknesses by comparing the ratios to those of the same company in prior periods, other similar companies, sector averages and market averages.

However, ratio analysis does have its limitations:

1. As financial statements contain historic data, ratios are not predictive, indeed occasionally historic figures can be restated in later periods, making comparison difficult.
2. Because there is no regulatory method of calculation for most ratios, comparison must only be made when the calculation methods do not differ.

The ratios required for the examination follow, first an explanation of key subsets of the ratios to meet the examiner's requirement that the candidate 'understands' the ratios, followed by the formulae so that the candidate can also 'calculate' the specified ratios.

5.1 ROCE AND PROFITABILITY RATIOS

LEARNING OBJECTIVE

6.5.1 Understand the following key ratios: profitability ratios (gross profit and operating profit margins); Return on Capital Employed

5.1.1 ROCE and Profitability Ratios Explained

Profitability ratios look at the percentage return that the company generates relative to its revenues. The **gross profit** looks at the percentage of revenues that the company earns after considering just the costs of sales. The **operating profit margin** looks at the percentage of revenues that the company earns after considering costs of sales and other operating costs (such as distribution costs and administrative expenses). Clearly, all other things being equal, a greater profit margin is preferable to a lesser profit margin.

Return on Capital Employed (ROCE) is widely seen as the best ratio for measuring overall management performance, in relation to the capital that has been paid into the business.

It looks at the amount of return (profit) that is being generated as a percentage of the finance put into the business (the capital employed). The amount of capital employed is the equity plus the long term debt. This is the money that the company holds from shareholders and debt providers, and it is from this money that the management should be able to generate profits.

5.1.2 ROCE and Profitability Ratios Calculations

Effectively, the ROCE gives a yield for the entire company. It compares the money invested in the company with the generated return. This annual return can then be compared to other companies, or less risky investments.

The formula is:

$$\textbf{Return on Capital Employed (ROCE)} = \frac{\textbf{operating profit}}{\textbf{capital employed}} \times 100$$

where operating profit is the profit before financing and tax on the income statement, and capital employed is the total for equity on the balance sheet plus the total for non-current liabilities from the balance sheet.

Using the example accounts for A plc encountered earlier:

ROCE = 2100/(12,280 + 2000) x 100 = 14.7%

The figures for the profitability ratios are drawn from the income statement. The formulae for the profitability ratios are:

Gross Profit Margin (%) = (Gross Profit / Revenues) x 100

Operating Profit Margin (%) = (Operating Profit/Revenues) x 100

Using the example from A plc earlier:

Gross Profit Margin (%) = (2500 / 9500) x 100 = 26.3%

Operating Profit Margin (%) = (2100/9500) x 100 = 22%

5.2 FINANCIAL GEARING RATIOS

LEARNING OBJECTIVE

6.5.2 Understand the following financial gearing ratios: Investors' Debt to Equity Ratio; Net Debt to Equity Ratio; Interest Cover

5.2.1 Financial Gearing Ratios Explained

Financial gearing is a measure of **risk** within a company. It is determined by examining the amount of a company's financing that comes from debt, and the amount that comes from shareholders' funds or equity – the debt to equity ratio.

The higher the proportion of debt finance, the higher the risk that the company will not be able to meet its financing commitments. This is because interest on debt must be paid every year and the debt must be repaid at some point, whereas dividends on shares need only be paid in profitable years and share capital never has to be repaid. It is the inability to service and repay debt that brings about company failure. However, high levels of borrowing under some circumstances can be positive for the shareholders because, if the debt interest is fixed, what is left after paying debt interest is the entitlement of the equity holders so, in years where the firm earns substantial returns, all of the excess belongs to the equity holders.

Whether debt levels are excessive is a matter of judgment, but gearing ratios tend to look at the total debt compared to equity. Sometimes this ratio may be less useful because, as well as holding substantial amounts of debt, the company also holds substantial cash and short-term investments that could be used to repay the debt – it is in these circumstances where **net debt to equity** is used.

Another way that can be used to assess whether debt levels are excessive is to look at the extent to which profits are being made to cover the interest burden on that debt – the **interest cover**.

5.2.2 Financial Gearing Ratio Calculations

5.2.2.1 Debt to Equity = Debt/Equity

Both figures for debt and equity are drawn from the balance sheet of a company such as A plc as illustrated in the earlier discussion. All non-current liabilities are generally considered to be **debt**, and the total of the equity portion of the balance sheet is considered to be equity. The ratio is either stated as a simple proportion: debt to equity is 0.6; or, as a percentage: debt is 60% of the equity.

Using the example of A plc from earlier in the chapter:

Debt to Equity = 2000/12280 = 0.163 or 16.3%

5.2.2.2 Net Debt to Equity = (Debt less cash and short-term investments)/Equity

Net debt is simply the debt as in the debt to equity ratio, less the cash and short-term investments that are within the current assets on the balance sheet.

Using the example of A plc from earlier in the chapter:

Net Debt to Equity = (2000 – 860)/12280 = 0.093 or 9.3%

5.2.2.3 Interest cover = Operating Profit/Interest Costs

Interest cover figures are drawn from the income statement. The operating profit is simply divided by the interest costs (the financing costs line on the income statement).

Using the example of A plc from earlier in the chapter:

Interest cover = 2100/230 = 9.13 times

5.3 INVESTORS' RATIOS EXPLAINED

LEARNING OBJECTIVE

6.5.3 Understand the following investors' ratios: Earnings per share; Price Earnings Ratio (both historic and prospective); Enterprise value to EBIT; Enterprise value to EBITDA; Net dividend yield; Net dividend cover

Overview

Existing and potential investors look at a variety of ratios to assess whether or not a company is likely to be a good investment. These ratios look to establish:

- how expensive the shares are, in order to reach a conclusion on the likelihood of capital growth;
- how much in dividends the shares pay, and how easily the company is able to bear the payment of those dividends, to reach a conclusion on the income those shares are likely to generate.

5.3.1 Earnings Per Share

The earnings per share ratio, or EPS, is one of the most useful and often cited ratios used in the investment world. It is used universally and more or less has the same meaning in most jurisdictions, but is one ratio for which there are prescribed rules in the UK regarding its calculation. These are laid out in IAS 33, which essentially defines the EPS as follows:

$$\textbf{EPS} = \frac{\textbf{Net profit /loss attributable to ordinary shareholders}}{\textbf{Average weighted number of ordinary shares outstanding in a period}}$$

EPS is expressed in pence and reveals how much profit was made during the year that is available to be paid out to each share. As a figure for 'profit per share', it can be divided into the current share price to assess how many times the profit per share must be paid to buy a share – in effect, how expensive (or cheap) those shares are. This is the **price/earnings ratio**.

Furthermore, investors are particularly interested in the earnings each share will generate in the future, rather than generated in the past. As a result, stockbrokers' research departments will endeavour to anticipate what the earnings per share will be, the **prospective earnings per share**, rather than what the earnings per share were in the last reported set of results, the **historic earnings per share**.

5.3.2 Diluted Earnings Per Share (EPS)

The purpose of publishing a separate figure for diluted earnings per share is to warn shareholders of potential future changes in the earnings per share figure as a result of events that actually may have, or theoretically could have, taken place.

EPS, as previously defined, is potentially misleading in instances where the company has substantial quantities of instruments in issue that are convertible into shares. These may be convertible bonds or share options issued to the senior management of the company. If the EPS is calculated in the usual way – by simply dividing the net income for the period by the number of issued shares – the users of the accounts are not incorporating the impact that convertible instruments might have – in particular their dilutive impact on the earnings per share. The issuance of more shares will mean a lower earnings per share. As a result, for companies with significant convertible instruments in issue, an adjusted figure for earnings per share is required to be disclosed that takes this into account. This ratio is called the 'diluted earnings per share'.

The reason why the term 'theoretically' is used in this context is because there is only a possibility – legally certain rights have been granted which could be exercised and require further issues of shares – and the prudent method of accounting is to assume, from the point of view of share dilution, the worst case scenario.

There are two possible factors that could cause share dilution and which need to be covered in the method of conservatively calculating a true and accurate picture of the EPS. A company may have either or both of the following kinds of securities outstanding:

- It may have issued convertible loan stock or convertible preference shares.
- It may have issued options or warrants.

Each of these circumstances may potentially result in more shares being issued, and thereby qualifying for a dividend in future years which would have the material effect of diluting the current earnings per share.

The diluted EPS figure is considered of such importance to the reader of the accounts and a potential investor, that its calculation and disclosure is required by IAS 33 – Earnings Per Share (FRS 22 in the UK).

5.3.3 Price Earnings Ratio

The price earnings (P/E) ratio is calculated as follows.

$$\textbf{Price/Earnings Ratio} = \frac{\textbf{Current market price per share}}{\textbf{Earnings per share}}$$

Let us suppose that the ordinary shares for a company are currently trading at £2.50 per share and that the EPS are 20p: the P/E ratio is £2.50/£0.20 = 12.5.

The P/E ratio informs as to how many years of earnings the current earnings will equal the current share price and in this case it is 12.5 years.

The price per share in the numerator is the market price of a single share of the stock. The earnings per share in the denominator of the formula can vary according to the 'type' of P/E that is being offered for consideration.

Essentially, analysts will tend to look at two types of earnings for the denominator – backward-looking and forward-looking. The latter require forecasting which can be notoriously unreliable and is often based on a company's own projections.

Trailing P/E

Also known as 'P/E (ttm)', this is the version that has already been described in the formula – although it can be updated inbetween issuing a separate income statement. It is customary in the analyst community to take for earnings the net income of the company for the most recent 12-month period divided by the number of shares outstanding. This is the most common meaning of 'P/E' if no other qualifier is specified.

Forward P/E

This is also known as 'P/E f ' or estimated P/E, and is based on estimation of net earnings over the next 12 months. Estimates are typically derived as the mean of a select group of analysts. In times of rapid economic dislocation, such estimates become less relevant as the macro-environment changes (eg, new economic data is published and/or the basis of their forecasts become obsolete) more quickly than analysts adjust their forecasts.

Companies with losses (negative earnings) or no profit have an undefined P/E ratio (usually shown as 'not applicable' or 'N/A').

Uses of the P/E Ratio

By comparing price and earnings per share for a company, one can analyse the market's stock valuation of a company and its shares relative to the income the company is actually generating. Stocks with higher (and/or more certain) forecast earnings growth, will usually have a higher P/E, and those expected to have lower (and/or riskier) earnings growth, will, in most cases, have a lower P/E.

Investors can use the P/E ratio to compare the relative valuations of stocks. Too simplistically one might claim, that if one stock has a P/E twice that of another stock, all things being equal, it is a less attractive investment. Companies are rarely equal, however, and comparisons between industries, companies, and time periods can be very misleading.

P/E ratios are closely followed by the investment community and financial analysts. Indeed the P/E ratio of stock market indices or averages are often used to determine whether or not the overall market is considered to be expensive, priced in line with historical norms or is cheap. For example, in the US the S&P 500 index has a mean historical P/E ratio, over the last fifty years of approximately 18 but has fluctuated rather considerably from that mean. When analysing the ratio it is customary to use the last 12 months of earnings of the constituent stocks of the index and this is referred to as the trailing average.

During the recession in the early 1980s the trailing P/E Ratio for the S&P index reached below 8 at times and in the early part of 2000, just prior to the collapse of the dot com stocks, the P/E ratio reached above 40 measured on a trailing 12 month basis. In mid-2010, the P/E Ratio is approximately 18 and, therefore, approximately priced in accordance with the long term historical norm. Forward looking earnings are also often factored into the ratio so that some analysts are more interested in the forward ratio than the trailing ratio.

One factor which can influence the criterion used to assess whether the overall market is over-priced, fairly priced or under-priced is the interest rate environment as well as the annual rate of inflation. During periods when short term interest rates are relatively low, and inflation is considered to be benign, a larger P/E ratio is supportable as there is less competition for equities coming from the income obtainable from fixed income securities and vice versa.

Companies in different sectors of the economy will also tend to exhibit generically contrasting P/E ratios. This will itself be largely based upon the market's expectations as to future earnings growth in different sectors. For example, a relatively young technology company which has bright prospects will often be rewarded by investors with a relatively high P/E ratio as the earnings are expected to grow dynamically. On the other hand a mature utility company which has fairly predictable future earnings potential will tend to have a relatively lower P/E ration based on more conservative growth estimations.

Another useful application of the P/E ratio is to consider the relationship between the P/E ratio on an individual company's security and the P/E ratio of the stock market average or of the sector average. Some investors will be attracted to companies with a low P/E ratio as it suggests that the company may be undervalued. Once again this needs to be placed into the context of which sector a possible acquisition candidate occupies so, for example, a company interested in taking over a technology company will almost certainly have to pay an above average market P/E multiple but will look for one that is still attractively priced within that sector of the market.

5.3.4 Enterprise Value to EBIT

This ratio consists of two other metrics – enterprise value (EV) and EBIT which is an acronym which represents a company's earnings before interest and tax and is explained further below.

Enterprise value is a measure of a company's value and is often used as an alternative to straightforward market capitalisation. A firm's EV is calculated as its market capitalisation plus all of its outstanding debt, minority interest(s) and preferred shares, minus all of the cash and cash equivalents.

From a slightly different perspective, EV is the sum of the claims of all of a company's security-holders which includes all of the debt-holders, preferred shareholders, minority shareholders, common equity holders, and others. EV is one of the fundamental metrics used in business valuation, financial modelling, accounting, and portfolio analysis.

A simplified and intuitive way to understand enterprise value is to envisage purchasing an entire business. If you settle with all the security-holders, you have essentially purchased the company at its enterprise value.

EBIT is an acronym which represents 'Earnings Before Interest and Tax'. It is another fairly widely used indicator of a company's financial performance and is calculated in the following simple calculation:

EBIT = Revenue less expenses (excluding tax and interest)

5.3.4.1 Comparison of EV/EBIT with P/E Ratio

Price earnings ratios provide a measure of the expensiveness, or cheapness, of a particular company's shares. As an alternative, enterprise value multiples look at the whole company, incorporating both the equity and the debt. Simplistically, the smaller the enterprise value to the earnings, the cheaper the company is, which could highlight a buying opportunity for investors.

5.3.5 Enterprise Value to EBITDA

This ratio, once again, is used as a measure of the profitability of a business and also uses the enterprise value as the numerator in the ratio as defined above.

EBITDA is essentially net income with interest, taxes, depreciation, and amortisation reversed and added back to become a variant of net income. EBITDA has been used by some in the financial world to compare profitability between companies because it eliminates the effects of financing and accounting decisions. However, it must be clearly understood that this is a non-GAAP measure. The criticism that is often made about the value is that it allows too much discretion as to what is (and is not) included in the calculation. This also means that companies often change the items included in their EBITDA calculation from one reporting period to the next.

EBITDA does not represent cash earnings: it may be a useful metric to evaluate profitability, but not cash flow. EBITDA also leaves out the cash required to fund working capital and the replacement of old equipment, which can be significant.

EBITDA = Revenue less Expenses (excluding tax, interest, depreciation and amortisation)

5.3.6 Net Dividend Yield

The net dividend yield expresses the total dividends per share paid out over the last year as a percentage of the current share price.

A high yield may indicate that the share price is relatively low in comparison with the return it offers. This suggests that the market does not have confidence that the dividends paid in the past will continue to be paid in the future. Conversely, a low dividend yield indicates high market confidence in the company's ability to increase dividends.

5.3.7 Net Dividend Cover

The dividend cover can be used to assess how well a company covered their dividend payout with the profits they made. In other words, how easy was it for the company to pay these dividends?

Dividend cover compares the earnings of the company (net income in relation to the year's activity) with the dividends paid in the year. This also reveals the proportion of profits that were reinvested in the company – if dividend cover was two times, then half of the profits are paid out to shareholders and half are retained.

A dividend cover of less than one is known as uncovered dividend, meaning the year's profits were not enough to cover the dividend.

5.4 CALCULATING INVESTORS' RATIOS

LEARNING OBJECTIVE

6.5.4 Be able to calculate the following investors' ratios: earnings per share; diluted earnings per share; price earnings ratio (both historic and prospective); net dividend yield; net dividend cover; corporation tax

5.4.1 Earnings per share

To calculate the earnings per share (EPS), one simply divides the value of net income or earnings (which is the net income for the financial year) by the number of ordinary shares in issue.

$$\textbf{EPS} = \frac{\textbf{Earnings or net income}}{\textbf{Number of ordinary shares in issue}}$$

Note that if the company has preference shares in issue, the earnings are after the preference shareholders' dividend, but before the ordinary shareholders' dividend. For a group of companies preparing **consolidated accounts**, the earning line would also be after any **minority interests**. Minority interests are the profits that belong to shareholders of any subsidiary companies that are not shareholders in the holding company.

The following illustration for an imaginary company, XYZ plc, shows how one can calculate the earnings per share.

ILLUSTRATION

XYZ plc has net income or earnings of £898,000 for its most recent fiscal year and, at the time of preparing the EPS estimate, has 5 million outstanding ordinary shares.

The EPS is £898,000/5,000,000 shares = 18p per share

5.4.2 Diluted earnings per share

The following illustration for the same imaginary company shows how one can calculate the diluted earnings per share.

ILLUSTRATION

The debt financing of XYZ plc at the year end 2008 includes £250,000 of 10% convertible loan stock, which was issued on 30 June 2008. The terms of conversion for every £100 nominal value of loan stock as of the following conversion dates are as follows:

- **31 December 2008 – conversion factor is 120**
- **31 December 2009 – conversion factor is 115**
- **31 December 2010 – conversion factor is 110**

Since the £250,000 of convertible loan stock is still in issue at year end 2008, the convertible stockholders have not taken the option of converting at a conversion factor of 120 shares.

XYZ plc Fully Diluted EPS Calculation			
	Basic earnings as of 31 December, 2008 in £000s		898
Dilution event	If convertible exercised	Period	
	interest saved for one half year	6/12	
	£250,000 @ 10%	12,500	
	Tax at 30%	–3750	
			8.75
Earnings following dilution event			906.75

The best option that remains for them is to convert in 2009 at a rate of 115 shares. So, assuming the most dilutive possibility as the one required for the IAS 33 rule, the maximum number of new ordinary shares that would be issued is [250,000/100] x 115 = 287,500 shares.

Number of shares pre-dilution		Period	5,000,000
	Conversion of 250,000 at a rate of	6/12	
	115/100	143,750	143,750
Fully diluted ordinary shares			5,143,750

The dilution is only assumed to occur for half a year, since the convertibles were only issued six months into 2008. In subsequent years, the dilution calculation would assume dilution for the whole year.

As shown above, pre-dilution, the EPS is £898,000/5,000,000 shares = 18p per share; fully diluted the EPS is £906,750/5,143,750 shares = 17.6p

5.4.3 P/E Ratio

The **price/earnings ratio**, or **P/E**, is calculated by dividing the current market price of the ordinary shares by the earnings per share.

$$\textbf{P/E ratio} = \frac{\textbf{Current market price of ordinary shares}}{\textbf{Earnings per share}}$$

Historic P/E ratios use the last published earnings per share from the financial statements, whereas prospective P/E ratios use forecasts of the next earnings per share that the company is likely to deliver.

Continuing with the illustration from above of XYZ plc, if the ordinary shares are currently trading at £1.60 each, and there is a forecast EPS for the next fiscal year for XYZ plc of 17p, the P/E ratios for the company would be as follows:

Historic P/E = 160/18 = 8.89 (this is based on the pre-diluted EPS of 18p.)

Prospective P/E = 160/17 = 9.41 (this is based on the forecast EPS of 17p.)

5.4.4 Net dividend yield

To calculate net dividend yield, simply divide the net dividend per share by the current share price and multiply it by 100.

$$\textbf{Net dividend yield} = \frac{\textbf{Net dividend}}{\textbf{Current share price}} \times 100$$

For XYZ plc, let us assume that the board of directors decides to distribute £400,000 to shareholders in the form of a dividend and retain the rest of net income on its balance sheet. The net dividend per share would be £400,000 divided by 5 million shares = 8p.

The net dividend yield would be:

Net dividend yield = 8/160 x 100 = 5%

5.4.5 Dividend Cover

To calculate the dividend cover for the imaginary XYZ plc, one would take the company's earnings per share and divide it by the net dividends per share.

$$\textbf{Dividend cover} = \frac{\textbf{EPS}}{\textbf{Net dividends per share}}$$

Using the figures from above, the dividend cover for XYZ plc would be 18/8 = 2.25 times.

5.4.6 Corporation Tax – Effective Tax Rate

It would be logical to expect the tax authorities to simply tax the company on its income before taxation as presented in the Income Statement. However, the reality is not quite so simple. For example, the UK's tax authority, Her Majesty's Revenue & Customs (HMRC) has detailed requirements designed to prevent a company from evading tax by artificially reducing its taxable profits.

Normal expenses such as wages and bills are accepted as deductions from income to arrive at taxable profits. However, costs such as entertainment costs are not deemed deductible; they are termed disallowed expenses.

Depreciation cannot be counted as an allowable expenditure for tax purposes because the company may be tempted to set artificially high rates of depreciation to reduce taxable profits. Instead of using depreciation to account for the using up of an asset, the company can make a standard deduction, determined by HMRC rules, called a capital allowance.

The result is that the tax charge in the income statement is not necessarily the percentage of income that the tax rate would suggest. The effective tax rate is commonly calculated to ascertain how effective a company is at planning and controlling the tax it pays.

Effective tax rate = (tax charge from the income statement/income before tax) x 100

For the example A plc encountered earlier:

Effective tax rate = (555/1990) x 100 = 27.9%

The rates of corporation tax that a company is liable to pay change each year and the main Corporation Tax Rates for financial years covering the period from April 2008 to the time of writing are as follows:

Profits	Rate applied	Financial years starting 1 April			
		2008	2009	2010	2011
Up to £300,000	Small profits rate	21%	21%	21%	20%
£300,001 – £1,500,000	Marginal relief from main rate	Between 21% and 28%	Between 21% and 28%	Between 21% and 28%	Between 20% and 27%
Over £1,500,000	Main rate	28%	28%	28%	27%
	Special rate for unit trusts and open-ended investment companies	20%	20%	20%	

5.4.7 Emergency Budget – June 22, 2010

From April 2011, the corporation tax rate known as the 'small profits rate' will drop to 20 % for all companies making profits of up to £300,000.

Around 850,000 firms will benefit from the tax cut, which Treasury forecasts say will trim a total of £3.8 billion from their tax bills over the next four years.

The main change to Corporation Tax proposed in the emergency budget in June 2010 will be the reduction of the main rate by 1% to 27% in tax year commencing April 1, 2011, a further reduction to 26% in tax year 2012, a further reduction to 25% in 2013 and then a final reduction to 24% in tax year 2014.

CHAPTER SEVEN

RISK AND REWARD

This syllabus area will provide approximately 6 of the 100 examination questions

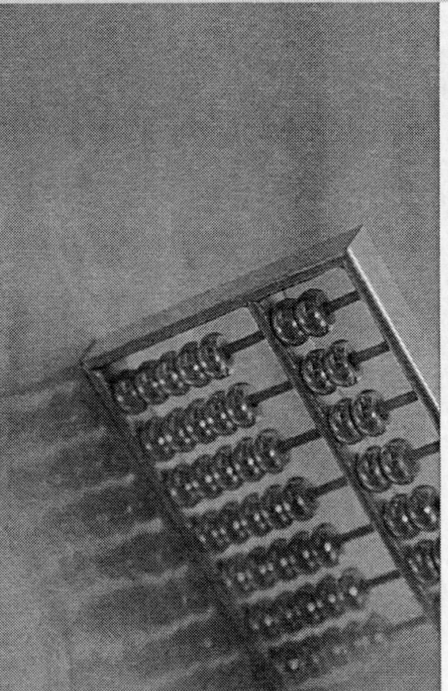

1. INVESTMENT MANAGEMENT

1.1 EQUITIES

LEARNING OBJECTIVE

7.1.1 Understand the risk and reward of investment in equities: risk/reward profile; effect of longer term; can offer income and capital appreciation

Equities are shares in companies that give the investor an ownership stake in the company alongside the attraction of limited liability. If the issuing company collapses, the shareholders' loss is simply the amount paid for the shares. As a part owner of the company, the investor has the opportunity to share in the company's profits and vote at general meetings. Indeed, most investors are attracted to equities in the hope that the value of the shares increases (**capital appreciation**), and this may be combined with income in the form of regular, and perhaps increasing, dividends.

Risk/Reward Profile

The risk/reward profile is often seen as a trade off between the risk associated with an investment or holding and the reward attached to it.

Equity investments are generally considered to be risky, relative to other investments, such as bonds and money market instruments. Medium levels of risk are attached to larger, well-established company shares, and high levels of risk attached to smaller company shares and start-up company shares. However, equity investments offer the potential to deliver high returns if held long-term.

Equity Risk Premium

For equity investors there is an equity risk premium which effectively is a higher rate of return that is required to entice investors to take on the risk of owning shares or equity as opposed to holding a secured asset such as a bond. If one is seeking the most secure form of investment this will usually be available in the form of a government bond or short term instrument. The risk-free rate is the rate on government bonds and short term debts because of the low chance that the government will default on its loans. An investment in stocks or equities has far more risk associated with it as it is a non-secured asset and companies can suffer from adverse business conditions or go bankrupt in which case shareholders often receive no residual value.

As an example,if the total return on a stock is 10% over a given period and the risk-free rate over the same period is 5%, the equity-risk premium would be 5%.

1.2 MONEY MARKET INSTRUMENTS

LEARNING OBJECTIVE

7.1.2 Understand the risk and reward of investment in money market instruments: risk/reward profile; use as short term investment

For investment horizons that are very short (eg, the next six months rather than the next 20 years), there is the potential for investors to keep their funds in cash and place them on interest earning deposit, or to invest in short-term money market instruments, like Treasury bills. These investments are low risk, relatively secure and deliver income, but provide little scope for capital growth. For investors that do not want their money tied-up for long periods, the predictable value and liquidity of these short-term investments is important.

Prices of money market instruments fluctuate and can in moments of financial crisis become quite erratic. Many investors will want to hold the shortest term instruments such as Treasury bills during periods when the money markets are not functioning 'normally'. During the financial crisis which became especially acute in September and October of 2008 many institutions wanted to replace all of their other money market holdings with the shortest duration Treasury bills. This can have the perverse consequence on extreme occasions of making such instruments, which are priced on a discount basis, yield a negative return or at a rate which is far below that which would normally be expected. The desire to move into such short-term paper during moments of crisis is referred to as a 'flight to safety'.

While some institutional investors, such as pension funds, seek out longer dated maturities in fixed income markets, there are many that prefer shorter and medium term assets.

There is often a trade off and calculation to be made between the value of a long term income stream from such instruments versus the greater volatility in the prevailing prices of longer dated paper. Duration of bond portfolios is a special issue for pension funds, for example, which have to match their assets and liabilities

1.3 DEBT INSTRUMENTS

LEARNING OBJECTIVE

7.1.3 Understand the risk/reward profile of investment in debt (fixed interest, floating rate and index linked): compared to equities; effect of holding to maturity; can combine low risk and certain return; can provide a fixed income; inflation risk; interest rate risk; default risk

Bonds are fixed-interest loan instruments, predominantly issued by companies, governments, government agencies and supranationals like the World Bank, providing the issuer with debt finance. Their attractiveness to investors is driven by the fixed-income that they offer from regular, pre-determined coupons, combined with the relative certainty of the principal amount to be repaid at redemption.

The coupons can be fixed (at a percentage of nominal value), they can float depending upon a published interest rate such as the London Inter-Bank Offered Rate (LIBOR) or they can be tied to inflation by being index-linked (eg, to the Consumer Price Index). The principal amount paid at maturity is generally the par or nominal value, although with index linked bonds it will be uplifted for inflation. They are generally less risky than equities, but offer less potential for substantial returns. Indeed, for highly rated bonds like gilts where the risk of default is low, investors can be virtually certain of the yield that their investment will deliver as long as they hold their bonds to maturity. If the bonds are sold before they reach maturity, there is a danger that their market value may be below their nominal value, bringing about a capital loss and the potential to adversely impact the investor's yield.

Interest rate risk is the risk that an interest rate movement brings about an adverse movement in the value of an investment. It is particularly acute when the investment is a fixed-interest bond and the interest rate rises. Because of the inverse relationship between bonds and interest rates, the value of the bond will fall. Interest rate risk is largely removed if the bond is floating rate, since the coupon will be reset in line with the higher market interest rate.

Inflation risk arises when inflation is more substantial than the investor expected, the value of the investments held may fall. Generally, bonds will suffer because the fixed cash payments that they deliver are less valuable. Floating rate bonds will suffer less because the higher inflation will bring about a higher interest rate, but the real value of the principal at redemption will fall. Index-linked bonds will not suffer. The coupon and the principal are linked to a measure of inflation (increases in the Retail Price Index) so the investor will not lose out.

In contrast to debt instruments, equities and property cope reasonably well with unexpected inflation. Companies are able to increase their prices and deliver larger dividends, and the property market as a whole tends to reflect the inflationary increases.

Investors in bonds face **default risk**. This is the probability of the issuer defaulting on their payment obligations. Default risk (often referred to as **credit risk**) can be assessed by reference to the independent credit rating agencies, mainly Standard and Poor's, Moody's and Fitch IBCA.

The rating agencies split bonds into two distinct classes: **investment grade** (alternatively referred to as **prime**) and **sub-investment grade** (alternatively referred to as **speculative**, **non-prime** or even **junk**).

The three rating agencies apply similar criteria to assess whether the borrower will be able to service the required payments on the bonds. Then the bonds are categorised according to their reliability. **AAA** tends to be the best and the next best is **AA** (although the rating agencies can have lesser notches such as pluses and minuses). The categorisation is broadly as follows:

Bond Credit Ratings				
Credit Risk		Moody's	Standard & Poors	Fitch Ratings
Investment Grade				
Highest Quality		Aaa	AAA	AAA
High Quality	Very Strong	Aa	AA	AA
Upper Medium Grade	Strong	A	A	A
	Medium Grade	Baa	BBB	BBB
Non-Investment Grade				
Lower Medium Grade	Somewhat Speculative	Ba	BB	BB
Low Grade	Speculative	B	B	B
Poor Quality	May Default	Caa	CCC	CCC
Most Speculative		Ca	CC	CC
No interest being paid or bankruptcy petition filed		C	D	C
In default		C	D	D

Very few organisations, except western governments and supranational agencies, have **AAA** ratings, but most large companies boast an investment grade rating. Issues of bonds categorised as sub-investment grade are alternatively known as 'junk bonds' because of the high levels of credit risk.

If the rating agencies **downgrade** the issuer of a bond, potential investors will look to compensate for the increased risk by demanding a greater yield on the issuer's bonds. This will inevitably **result in a lower price for the bond**. Some issuers of bonds utilise 'credit enhancements' to enable their bonds to be rated more highly by the credit rating agencies. Examples of credit enhancements would be bonds guaranteed by another group company, or bonds with a fixed charge over particular assets.

1.4 OVERSEAS EQUITIES AND BONDS

LEARNING OBJECTIVE

7.1.4 Understand risk/reward profile of investment in overseas shares and debt: country risk; exchange rate risk

To lessen the risk that a particular company, or issuer of a bond, delivers poor returns due to problems in the domestic economy, investors can invest in overseas companies' equities, or overseas bond issues. Like domestic equities and bonds, these overseas investments may offer the possibilities of income and capital appreciation.

However, the investor may be less knowledgeable about the overseas company/issuer and there may be particular idiosyncrasies in some overseas markets, for example, local custodians may not be required to give the holder access to corporate actions. These overseas investments are also higher risk than their domestic equivalents because of the additional risk that is created by the possibility of exchange rates moving against the investor.

Currency (or Exchange Rate) Risk

For investments that are denominated in a currency other than £ sterling, an adverse exchange rate movement will create an adverse movement in the value of the investment. Clearly, this is particularly relevant for overseas investments. It can also be problematic if the investment is in a UK company that has substantial overseas business interests.

1.5 TYPES OF RISK

LEARNING OBJECTIVE

7.1.5 Understand the risks facing the investor: specific/unsystematic; market/systematic

Risk can be categorised in a number of different ways, but the over-riding rule for investment is that the potential for spectacular return can only arise if the investor takes a large amount of risk: the **risk-return relationship**.

Market (or Systematic) Risk

As seen above, this is the risk that the whole market moves in a particular direction. It is typically applied to equities and brought about by economic and political factors. It cannot be diversified away. For example, political crises or general recessions will tend to bring about falls in the market value of all shares, although they may affect different company shares to different degrees.

Specific (or Unsystematic) Risk

As seen earlier, this is the risk that something adverse impacts the value of a particular investment, but the adverse impact is not market-wide. An obvious example is a company's management making some sort of error – perhaps producing a defective product with resultant impact on profits and customer goodwill. Specific risk can be diversified away by holding many investments.

1.6 CORRELATION/DIVERSIFICATION

LEARNING OBJECTIVE

7.1.6 Understand how to optimise the risk/reward relationship through the use of: correlation; diversification

Investors generally choose to avoid unnecessary risk in their portfolios by holding appropriate proportions of each class of investment. The more conservative investor will hold a greater proportion of low risk bonds and money market instruments. These lower risk investments are likely to give rise to lower, but more predictable, returns. The more adventurous investor will hold a greater proportion of medium and high-risk equity investments, because higher risk means greater potential for higher returns. Essentially, the choice of investments is driven by the investor's attitude to risk and the fact that there is a trade off between risk and return. However, diversification can remove some of the general investment risk without having to remove all high-risk investments from a portfolio.

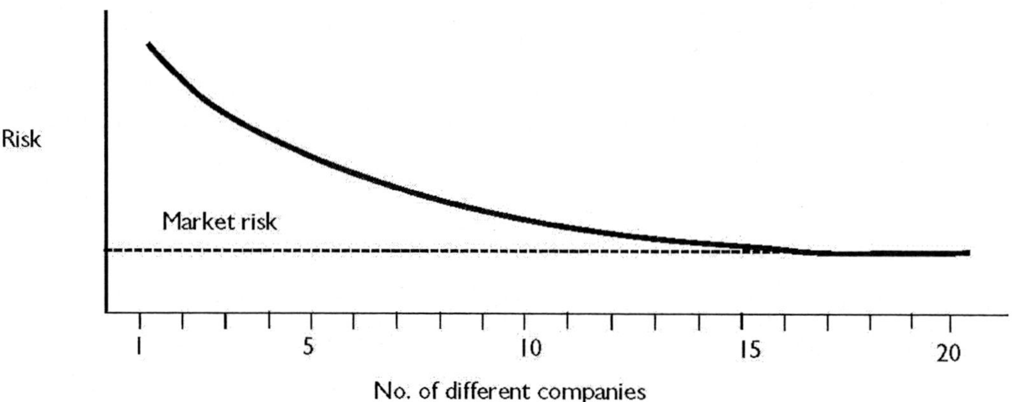

For example, an investor's portfolio might contain high risk equity investments but as the portfolio diversifies, ie, as the investor includes a wider range of companies' shares, risk diminishes, because unexpected losses made on one investment are offset by unexpected gains on another.

Diversification benefits are maximised by holding investments with uncorrelated returns (where the returns do not tend to move in the same direction and to the same degree). It is not necessary for the investments to be negatively correlated, with combinations of investments that are positively correlated still providing diversification benefits. It is only a combination of investments that are perfectly positively correlated that will offer no diversification benefits. However, diversification cannot remove all of the risk. There are certain things, such as economic news, that tend to impact the whole market. The risk that can be removed is known as the specific or unsystematic risk and the risk that cannot be diversified away is the market or systematic risk.

1.7 HEDGING

LEARNING OBJECTIVE

7.1.7 Know the role of hedging in the management of investment risk

The risks that are inevitable when investing in shares, bonds and money market instruments can be largely removed by entering into **hedging**. Unfortunately, the hedging strategies will have a cost that inevitably impacts investment performance.

Hedging is usually achieved by using derivatives, for example, options, futures and forwards. Buying put options on investments held will enable the investor to remove the risk of a fall in value, but the investor will have to pay a premium to buy the options.

Futures, such as stock index futures, can be used to hedge against equity prices falling – but the future will remove any upside as well as downside.

Forwards, such as currency forwards, could be used to eliminate exchange rate risk – but, like futures, the upside potential will be lost in order to hedge against the downside risk.

2. INSTITUTIONAL INVESTMENT ADVICE

2.1 INSTITUTIONAL CLIENT PROFILES

LEARNING OBJECTIVE

7.2.1 Know the differences between institutional client profiles including: pension funds; life and general insurance funds; hedge funds; regulated mutual funds; banks

There are a number of institutional investors, including pension funds, the providers of life assurance, the providers of general insurance and banks.

Pension Funds are set up with the aim of providing retirement funds for the beneficiaries. They may be sponsored by an employer, be solely dependent on contributions from the workforce, or a combination of the two. Pension funds tend to be approved by tax authorities (such as HMRC in the UK), and can then accumulate income and capital gains tax-free. The money in the fund is invested by fund managers and, because pension funds have a relatively long investment horizon, they can take risks and have tended to invest heavily in equities.

Pension funds can be divided into two broad classes: those that define the benefits they will pay out (**defined benefit schemes** or **final salary schemes**), and those where the benefit is driven by the contributions made and the investment performance (**defined contribution schemes**).

Life assurance business: Life assurance arises from insurance contracts written by an insurance company on the life of an individual. They mainly comprise:

- term assurance policies which, in exchange for a regular premium, only pay out if the individual dies before the end of a set policy term;
- whole of life policies which simply pay out on death in exchange for regular premiums;
- endowment policies which are term assurance policies with a significant investment element that depends on the performance of the insurance company's fund;
- single premium life assurance bonds which are single premium endowments; again they have a significant investment element.

Like pension funds, because of the long-term nature of life assurance business, the funds tend to be willing to invest in higher risk investments involving a heavy weighting in equity investments. Unlike pension funds, the income and the gains made within life assurance funds are subject to tax.

General insurance is where insurance is written by an insurance company against short-term personal and commercial risks, such as car or household contents insurance. Because of the short-term nature of the liabilities, the funds from the premiums tend to be invested in low-risk, liquid, short-term assets such as money market instruments. Like life assurance funds, general insurance funds are subject to tax on the income and gains within the fund.

Banks: If banks hold surplus cash at the end of each business day, they will place the funds on deposit with other banks (in the inter-bank market) and invest in eligible money market instruments (such as treasury bills and commercial paper) – relatively risk-free investments to cover the short-term nature of the banks' liabilities to depositors. An eligible money market instrument means that the Bank of England will accept it as collateral against loans. As with insurance companies, banks are taxed on income and gains they generate from their investments.

The following table provides a summary of the key distinctions and similarities across the institutional investors:

Institution	Investment horizon	Proportion of equity investments	Proportion of money market investments	Relative risk profile
Pension fund	Long-term	High	Low	High
Life assurance fund	Long-term	High	Low	High
General insurance fund	Short-term	Low	High	Low
Bank	Short-term	Low	High	Low

Regulated Mutual Funds

We have seen that diversification of shareholdings reduces risk, but for a private client with a relatively modest amount to invest, this would be prohibitively expensive. One way of avoiding the high cost of investing in many different companies is to invest in a pooled fund where a fund manager handles the money of a group of investors. As a result, the portfolio is conveniently and cheaply diversified. There are four major vehicles that enable individuals to diversify collectively with others. They are unit trusts, investment trusts, open-ended investment companies and exchange traded funds (ETFs).

Questions on collective investment vehicles will refer to some schemes as being **regulated** and others as being **unregulated**. This refers to authorisation by the regulator – such as the FSA in the UK. Regulated schemes can be freely marketed; unregulated schemes cannot be **freely marketed**.

Certain schemes are also granted UCITS (Undertaking for Collective Investment in Transferable Securities) status. UCITS status allows the scheme to be marketed across the **EU**.

An unauthorised collective investment scheme can still be marketed but with restrictions, eg, only to relatively large customers, more sophisticated investors or those who already hold such an investment.

Hedge Funds

Hedge funds are **unauthorised** investment vehicles that are free to invest in **high risk** strategies, including highly-geared **derivatives** and **arbitrage**, such as going long in some investments and short in others (a **long/short** strategy). Most hedge funds are offshore investments, with the fund domiciled in the most tax-efficient location. Unlike most of the conventional collective investment vehicles (such as unit trusts, investment trusts, OEICs and ETFs) that are restricted to a 'long only' investment strategy, hedge funds can be more flexible and take substantial short positions. The term 'hedge' fund comes from the fact that the unconventional nature of their investments means they can produce positive returns when the general market is suffering. For example, a long/short strategy will potentially generate positive returns regardless of the general market – it is described as a 'market-neutral strategy'.

Because of their unauthorised nature, nothing prevents hedge funds from borrowing money and 'gearing up' the returns for their shareholders. Indeed, many hedge funds have substantial amounts of borrowed funds and are highly geared.

Because they are not authorised, they cannot be freely marketed. This, combined with the requirement to invest substantial minimum amounts, means that hedge funds tend to be accessible only to institutional investors and high net worth individuals.

2.2 ACTIVE AND PASSIVE INVESTMENT MANAGEMENT METHODOLOGIES

LEARNING OBJECTIVE

7.2.2 Know what are active and passive investment management methodologies and the advantages and disadvantages of each

2.2.1 Active Management

Active management (also called active investing) refers to a method of portfolio management where the manager's strategy is designed to outperform the returns available from an investment benchmark index. For example, an active portfolio manager focused on investing in UK equities would be seeking to realise superior returns to those available from a simple method/strategy of buying and holding all of the constituents of the FTSE 100.

It is worth pointing out that purchasing a simple derivative, such as a FTSE 100 futures contract, would not reflect the total returns available to an investor in the actual index, as the futures would only capture changes in the price level of the index and not dividend income. More complex derivative products can emulate the total returns without requiring an outright purchase of all 100 stocks in the index.

2.2.2 Passive Management

Passive managers are those that do not aspire to create a return in excess of a benchmark index. They will often follow exactly the course just outlined and invest in an index fund or derivative that replicates as closely as possible the investment weighting and returns of a selected benchmark index such as the FTSE 100, or if they seek to match the returns of the US market they may invest in an instrument which exactly tracks the total returns of the S&P 500 index.

2.2.3 Management Strategy and the Efficient Markets Hypothesis (EMH)

The efficient markets hypothesis (EMH) is an investment theory stating that it is impossible to 'beat the market' because stock market efficiency causes existing share prices to always incorporate and reflect all relevant information. According to the EMH, this means that stocks always trade at their fair value on stock exchanges, making it impossible for investors to either purchase undervalued stocks or sell stocks for inflated prices. As such, it should be impossible to outperform the overall market through expert stock selection, technical analysis, or market timing, and that the only way an investor can possibly obtain higher returns is by purchasing riskier investments. This would be in accordance with the view of the CAPM that only higher beta stocks will deliver higher returns, but with increased risk.

Passive fund management is consistent with the idea that markets are efficient and that no mispricing exists. If the EMH is an accurate account of the way that capital markets work, then there is no benefit to be had from active trading. Such trading will simply incur dealing and management costs for no benefit. Investors who do not believe that they can identify active fund managers whom they are confident can produce returns above the level of charges for active management, will often elect to invest in passive funds or index trackers.

An active manager will try to achieve the desired goal of outperforming a designated benchmark by seeking out market inefficiencies and by purchasing securities (stocks, etc) that are undervalued or by short selling securities that are overvalued. Either of these methods may be used alone or in combination. Depending on the goals of the specific investment portfolio, active fund management may also serve to create less volatility (or risk) than the benchmark index. The reduction of risk may be instead of, or in addition to, the goal of creating an investment return greater than the benchmark.

Active portfolio managers can use various strategies to construct their portfolios with a view to superior performance than that available from index tracking. For example, the manager could focus on selecting securities based on research and quantitative analysis focused on measures such as P/E ratios and Price Earnings Growth (PEG) ratios, sector investments that attempt to anticipate long-term macroeconomic trends (such as a focus on energy or housing stocks), and purchasing stocks of companies that are temporarily out of favour or selling at a discount to their intrinsic value. Certain actively managed funds will also pursue more specialised strategies such as merger arbitrage, option writing, and other kinds of statistical arbitrage involving more exotic securities such as derivatives and convertible securities.

2.2.4 Performance

The effectiveness of an actively-managed investment portfolio will clearly depend on the skill (or good fortune) of the manager and research staff. In reality, the majority of actively managed collective investment schemes rarely outperform their index counterparts over an extended period of time, assuming that they are benchmarked correctly. For example, research from the US shows that the Standard & Poor's Index Versus Active (SPIVA) quarterly scorecards demonstrate that only a minority of actively managed mutual funds have gains better than the Standard & Poor's (S&P) index benchmark. As the time period for comparison increases, the percentage of actively-managed funds whose gains exceed the S&P benchmark declines further.

2.2.5 Advantages of Active Management

The primary attraction of active management is that it allows selection of a variety of investments instead of investing in the market as a whole. Investors may have a variety of reasons for not wanting to simply track an index. Investors may, for example, be sceptical of the EMH, or believe that some market segments are less efficient in creating profits than others. They may also want to reduce volatility by investing in less-risky, high-quality companies rather than in the market as a whole, even at the cost of slightly lower returns. Conversely, some investors may want to take on additional risk in exchange for the opportunity of obtaining higher-than-market returns. Investments that are not highly correlated to the market are useful as a portfolio diversifier and may reduce overall portfolio volatility. Some investors may wish to follow a strategy that avoids or under-weights certain industries compared to the market as a whole, for instance, an employee of a high-technology growth company who receives company stock or stock options as a benefit, might prefer not to have additional funds invested in the same industry.

2.2.6 Disadvantages of Active Management

The most obvious disadvantage of active management is that the fund manager may make bad investment choices or follow an unsound theory in managing the portfolio. The fees associated with active management are also higher than those associated with passive management, even if frequent trading is not present. Those who are considering investing in an actively-managed fund should evaluate the fund's prospectus carefully.

Active fund management strategies that involve frequent trading generate higher transaction costs which diminish the fund's return. In addition, the short-term capital gains resulting from frequent trades often have an unfavourable income tax impact when such funds are held in a taxable account.

More specialised tracker funds can also be linked to the performance of securities in emerging markets, and specific industry sectors. Increasingly the proliferation of exchange traded funds (ETF's), allows investors to purchase shares in a fund which trades actively on a major exchange and which provides exposure to certain kinds of securities and where the minimal management fees are incorporated into the actual price of the shares of the ETF. The benefit to an investor purchasing such exchange traded funds is that there is usually a high degree of liquidity, the asset values of the fund constituents as well as the price of the ETF shares is updated on a real time basis and the costs for the packaging of the securities is minimal.

When the assortment of assets of an actively-managed fund becomes too large, it begins to take on index-like characteristics because it must invest in an increasingly broad selection of securities which, in the limiting case, will tend to perform exactly in line with the overall market. In such a situation the fund becomes a pseudo-tracker, and an investor in such a fund is paying active management fees when the actual style is effectively passive. This last factor is why some fund managers close their funds to new investors after the fund reaches a certain size so that they can avoid having to be so broadly diversified as to deviate from their original selection criteria underlying their active strategic focus.

2.2.7 Advantages of Passive Management

To a large extent, the advantages and disadvantages of a passive approach to portfolio management will tend to be the converse of the respective positions with respect to active management that were discussed above.

Indeed, the most frequently cited advantage of a passive approach to asset management is that the performance of the fund is not dependent on the manager's ability to make investment choices which, it is contended by the active manager, will out-perform the broad market, but which in fact may well prove not to be the case and will lead to a less rewarding performance than simply investing in a tracker fund.

Subscribers to the EMH will tend to favour the use of index trackers if they are seeking out a risk/reward ratio which is in accordance with the overall performance of the market. By investing in a fund which tracks a broad benchmark, such as the S&P 500 index or FTSE 100 index, the investor is only exposed to the systematic risk within the market and can avoid the risks (and potential rewards) of non-systematic risk.

Several research studies have provided evidence that the majority of actively-managed large and mid-cap stock funds in US have failed to outperform their passive index counterparts.

Investors in a passively managed fund, which most commonly takes the form of 'index tracking', in which the portfolio constituents are required to replicate the performance of a broad market index such as the FTSE 100 Index, can also avoid incurring the fees associated with active management. A passive fund management strategy can avoid the frequent trading which is more likely under an active management approach and transaction costs will be lower which, relatively speaking, will enhance the fund's return. Also, a strategy of buy-and-hold which is typically the outcome of a passive strategy, is far less likely to incur frequent short-term capital gains resulting from the larger focus on short-term trading activities of active management, and, to that extent, will also be able to avoid the unfavourable income tax impact when such funds are held in a taxable account.

Another significant advantage of a passive management style is the fact that the total expense ratio will be considerably lower than for many actively managed funds, such as hedge funds which operate with both fees charged for funds under management and also incentive fees. With regard to unit trusts and mutual funds, it is also the case that index tracker funds will have lower expense ratios and, somewhat ironically, they may not differ in their performance and fund composition than the actively managed funds. This can arise when the asset composition of an actively-managed fund becomes too large that it begins to take on index-like characteristics. The largest funds have to invest in an increasingly diverse set of investments instead of those limited to the fund manager's specific asset selection acumen. In such cases, the actively managed fund, while it may not have set out with the intention, becomes, in effect, a closet index tracker. To avoid this situation, some large fund companies close their funds before they reach this point, but there is potential for a conflict of interest between the fund management and the unit-trust holders as closing the fund will result in a loss of income (management fees) for the fund managers.

Passive management has recently become more appealing to a broad range of investors because innovative investment products, introduced in recent years, now allow investors to investor in 'sector trackers'. For example, specialised exchange traded funds (ETFs) can be linked to the performance of securities in emerging markets, and specific industry sectors. Increasingly, the proliferation of ETFs allows investors to purchase shares in a fund which trades actively on a major exchange and which provides exposure to certain kinds of securities and where the minimal management fees are incorporated into the actual price of the shares of the ETF.

2.2.8 Disadvantages of Passive Management

Disadvantages of passive management include the fact that performance is always dictated by a benchmark or index, meaning that investors must be satisfied with market returns. In addition, the inherent lack of control dictated by being passive, thereby prevents defensive measures if it appears that a certain class of asset prices, specifically equities, may be heading for turbulent trading conditions and possible capital losses.

The investor in a passively managed fund should only expect to realise similar returns to those that are available from the broad market or sector index upon which the passively managed fund is based. So, while the investor's returns will be 'acceptable' from a relative perspective, ie, they will be highly correlated with the broad market return, they may still be 'unacceptable' from an absolute perspective in the sense that losses will arise if the broad market sustains such losses.

The main disadvantage of passive management is that it lacks the potential to generate alpha or above market returns. The investor in a passively managed fund foregos the opportunity to have exposure to a variety of investments which could out-perform a broad benchmark index and which may have other desirable attributes providing diversification and lower correlation elements that simply investing in the market as a whole.

Investors may have a variety of reasons for not wanting to simply track an index. Those opposed to passive management may have serious reservations regarding the validity of the EMH and believe that some market segments are more efficient in creating profits than others. They may also want to reduce volatility by investing in less-risky, high-quality companies rather than in the market as a whole, even at the cost of slightly lower returns. Conversely, some investors may want to take on additional risk in exchange for the opportunity of obtaining higher-than-market returns and such investors would be willing to seek out higher beta stocks (by definition a broad benchmark based portfolio should have a beta of approximately one) in exchange for the possibility of above average potential gains (and losses). Investments that are not highly correlated to the market, eg, certain commodities such as gold, are useful as a portfolio diversifier and may reduce overall portfolio volatility. Some investors may wish to follow a strategy that avoids or under-weights certain industries compared to the market as a whole as part of a deliberate diversification strategy. For example, someone employed in the financial services industry whose own compensation is closely tied to company stock or the stock options of his/her employer may prefer not to have any additional funds invested in the same sector.

2.2.9 Active Management with Manager Participation

Many funds do not have either the manager or directors with an equity stake in the fund that the manager is running. Another meaning sometimes given to active management, is when the managers/ directors have a vested interest in the success of the fund. Private-equity is often real active management since a privately owned company usually has just one owner that make strategy decisions at the board level.

The advantage to an investor in a fund where the management is personally at risk by holding a stake in the fund under management is that the manager's interests will be perfectly aligned with the investors as he/she has what is known as 'skin in the game'.

2.2.10 Active Bond Strategies

Generally speaking, active based strategies are used by those portfolio managers who believe the bond market is not perfectly efficient and, therefore, subject to mispricing. If a bond is considered mispriced, then active management strategies can be employed to capitalise upon this perceived pricing anomaly.

Bond switching, or bond swapping, is used by those portfolio managers who believe they can outperform a buy-and-hold passive policy by actively exchanging bonds perceived to be overpriced for those perceived to be underpriced.

Bond switching takes three forms:

- **Anomaly switching** – this involves moving between two bonds similar in all respects apart from the yield and price on which each trades. This pricing anomaly is exploited by switching away from the more to the less highly priced bond.

- **Policy switching** – when an interest rate cut is expected but not implied by the yield curve, low duration bonds are sold in favour of those with high durations. By pre-empting the rate cut, the holder can subsequently benefit from the greater price volatility of the latter bonds.
- **Inter-market spread switch** – when it is believed that the difference in the yield being offered between corporate bonds and comparable gilts, for example, is excessive given the perceived risk differential between these two markets, an inter-market spread switch will be undertaken from the gilt to the corporate bond market. Conversely, if an event that lowers the risk appetite of bond investors is expected to result in a flight to quality, gilts would be purchased in favour of corporate bonds.

Active management policies are also employed where it is believed the market's view on future interest rate movements, implied by the yield curve, are incorrect or have failed to be anticipated. This is known as market timing.

Riding the yield curve is an active bond strategy that does not involve seeking out price anomalies but instead takes advantage of an upward sloping yield curve.

EXAMPLE

If a portfolio manager has a two-year investment horizon then a bond with a two-year maturity could be purchased and held until redemption. Alternatively, if the yield curve is upward sloping and the manager expects it to remain upward sloping without any intervening or anticipated interest rate rises over the next two years, a five-year bond could be purchased and sold two years later when the bond has a remaining life of three years.

Assuming that the yield curve remains static over this period, the manager would benefit from selling the bond at a higher price than that at which it was purchased as its GRY falls.

2.2.11 Passive Bond Strategies

Passive bond strategies are employed either when the market is believed to be efficient, in which case a buy-and-hold strategy is used, or when a bond portfolio is constructed around meeting a future liability fixed in nominal terms.

Immunisation is a passive management technique employed by those bond portfolio managers with a known future liability to meet.

An **immunised bond portfolio** is one that is insulated from the effect of future interest rate changes. Immunisation can be performed by using either of the following techniques, cash matching or duration based immunisation.

Cash matching involves constructing a bond portfolio, whose coupon and redemption payment cash flows are synchronised to match those of the liabilities to be met.

Duration-based immunisation involves constructing a bond portfolio with the same initial value as the present value of the liability it is designed to meet and the same duration as this liability. A portfolio that contains bonds that are closely aligned in this way is known as a bullet portfolio.

Alternatively, a **barbell strategy** can be adopted. If a **bullet portfolio** holds bonds with durations as close as possible to ten years to match a liability with ten-year duration, a barbell strategy may be to hold bonds with a durations of five and 15 years. Barbell portfolios necessarily require more frequent rebalancing than bullet portfolios.

Finally, a ladder portfolio is one constructed around equal amounts invested in bonds with different durations. So, for a liability with ten-year duration, an appropriate ladder strategy may be to hold equal amounts in bonds with one-year duration, two-year duration right through to 20 years.

ABBREVIATIONS

The following list, arranged in alphabetical order, contains abbreviations that may be useful:

ADR	American Depository Receipt
AESP	Automatic Execution Suspension Period
AGM	Annual General Meeting
AIM	Alternative Investment Market
ASB	Accounting Standards Board
ASC	Accounting Standards Committee
BBA	British Bankers' Association
CAD	Cash Against Delivery
CAT	Charges, Access, Terms
CBO	Collateralised Bond Obligation
CC	Competition Commission
CCSS	CREST Courier and Sorting Service
CDI	CREST Depositary Interest
CDO	Collateralised Debt Obligation
CGT	Capital Gains Tax
CLO	Collateralised Loan Obligation
CLS	Continuous Linked Settlement
CP	Committed Principals
CSD	Central Securities Depository
CTF	Child Trust Fund
DBV	Delivery By Value
DIE	Designated Investment Exchange
DMO	Debt Management Office
DTCC	Depository Trust Clearing Corporation

DTI	Department of Trade and Industry
DVP	Delivery Versus Payment
ECN	Electronic Communication Network
EDGAR	Electronic Data Gathering And Retrieval System
EGM	Extraordinary General Meeting
EPS	Earnings Per Share
ETF	Exchange-Traded Fund
EVA	Economic Value Added
FIFO	First In, First Out
FRS	Financial Reporting Standard
FSA	Financial Services Authority
FSMA	Financial Services and Markets Act
GDP	Gross Domestic Product
GEMM	Gilt-Edged Market Maker
GRY	Gross Redemption Yield
GUI	Graphical User Interface
HMRC	Her Majesty's Revenue & Customs
ICVC	Investment Company with Variable Capital
ICMA	International Capital Market Association (formally known as the International Securities Market Association (ISMA))
IDB	Inter-Dealer Broker
IHT	Inheritance Tax
IPA	Individual Pension Account
IPO	Initial Public Offering
IRS	International Retail Service
ISA	Individual Savings Account

IV	Intrinsic Value
JGB	Japanese Government Bond
KFI	Key Features Information
LCH	London Clearing House
LIBOR	London Interbank Offered Rate
LIFO	Last In, First Out
LSE	London Stock Exchange
MQP	Mandatory Quote Period
MQS	Minimum Quote Size
NASDAQ	National Association of Securities Dealers Automated Quotations
NMS	Normal Market Size
NRV	Net Realisable Value
NRY	Net Redemption Yield
NYSE	New York Stock Exchange
OEIC	Open Ended Investment Company
OFT	Office of Fair Trading
OTC	Over-The-Counter
P&L	Profit and Loss
P/E	Price/Earnings Ratio
PAT	Profit After Tax
PAYE	Pay As You Earn
PBIT	Profit Before Interest and Tax
PEP	Personal Equity Plan
POTAM/PTM	Panel On Takeovers And Mergers
PSBR	Public Sector Borrowing Requirement
PSNCR	Public Sector Net Cash Requirement

PVP	Payment Versus Payment
RCH	Recognised Clearing House
RIE	Recognised Investment Exchange
ROCE	Return On Capital Employed
RPI	Retail Price Index
RPIX	RPI, excluding mortgage interest payments
RUR	Register Update Request
SAR	Substantial Acquisition Rule
SBLI	Stock Borrowing and Lending Intermediary
SDRT	Stamp Duty Reserve Tax
SEAQ	Stock Exchange Automated Quotation system
SEATS plus	Stock Exchange Alternative Trading Service
SEC	Securities and Exchange Commission
SEDOL	Stock Exchange Daily Official List
SETS	Stock Exchange Electronic Trading Service
SIPP	Self-Invested Personal Pension scheme
SPV	Special Purpose Vehicle
SRO	Self Regulating Organisation
SSAP	Statement of Standard Accounting Practice
STRIPS	Separate Trading of Registered Interest and Principal of Securities
TV	Time Value
UCITS	Undertaking for Collective Investment in Transferable Securities
UKLA	United Kingdom Listing Authority
WACC	Weighted Average Cost of Capital
WPA	Worked Principal Agreement

Syllabus Unit/ Element		Chapter/ Section
ELEMENT 1	**SECURITIES**	**CHAPTER 1**
1.1	**Shares**	
	On completion, the candidate should be able to:	
1.1.1	know the principal features and characteristics of ordinary shares and non-voting shares:	1
	• 'A' ordinary shares	
	• 'B' shares	
	• preference shares	
	• bearer shares	
	• partly paid shares and calls	
	• ranking for dividends	
	• ranking in a liquidation	
	• voting rights	
	• purpose of non-voting shares	
1.1.2	understand the differences and principal characteristics of the following classes of preference shares:	1.2
	• cumulative	
	• participating	
	• redeemable	
	• convertible	
1.1.3	know the broad composition and geographical scope and use of the following stock indices:	1.3
	• DJ STOXX	
	• FTSE Eurofirst 300	
	• MSCI World	
	• FTSE 100	
	• Dow Jones Industrial Average	
	• Nikkei Stock 225	
	• Hang Seng	
	• CAC 40	
	• DAX	
	• S&P 500	
	• FTSE Allshare	
	• NASDAQ	
1.1.4	understand the use of a tax credit on a dividend	1.4
1.1.5	know the implications of free float on market capitalisation	1.5
1.2	**Debt instruments**	
	On completion, the candidate should:	
1.2.1	know the principal features and characteristics of debt instruments	2.1
1.2.2	understand the uses and limitations of the following:	2.2
	• flat yield	

Syllabus Unit/ Element		Chapter/ Section
	• gross redemption yield (using internal rate of return)	
	• net redemption yield	
	• modified duration	
	• calculation of price change	
	• convexity	
1.2.3	be able to calculate:	2.3
	• simple interest income on corporate debt	
	• conversion premiums on convertible bonds	
	• flat yield	
	• accrued interest (given details of the day count conventions)	
1.2.4	understand the concept of spreads and be able to convert spread over a Government benchmark to a LIBOR-based spread	2.4
1.2.5	understand the role of the yield curve and the relationship between price and yield with reference to the yield curve (normal and inverted)	2.5
1.2.6	be able to calculate the present value of a bond (maximum 2 years) with annual coupon and interest income	2.6
1.3	**Government Debt**	
	On completion, the candidate should:	
1.3.1	know the principal features and characteristics of the following classes of government debt:	3.1
	• short-, medium-, long-dated	
	• dual dated	
	• undated	
1.3.2	understand the following features and characteristics of government debt:	3.2
	• redemption price	
	• interest payable	
	• accrued interest	
	• effect of changes in interest rates	
1.3.3	understand the following features and characteristics of index linked debt:	3.3
	• index-linking	
	• the retail price index and index-linking	
	• effect of the index on price, interest and redemption	
	• return during a period of zero inflation	
1.3.4	know the features and characteristics of French, German, Japanese and US bonds:	3.4
	• settlement periods	
	• coupons	
	• terms and maturities	

Syllabus Unit/ Element		Chapter/ Section
1.4	**Corporate Debt**	
	On completion, the candidate should:	
1.4.1	understand the principal features and uses of secured debt:	4.1
	• fixed charges and floating charges	
	• asset backed securities	
	• mortgage backed securities	
	• securitisation process	
1.4.2	understand the role of the Trustee, rating agency, cash manager and servicer in a secured debt transaction	4.1.4
1.4.3	understand the principal features and uses of unsecured debt:	4.2
	• subordinated	
	• guaranteed	
	• convertible bonds	
1.4.4	understand the principal features and uses of credit ratings:	4.3
	• rating agencies	
	• impact on price	
	• use of credit enhancements	
	• difference between investment grade and sub-investment grade bonds	
1.4.5	know the principal features and uses of Commercial Paper	4.4
	• issuers, including CP Programmes	
	• investors	
	• discount security	
	• unsecured	
	• asset backed	
	• rating	
	• normal life	
	• method of issuance	
	• role of dealer	
1.5	**Money Markets**	
	On completion, the candidate should:	
1.5.1	understand the features and characteristics of Treasury Bills:	5
	• issuer	
	• purpose of issue	
	• minimum denomination	
	• normal life	
	• no coupon and redemption at par	
	• redemption	
1.5.2	understand the basic purpose and characteristics of the repo markets	5.2
	• sale and repurchase at agreed price, rate and date	
	• reverse repo – purchase and resale at agreed price and date	

Syllabus Unit/ Element		Chapter/ Section
	• documentation	
	• benefits of the repo market	
1.6	**Eurobonds**	
	On completion, the candidate should:	
1.6.1	understand the principal features and uses of Eurobonds	6.1
	• issued through syndicates of international banks	
	• concept of continuous pure bearer	
	• immobilised in depositories	
	• ex-interest date	
	• accrued interest	
	• interest payments	
1.7	**Other securities**	
	On completion, the candidate should:	
1.7.1	know the principal features and characteristics of Depositary Receipts:	7.1
	• American Depositary Receipts	
	• Global Depositary Receipts	
	• transferability	
	• means of creation including pre-release facility	
	• how registered	
	• rights attached	
	• dividends	
	• transfer to underlying shares	
1.7.2	know the rights, uses and differences between warrants and covered warrants	7.2
	• benefit to the issuing company and purpose	
	• issuer	
	• right to subscribe for capital	
	• effect on price of maturity and the underlying security	
	• detachability	
	• exercise and expiry	
	• the calculation of the conversion premium (discount) on a warrant (warrant price + exercise price minus the share price)	
1.8	**Foreign Exchange**	
	On completion, the candidate should:	
1.8.1	know the principal features and uses of spot, forward and cross rates:	
	• quotation as bid-offer spreads	8.1
	• forwards quoted as bid-offer margins against the spot	
	• quotation of cross rates	
1.8.2	be able to calculate spot and forward settlement prices using:	8.2
	• premiums or discounts	
	• interest rate parity	

Syllabus Unit/ Element		Chapter/ Section
1.9	**Prime brokerage and equity finance**	
	On completion, the candidate should:	
1.9.1	know the main services provided by an Equity and Fixed Income prime broker, including:	9.1
	• securities lending and borrowing	
	• leverage trade execution	
	• cash management	
	• core settlement	
	• custody	
	• rehypothecation	
1.9.2	know the use of the main sources of equity financing:	9.2
	• stock borrowing and lending	
	• repurchase agreements	
	• collateralised borrowing	
	• tri-party repos	
	• synthetic financing	
1.9.3	know the uses of, requirements and implications of stock lending:	9.3
	• what is stock lending	
	• purpose for the borrower	
	• purpose for the lender	
	• function of market makers and stock borrowing and lending intermediaries	
	• effect on the lender's rights	
	• lender retains the right to sell	
	• collateral	
ELEMENT 2	**NEW ISSUES**	**CHAPTER 2**
2.1	**The Primary and Secondary markets**	
	On completion, the candidate should:	
2.1.1	know the principal characteristics of, and the differences between, the primary and secondary markets. In particular:	1
	• the role of the listing authority	
	• users of the primary market and why	
	• users of the secondary market and why	
2.2	**Stock Exchanges**	
	On completion, the candidate should:	
2.2.1	know the purpose, role and main features of the major stock exchanges. In particular	2.1
	• scope	
	• provision of liquidity	
	• price formation	
	• brokers versus dealers	
	• different types of stock exchanges	

Syllabus Unit/ Element		Chapter/ Section
	• electronic	
	• 'open outcry'	
	• major exchanges	
	• Deutsche Börse	
	• London Stock Exchange	
	• NASDAQ	
	• NYSE Euronext	
	• Tokyo Stock Exchange	
2.2.2	know the role of advisors	3
	• Listing Agent	
	• Corporate Broker	
2.2.3	know the Issuer's obligations	3
	• corporate governance	
	• reporting	
2.3	**London Stock Exchange**	
	On completion, the candidate should:	
2.3.1	know the regulatory framework for the LSE	4
	• Companies Act	
	• FSA	
	• Exchange Rule Book	
2.3.2	know the admissions criteria for listing	4.1
	• trading record	
	• amount raised	
	• percentage in public hands	
	• market capitalisation	
2.4	**AIM**	
	On completion, the candidate should:	
2.4.1	know the admissions criteria	4.2
	• appointment and role of a nominated advisor	
	• appointment and role of a broker	
	• transferability of shares	
	• no minimum shares in public hands	
	• no trading record required	
	• no shareholder approval needed	
	• no minimum market capitalisation	
2.4.2	know the issuer's obligations	4.2
	• corporate governance	
	• reporting	
2.4.3	know the regulatory framework for AIM	4.2
	• London Stock Exchange	
	• AIM Rules	

Syllabus Unit/ Element		Chapter/ Section
	• Companies Act	
	• FSA	
2.5	**Listing Securities**	
	On completion, the candidate should:	
2.5.1	understand the role of the Origination Team	5.1
2.5.2	understand the role of the Syndicate Group	5.2
	• different roles within a Syndicate	
	• bookrunner	
	• co-lead	
	• co-manager	
	• marketing and bookbuilding	
2.5.3	understand the purpose and practice of underwriting, rights and responsibilities of the underwriter	5.3
	• benefits to the issuing company	
	• risks and rewards to the underwriter	
2.5.4	understand stabilisation and its purpose:	5.4
	• governing principles and regulation with regard to stabilisation activity	
	• who is involved in stabilisation	
	• what does stabilisation achieve	
	• benefits to the issuing company and investors	
2.5.5	understand the use of an initial public offering	5.5
	• why would a company choose an IPO	
	• structure of IPO – base deal plus greenshoe	
	• stages of an IPO	
	• underwritten versus best efforts	
2.5.6	understand the use of follow on offerings	5.6
	• why would a company choose a follow on offering	
	• structure of follow on – base deal plus greenshoe	
	• stages of follow on offering	
	• underwritten versus best efforts	
2.5.7	understand the use of open offers and offers for subscription	5.7
	• why would a company choose an open offer	
	• structure of offer	
	• stages of offer	
	• tenders, strike price, who is involved in the offer process	
2.5.8	understand the use of offers for sale	5.8
	• why would a company choose an offer for sale	
	• structure of an offer for sale	
	• stages of an offer for sale	
	• tenders, strike price, who may receive an allotment, who is involved in the offer process	

Syllabus Unit/ Element		Chapter/ Section
2.5.9	understand the basic process and uses of selective marketing and placing:	5.9
	• advantages to the issuing company	
	• what is a placing	
	• what is selective marketing	
	• how is a placing achieved	
	• how is selective marketing achieved	
2.5.10	understand the use of Introductions	5.10
	• why would a company undertake an Introduction	
	• structure of a introduction	
	• stages of a introduction	
2.5.11	understand the use of exchangeable / convertible bond offerings	5.11
	• the difference between exchangeable and convertible Bonds	
	• structure of offering – base deal plus greenshoe	
	• stages of offering	
	• underwritten versus best efforts	
2.6	**Bond offerings**	
	On completion, the candidate should:	
2.6.1	know the different types of issuer:	6.1
	• supranationals	
	• governments	
	• agency	
	• municipal	
	• corporate	
	• financial institutions & special purpose vehicles	
2.6.2	understand the seniority of debt and how they rank in default:	6.2
	• senior	
	• subordinated	
	• mezzanine	
	• PIK	
2.6.3	understand the pricing benchmarks:	6.3
	• spread over government bond benchmark	
	• spread over/under LIBOR	
	• spread over/under swap	
2.6.4	know the methods of issuance:	6.4
	• scheduled funding programmes and opportunistic issuance (eg, MTN)	
	• auction/tender	
	• reverse inquiry (under MTN)	
2.6.5	understand the role of the Origination team including:	6.5
	• pitching	

Syllabus Unit/ Element		Chapter/ Section
	• indicative bid	
	• mandate announcement	
	• credit rating	
	• roadshow	
	• listing	
	• syndication	
2.6.6	understand methods of raising new capital to finance takeovers:	6.6
	• follow on offerings	
	• rights issues	
	• convertible bond offerings	
2.7	**Share capital and changes to share ownership**	
	On completion, the candidate should:	
2.7.1	understand why are share buybacks undertaken:	7.1
	• governing regulation	
	• resolution at AGM	
	• limits on percentage of shares and price	
	• use of company's own money	
	• key aspects of share buybacks – criteria to comply with	
	• different structures regarding block trades	
	• accelerated bookbuild – best efforts basis	
	• accelerated bookbuild – back stop price	
	• bought deal	
2.7.2	understand how and why stake building is used:	7.2
	• strategic versus acquisition	
	• direct versus indirect	
	• direct – outright purchase	
	• indirect – CFDs	
	• disclosure thresholds, including mandatory takeover threshold	
2.8	**Corporate Actions**	
	On completion, the candidate should:	
2.8.1	understand the use of rights issues	8.1
	• reasons for a rights issue	
	• structure of rights issue	
	• stages of rights issue	
	• pre-emptive rights	
	• ability to sell nil paid	
2.8.2	be able to calculate the impact of a rights issue on the share price	8.1.4
2.8.3	understand the use of scrip (also known as bonus or capitalisation) issues and why a company will undertake a scrip issue	8.2
2.8.4	be able to calculate the impact of a scrip issue on the share price	8.2.1

Syllabus Unit/ Element		Chapter/ Section
2.8.5	be able to calculate the maximum nil paid rights to be sold to take up the balance at nil cost	8.3
2.8.6	be able to calculate the value of nil paid rights	8.4
2.8.7	understand the difference between a stock split and a scrip issue	8.5
ELEMENT 3	**PRIMARY AND SECONDARY MARKETS**	**CHAPTER 3**
3.1	**Methods of Trading and Participants**	
	On completion, the candidate should:	
3.1.1	understand the differences between quote driven and order driven markets and how they operate	1.1
3.1.2	know the functions and obligations of:	1.2
	• market makers	
	• broker/dealers	
	• inter-dealer brokers	
	• stock lending and borrowing intermediaries	
3.2	**Transaction Reporting**	
	On completion, the candidate should:	
3.2.1	understand the definition of a reportable transaction	2.1
3.2.2	understand the role and purpose of transaction reporting for the firm and the regulator.	2.2
3.2.3	know which party to a transaction is responsible for reporting including transactions carried out by overseas branches	2.3
3.2.4	know the reporting channels and systems	2.4
3.3	**London Stock Exchange (LSE) – UK Equity**	
	On completion, the candidate should:	
3.3.1	understand the rules, procedures and requirements applying to dealing through the Stock Exchange Electronic Trading System (SETS) in the following areas:	3.1
	• order book features	
	• order management	
	• worked principal agreements	
	• limitations and benefits of trading through SETS	
3.3.2	understand the following order types and their differences	3.2
	• limit	
	• at best	
	• fill or kill	
	• execute and eliminate	
	• iceberg	
	• multiple fills	
3.3.3	understand the operation and purpose of the LSE's Central Counterparty	3.3
	• LCH.Clearnet Limited	
	• x-clear	

Syllabus Unit/ Element		Chapter/ Section
	• benefits and any limitations	
3.3.4	know the LSE's right to call for a halt in trading in any listed security	3.4
	• for any reason	
	• length of trading halt	
3.3.5	know the features and requirements of SETSqx dealing	3.5
	• SETSqx as an order driven trading system	
	• relative illiquidity	
	• securities covered	
	• normal market size (NMS)	
	• minimum number of market makers	
3.4	**London Stock Exchange International Equity Market**	
	On completion, the candidate should:	
3.4.1	understand the rules, procedures and requirements applying to dealing through the International Order Book (IOB) in the following areas:	4.1
	• securities covered	
	• minimum and maximum trading sizes	
	• who can access the IOB	
3.4.2	understand the rules, procedures and requirements applying to dealing through the International Bulletin Board (ITBB) in the following areas	4.2
	• market makers' obligations	
	• when to enter two way prices	
	• price quotes during and outside the mandatory quote period	
	• who can access the ITBB	
3.4.3	understand the purpose of and firms' obligations towards the International Retail Service (IRS):	4.3
	• purpose of the IRS	
	• 'Committed Principals'	
	• Mandatory Quote Period for most European stocks	
	• currency of quotation	
3.5	**Other Equity Markets**	
	On completion, the candidate should:	
3.5.1	Know how trading on the NYSE compares with trading on the LSE:	5.1
	• specialists	
3.5.2	know the rules, procedures and requirements of trading securities on PLUS:	5.2
	• Recognised Investment Exchange	
	• securities covered	
	• PLUS listed	
	• PLUS quoted	
	• PLUS traded – listed or unlisted	

Syllabus Unit/ Element		Chapter/ Section
3.6	**Government Bonds**	
	On completion, the candidate should:	
3.6.1	understand the basic characteristics and purpose of government bond markets in the UK, US, Japan and the Eurozone:	6
	• ratings and the concept of 'risk free'	
	• currency, credit and inflation risks	
	• inflation indexed bonds	
3.6.2	know the functions, obligations and benefits of the following in relation to government bonds with respect to the UK, US, Japan and the Eurozone:	6.1
	• primary dealers	
	• broker dealers	
	• inter-dealer brokers	
	• Government issuing authority such as the UK Debt Management Office	
3.6.3	know the basic purpose and characteristics of the strip market	6.2
	• result of stripping a bond	
	• number of securities possible from a strippable bond	
	• zero coupon securities	
3.6.4	understand the broad mechanisms by which bond prices are driven by bond future prices	6.3
3.7	**Corporate Bond Markets**	
	On completion, the candidate should:	
3.7.1	understand the characteristics of corporate bond markets:	7.1
	• decentralised dealer markets and dealer provision of liquidity	
	• the impact of default risk on prices	
	• the differences between bond and equity markets	
	• dealers rather than market makers	
	• bond pools of liquidity versus centralised equity exchange	
3.8	**Dealing Methods**	
	On completion, the candidate should:	
3.8.1	know the different trading methods for bonds:	8.1
	• bond trading has moved from voice trading (ie by telephone) to e-trading using systems such as:	
	• OTC inter-dealer voice trading (eg, direct dealer to dealer, dealer to dealer via voice broker)	
	• inter-dealer (B2B) electronic market (eg, electronic trading platforms (ETPs) such as MTS, Brokertec)	
	• OTC customer to dealer voice trading	
	• customer to dealer (B2C) electronic market (eg, ETPs such as TradeWeb, BondVision, proprietary Single Dealer Platform (SDP))	

Syllabus Unit/ Element		Chapter/ Section
	• On-exchange trading	
3.8.2	understand the different trends between trading methods:	8.2
	• electronic methods characterised by the efficient trading of high liquidity and/or commoditised assets:	
	• government and agency	
	• debt and liquid corporate debt	
	• price driven via Inter-dealer brokers (IDB) – dealer to dealer	
	• request for quote (RFQ) –customer to dealer	
	• OTC methods characterised by trading in lower liquidity or higher volatility classes, or trades of unusual size:	
	• high yield	
	• ABS	
	• emerging markets	
3.8.3	know the factors that influence bond pricing:	8.3
	• Issuer factors	
	• yield to maturity	
	• seniority	
	• structure	
	• technical factors	
	• credit rating	
	• specific issuer prospects	
	• default risk	
	• liquidity	
	• benchmark bonds	
	• market factors	
	• benchmark bonds	
	• liquidity premiums for highly-traded bond issues	
	• indicative pricing versus firm two-way quotes	
	• bid/offer spreads	
	• availability of a liquid repo market and the difficulty in offering illiquid bonds	
	• inability to borrow or cover shorts	
	• impact of interest rates	
3.8.4	know the different quotation methods (ie, yield, spread, price) and the circumstances in which they are used	8.4
3.9	**Market Data**	
	On completion, the candidate should:	
3.9.1	understand the relationship between inflation and interest rate expectations	9.1
3.9.2	understand how interest rates impact securities pricing	9.2

Syllabus Unit/ Element		Chapter/ Section
3.10	**Regulatory Information and Financial Communications**	
	On completion, the candidate should:	
3.10.1	know the main sources of regulatory information and financial communications within UK equity	10.1
	• RNS, PIPS & SIPS	
	• Bloomberg, Reuters	
	• analyst research	
	• websites: FSA, LSE, EU (Europa, CESR)	
ELEMENT 4	**SETTLEMENT**	**CHAPTER 4**
	On completion, the candidate should:	
4.1.1	know the principal details of settlement in UK, EU, USA and Japan	1
	• DVP	
	• free delivery	
	• trade confirmation	
	• settlement periods	
	• instruments settled	
	• settlement systems	
	• Euroclear UK & Ireland	
	• LCH.Clearnet	
	• Clearstream	
	• DTCC	
	• Jasdec	
4.1.2	Know the concept of custody and the roles of the different types of custodian	2
	• Global	
	• Regional	
	• Local	
	• Sub-custodian	
4.1.3	understand the implications of registered title	3
	• registered title versus unregistered (bearer)	
	• legal title	
	• beneficial interest	
	• voting rights	
	• right to participate in corporate actions	
4.1.4	understand the basics of designated and pooled nominee accounts and their uses, and the concept of corporate nominees:	4
	• designated nominee accounts	
	• pooled nominee accounts	
	• details in share register	
	• function of corporate nominees	
	• legal ownership	

Syllabus Unit/ Element		Chapter/ Section
	• effect on shareholder rights of using a nominee	
4.1.5	know which securities may be subject to UK stamp duty/SDRT	5
4.1.6	know which transactions are exempt UK stamp duty	6
4.1.7	understand the concepts, requirements, benefits and disadvantages of deals executed cum, ex, special cum and special ex:	7
	• timetable	
	• effect of deals on the underlying right	
	• effect on the share price before and after a dividend	
	• the meaning of 'books closed', 'ex-div' and 'cum div', cum and ex-rights	
	• effect of late registration	
	• benefits that may be achieved	
	• disadvantages / risks	
	• when dealing is permitted	
4.1.8	understand what Continuous Linked Settlement (CLS) is and its purpose:	8
	• the settlement of currencies across time zones	
	• receiving and matching instructions	
	• advantages	
	• how it reduces settlement risk	
ELEMENT 5	**SPECIAL REGULATORY REQUIREMENTS**	**CHAPTER 5**
5.1	**Takeovers and Mergers**	
	On completion, the candidate should:	
5.1.1	know the implications of the EU Takeover Directive:	1
	• that some countries continue with their own rules as minimum standards and that takeover rules vary between states	
	• application to all EU companies trading on an EU regulated market	
	• requirement for a designated supervisory authority and scope for shared supervision	
	• general principles of the Directive (Art. 3)	
	• consequences of a mandatory bid and different mandatory bid thresholds	
	• publication of information on the bid (Articles 6 and 10)	
5.1.2	know the legal nature and purpose of the UK Takeover Code (Section 2 of the Introduction); the six General Principles; the definitions of 'acting in concert', 'dealings', 'interest in shares' and 'relevant securities'	2
5.2	**Disclosure of interests**	
	On completion, the candidate should:	
5.2.1	understand the principles behind disclosure of interest rules and why they are required	3.1

Syllabus Unit/ Element		Chapter/ Section
5.2.2	know the following disclosure of interest rules:	3.2
	• EU under the Transparency Directive:	
	• the disclosure thresholds	
	• to whom disclosure has to be made and within what time scale	
	• differing implementation of the Transparency Directive across EEA countries	
	• US Securities and Exchange Commission:	
	• the disclosure thresholds	
	• to whom disclosure has to be made and within what time scale	
	• UK under the Companies Act 2006, Section 793, in relation to company investigations	
5.3	**Specific regulations in US, Canada and Japan**	
	On completion, the candidate should:	
5.3.1	know that these markets restrict the promotion and sale of foreign equity	4.1
5.3.2	know that foreign dealer-brokers must be registered with the local regulator in these markets before they can disseminate research	4.2
ELEMENT 6	**ACCOUNTING ANALYSIS**	**CHAPTER 6**
6.1	**Basic principles**	
	On completion, the candidate should:	
6.1.1	understand the purpose of financial statements	1.1
6.1.2	understand the requirements for companies and groups to prepare accounts in accordance with applicable accounting standards:	1.2
	• accounting principles	
	• International Financial Reporting Standards (IFRS)	
	• IAS	
6.1.3	understand the differences between group accounts and company accounts and why companies are required to prepare group accounts. (Candidates should understand the concept of goodwill and minority interests but will not be required to calculate them.)	1.3
6.2	**Company Balance Sheets**	
	On completion the candidate should:	
6.2.1	know the purpose of the balance sheet, its format and main contents,	2.1
6.2.2	understand the concept of depreciation and amortisation	2.3
6.2.3	understand the difference between authorised and issued share capital, capital reserves and revenue reserves	2.4
6.2.4	know how loans and indebtedness are included within a balance sheet	2.5
6.3	**Income Statement**	
	On completion the candidate should:	
6.3.1	know the purpose of the income statement, its format and main contents	3.1
6.3.2	understand the difference between capital and revenue expenditure	3.2

Syllabus Unit/ Element		Chapter/ Section
6.4	**Cash Flow Statement**	
	On completion the candidate should:	
6.4.1	know the purpose of the cash flow statement, its format as set out in IAS 7	4.1
6.4.2	understand the difference between profit and cash and their impact on the long term future of the business	4.2
6.4.3	understand the purpose of free cash flow and the difference between enterprise cash flow and equity cash flow	4.3
6.5	**Financial Statements Analysis**	
	On completion the candidate should:	
6.5.1	understand the following key ratios:	5.1
	• profitability ratios (gross profit and operating profit margins)	
	• return on capital employed	
6.5.2	understand the following financial gearing ratios:	5.2
	• investors' debt to equity ratio	
	• net debt to equity ratio	
	• interest cover	
6.5.3	understand the following investors' ratios:	5.3
	• earnings per share	
	• diluted earnings per share	
	• price earnings ratio (both historic and prospective)	
	• enterprise value to EBIT	
	• enterprise value to EBITDA	
	• net dividend yield	
	• net dividend cover	
6.5.4	be able to calculate the following investors' ratios:	
	• earnings per share	5.4
	• price earnings ratio (both historic and prospective)	
	• net dividend yield	
	• net dividend cover	
	• corporation tax	
ELEMENT 7	**RISK AND REWARD**	**CHAPTER 7**
7.1	**Investment management**	
	On completion the candidate should:	
7.1.1	understand the risk and reward of investment in equities:	1.1
	• risk/reward profile	
	• effect of longer term	
	• can offer income and capital appreciation	
7.1.2	understand the risk and reward of investment in money market instruments:	1.2
	• risk/reward profile	
	• use as short-term investment	

Syllabus Unit/ Element		Chapter/ Section
7.1.3	understand the risk/reward profile of investment in debt (fixed interest, floating rate and index linked):	1.3
	• compared to equities	
	• effect of holding to maturity	
	• can combine low risk and certain return	
	• can provide a fixed income	
	• inflation risk	
	• interest rate risk	
	• default risk	
7.1.4	understand risk/reward profile of investment in overseas shares and debt:	1.4
	• country risk	
	• exchange rate risk	
7.1.5	understand the risks facing the investor:	1.5
	• specific/unsystematic	
	• market/systematic	
7.1.6	understand how to optimise the risk/reward relationship through the use of:	1.6
	• correlation	
	• diversification	
7.1.7	know the role of hedging in the management of investment risk	1.7
7.2	**Institutional Investment Advice**	
	On completion, the candidate should:	
7.2.1	know the differences between institutional client profiles including:	2.1
	• pension funds,	
	• life and general insurance funds,	
	• hedge funds,	
	• regulated mutual funds	
	• banks	
7.2.2	know what are active and passive investment management methodologies and the advantages and disadvantages of each	2.2

EXAMINATION SPECIFICATION

Each examination paper is constructed from a specification that determines the weightings that will be given to each element. The specification is given below.

It is important to note that the numbers quoted may vary slightly from examination to examination as there is some flexibility to ensure that each examination has a consistent level of difficulty. However, the number of questions tested in each element should not change by more than plus or minus 2.

		Questions
ELEMENT 1	SECURITIES	24
ELEMENT 2	NEW ISSUES	26
ELEMENT 3	PRIMARY AND SECONDARY MARKETS	22
ELEMENT 4	SETTLEMENT	6
ELEMENT 5	SPECIAL REGULATORY REQUIREMENTS	4
ELEMENT 6	ACCOUNTING ANALYSIS	12
ELEMENT 7	RISK AND REWARD	6
	TOTAL	100

CISI Membership

Studying for a CISI qualification is hard work and we're sure you're putting in plenty of hours, but don't lose sight of your goal! This is just the first step in your career, there is much more to achieve!

The securities and investments industry attracts ambitious and driven individuals. You're probably one yourself and that's great, but on the other hand you're almost certainly surrounded by lots of other people with similar ambitions. So how can you stay one step ahead during these uncertain times?

Entry Criteria:	Pass in either: • IAQ, IFQ, ICFA, CISI Certificates in, eg, Securities, Derivatives or Investment Management, Advanced Certificates • one or two CISI Diploma/Masters papers
Joining Fee:	£25 or free if applying via prefilled application form
Annual Subscription (pro rata):	£115
International Annual Subscription:	£86.25

Using your new CISI qualification* to become an Associate (ACSI) member of the Chartered Institute for Securities & Investment could well be the next important career move you make this year, and help you maintain your competence.

Join our global network of over 40,000 financial services professionals and start enjoying both the professional and personal benefits that CISI membership offers. Once you become a member you can use the prestigious ACSI designation after your name and even work towards becoming personally chartered.

(* ie, IAQ, IFQ, CISI Certificate Programme)

Turn over to find out more about CISI membership

CISI
CHARTERED INSTITUTE FOR
SECURITIES & INVESTMENT

Feedback to CISI

Have you found this workbook to be a valuable aid to your studies? We would like your views, so please email us (learningresources@cisi.org) with any thoughts, ideas or comments.

Accredited Training Providers

Support for examination students studying for the Chartered Institute for Securities & Investment (CISI) Qualifications is provided by several Accredited Training Providers (ATPs), including 7City Learning and BPP. The CISI's ATPs offer a range of face-to-face training courses, distance learning programmes, their own learning resources and study packs which have been accredited by the CISI. The CISI works in close collaboration with its accredited training providers to ensure they are kept informed of changes to CISI examinations so they can build them into their own courses and study packs.

CISI Workbook Specialists Wanted

Workbook Authors

Experienced freelance authors with finance experience, and who have published work in their area of specialism, are sought. Responsibilities include:

* Updating workbooks in line with new syllabuses and any industry developments
* Ensuring that the syllabus is fully covered

Workbook Reviewers

Individuals with a high-level knowledge of the subject area are sought. Responsibilities include:

* Highlighting any inconsistencies against the syllabus
* Assessing the author's interpretation of the workbook

Workbook Technical Reviewers

Technical reviewers provide a detailed review of the workbook and bring the review comments to the panel. Responsibilities include:

* Cross-checking the workbook against the syllabus
* Ensuring sufficient coverage of each learning objective

Workbook Proofreaders

Proofreaders are needed to proof workbooks both grammatically and also in terms of the format and layout. Responsibilities include:

* Checking for spelling and grammar mistakes
* Checking for formatting inconsistencies

Notes

Notes

Notes

Notes

Notes

Notes

Notes

Notes

Notes

Notes

Notes

Notes

Notes

Notes

Notes

Notes

Notes

Notes

Notes

Notes